MARX, MARXISM AND UTOPIA

For Carla

Marx, Marxism and Utopia

DARREN WEBB
Coventry University

LONDON AND NEW YORK

First published 2000 by Ashgate Publishing

Reissued 2019 by Routledge
2 Park Square, Milton Park, Abingdon, Oxon, OX14 4RN
52 Vanderbilt Avenue, New York, NY 10017

Routledge is an imprint of the Taylor & Francis Group, an informa business

Copyright © 2000, Darren Webb

All rights reserved. No part of this book may be reprinted or reproduced or utilised in any form or by any electronic, mechanical, or other means, now known or hereafter invented, including photocopying and recording, or in any information storage or retrieval system, without permission in writing from the publishers.

Notice:
Product or corporate names may be trademarks or registered trademarks, and are used only for identification and explanation without intent to infringe.

Publisher's Note
The publisher has gone to great lengths to ensure the quality of this reprint but points out that some imperfections in the original copies may be apparent.

Disclaimer
The publisher has made every effort to trace copyright holders and welcomes correspondence from those they have been unable to contact.

A Library of Congress record exists under LC control number:

ISBN 13: 978-1-138-72000-8 (hbk)
ISBN 13: 978-1-138-71998-9 (pbk)
ISBN 13: 978-1-315-19519-3 (ebk)

Contents

Acknowledgements	*vi*
Introduction	1
1 Marx's Critique of 'Utopian Socialism'	4
2 Marx's Description of the Lower Phase of Communism	36
3 Marx's Description of the Higher Phase of Communism	58
4 Materialistically Critical Socialism	79
5 Marx the 'Accidental' Utopian	109
Conclusion: Marxism and Utopia	138
Bibliography	*169*
Index	*182*

Acknowledgements

This book started life as a doctoral thesis. It has changed quite a bit since then but thanks are still very much due to those who helped me through my PhD. Anthony Arblaster and Mike Kenny deserve special mention here, as does Sarah Cook (the unsung heroine of the Sheffield University Politics Department). Vincent Geoghegan encouraged to me to turn my thesis into a book in spite of the fact that I take issue with many of his own positions. I am therefore particularly grateful for his support.

Introduction

Marx was not a utopian system-builder. He did not sit alone at night sketching plans for a better society, nor did he spend his time deliberating on the form that communism would (or should) take once the proletarians had victoriously shed their chains and gained the world. Marx's opposition to utopianism was total and unwavering. Those socialists who did construct utopian systems were criticised on the grounds that their political methodology implied an elitist process of prophetic messianism founded on nothing short of deceit. And yet, in spite of this, it cannot be denied that Marx himself was a 'utopian' of sorts. For he presented us with a vision of communism that has variously been described as 'more dazzling in its utopianism than that of even the most utopian of utopian socialists' (Kumar, 1987, p.53) and 'the grandest and noblest vision in human history' (Hunt, 1984, p.97). My primary aim in this book is to offer an interpretation of Marx which accounts for this apparent ambiguity in his thought.

That Marx was both a utopian and a critic of utopianism has long been recognised. Indeed, this paradox — neatly characterised by Steven Lukes as Marx's 'anti-utopian utopianism' (1984, p.155) — provides the intellectual framework around which most of the discussions concerning the relationship between Marxism and utopianism are constructed. But what does it actually mean to suggest that Marx was both a utopian and a critic of utopianism? What, in other words, do 'utopians' do and what do critics of 'utopianism' criticise? Here I follow J. Max Patrick when he suggests that:

> A Utopia should describe in a variety of aspects and with some consistency an imaginary state or society which is regarded as better, in some respects at least, than the one in which its author lives (cited in Sargent, 1975, p.140).

As it is to be used here, then, the term 'utopia' refers to a) an imaginary state or society which b) is regarded as better than the one in which its author lives and c) is described by that author in a variety of aspects and with some consistency. By logical extension, a utopia*n* becomes someone who creates and describes such a state or society and utopia*nism* refers to the general act of creating and describing such societies. Whilst some writers may quibble with this definition, most, I think, would agree that it adequately captures the main features of 'utopia' and the various terms derived from it. I am confident, therefore, that when we discuss what other people have had to say about these things we can avoid talking at cross-purposes.

With regards to what other people have in fact had to say, I think it fair to suggest that the utopia/anti-utopia paradox has seldom been considered a pivotal aspect or defining feature of Marx's thought. What I shall argue here, however, is that his 'anti-utopian utopianism' was symptomatic of the fundamental problems which confronted Marx throughout his life. The problems were those of generating radical hope without foreclosing the future; of capturing the spirit of revolution whilst remaining faithful to the principles of proletarian self-emancipation and self-determination. So important did Marx consider these problems that resolving them became his own political and theoretical 'project'.

Of course, we are now so used to the idea that there were 'multiple Marxes' (Carver, 1998), each of whom spoke in a different language and possessed a different 'spirit' (Derrida, 1994), that to ascribe *a* (in the singular) 'project' to Marx may appear rather old fashioned. If it does then so be it. In suggesting that Marx's ideas were framed and guided by a common purpose, however, I am not at all denying that Marx said different things at different times. I am merely suggesting that Marx's works were consistent in their *aims*, i.e., that they represented varied attempts to deal with the same problems. The fact that Marx sometimes said conflicting (and even contradictory) things does not, therefore, mean that these things were each spoken in a different language by a different Marx. It simply means that in attempting to solve the problems he was attempting to solve Marx sometimes proposed conflicting solutions.

The central thesis of this book is that the theoretical origins of Marx's 'anti-utopian utopianism' lie precisely in the conflicting solutions he proposed to the problems that he set himself. The problems were those of generating radical hope and of capturing the spirit of revolution whilst simultaneously avoiding the need for utopianism and all the paternalistic, elitist and messianic baggage that came with it. The solutions he proposed, however, were never quite adequate to the task. Indeed, on the basis of the solutions he proposed I come to the conclusion that Marx was an 'accidental' utopian. By this I mean that the visionary concepts which together define his 'utopia' were not the product of any conscious attempt on Marx's part to give concrete shape to an imaginary state or society which he regarded as better than the one in which he lived. Instead, these concepts each formed an integral (and ultimately indispensable) part of the historical models designed by Marx in order to overcome the need for utopianism. As such, the origins of Marx's utopianism lie, not in the utopian imagination he so persistently ridiculed, but rather in his failure to establish the logical coherency of his (anti-utopian) historical framework.

Having argued this, what I do in the Conclusion is offer some thoughts on the role to be played by utopian thought within contemporary Marxism. However, rather than mount a defence of political utopianism on the grounds that Marx failed to establish a coherent alternative, I focus instead on the power of Marx's critique and also on its continuing vitality. Rejecting the 'pro-utopian' position adopted by so many writers over recent years, I argue that utopianism conceived as a political tool cannot help but descend into the messianic elitism so accurately described by Marx. I also tentatively suggest that the future of socialism lies in its ability to harness, not the spirit of utopia, but the spirit of adventure.

1 Marx's Critique of 'Utopian Socialism'

Introduction

Commentators on Marx seem to have reached a broad consensus about something. Such a momentous event would call for celebration were it not for the fact that the consensus is based around the strangest interpretation of Marx. The 'something' about which there is general agreement is that Marx's critique of 'utopian socialism' did not — repeat did *not* — involve, incorporate or encompass a critique of 'utopianism'. So peculiar do I find this claim that I spend the first part of this chapter trying to understand it and the latter part disputing it. What I argue in its place is that Marx not only *did* criticise 'utopianism' but that he also attached a great deal of importance to his critique of it. For understood as both a theoretical framework and a political tool, utopianism only served to undermine the principles of proletarian self-emancipation and self-determination, principles which, if anything, helped define what Marx himself was trying to do.

As a starting point I fully accept that Marx's critique of 'utopianism' seldom found expression outside his rather more specific attack on the 'utopian socialists'. As Ruth Levitas correctly observes: 'The term utopia is in fact hardly ever used by Marx or Engels other than as the adjective 'utopian', generally in the terms 'utopian socialism' and 'utopian communism'' (1990, pp.35-36). What I argue against, however, is the idea that Marx divorced the adjective 'utopian' from the noun 'utopianism'. Instead, I believe that Marx's specific attack on those whom he used the adjective to describe was part and parcel of a more general attack on the activity to which the noun refers. I also believe that this will become clear if we consider *carefully* i) what Marx meant when he used the term 'utopian' to describe a particular group of socialist thinkers and ii) why he considered the utopianism so ascribed to be worthy of critique. Before I offer my own considerations, let us see what other commentators have had to say on the subject.

The Means/Ends Dichotomy Consensus

A substantial number of writers have challenged the very idea that Marx was 'anti-utopian'. None go quite so far as to deny that Marx *criticised* the utopian socialists, nor do they deny that Marx criticised them for what *he* considered to be their utopianism. Their point of contention, however, concerns the nature of what Marx meant by the term 'utopianism' and their basic argument is that his critique of it, however paradoxical this may sound, had nothing at all to do with a critique of the construction of utopias. I have termed the approach in question 'the means/ends dichotomy consensus' and the basic argument is this:

> It was not the ends that the utopian socialists sought that made them "utopian" in the Marxist sense, but rather the inadequacy of the means proposed to achieve those ends (Meisner, 1982, p.8).

> The difference between Marxism and utopian socialism does not ... rest on the existence or otherwise of an image of the socialist society to be attained, nor even on the content of that image. It rests upon disagreements about the process of transition (Levitas, 1990, p.45).

With regards to the first of the questions posed above — what Marx meant when he used the term 'utopian' to describe a particular group of socialist thinkers — the answer is clear: because the term referred neither to the ends that the utopian socialists sought nor to the content of their images of the socialist society to be attained, their supposed utopianism bore no relation whatsoever to their utopian descriptions of socialism. The term 'utopian' referred instead to the means by which the utopians hoped to achieve their ends and their ideas concerning the process of transition. The second question — why Marx criticised the utopianism of the 'utopian socialists' — then becomes inextricably tied to the first. For the means proposed by the 'utopian socialists' were only deemed by Marx to be 'utopian' because they were 'inadequate', so that Marx in effect offered a critical definition of utopianism: 'utopian socialists' were utopian because they forwarded an ineffective theory of the transitional process and inadequate means of attaining a set of ends with which Marx himself was in broad agreement.

Fredric Jameson argues along the same lines when he suggests that 'the indispensable feature supplied by the Utopian socialists to the Marxism-to-be of Marx's and Engels's time was simply their vision of the *future* itself' (1976, p.53). What made the utopian socialists 'utopian', however, was not the nature of their vision of the future but the inadequacy of the 'mechanism' they chose 'for implementing their vision' (ibid.). Richard T. De George offers a similar argument when he states that:

> The term "communism" is used by Marx (and Engels) in three different, although related ways. The term signifies a doctrine (communism$_d$), a movement (communism$_m$), and a stage of historical development (communism$_s$) (1981, p.11).

He then tells us that 'Communism$_d$ consists of a description of communism$_s$ and a theory of how communism$_s$ is to be achieved' (ibid., p.12), arguing of the latter that:

> It is this portion of Marxist theory that, according to Marx and Engels, raises communism$_d$ as a theory from the status of a utopian ideal to the status of science. This distinguishes scientific socialism from utopian socialism (ibid., p.15).

What distinguishes Marx from the utopian socialists, then, is not the fact that the former refused to describe the future, for such a description was an essential feature of communism$_d$. It is rather Marx's 'theory of *how* communism is to be achieved'. Marx's theory can be distinguished from utopian socialism, in other words, by virtue of his analysis of the *means* required to achieve his description of communism$_s$.

As to *why* the means proposed by the 'utopian socialists' were inadequate and henceforth 'utopian', Ruth Levitas supplies the answer:

> The real dispute between Marx and Engels and the utopian socialists is not about the merit or otherwise of goals or of images of the future but about the process of transformation, and particularly about the belief that propaganda alone would result in the realisation of socialism (1990, p.35).

Morris Zeitlin also says of the 'utopian socialists' that 'Marx and Engels disputed not their vision of life in socialist society but their unrealistic belief that propaganda alone would bring it about' (1996, p.23). According to both Levitas and Zeitlin, then, the 'utopian socialists' were utopian 'in the Marxist sense' because they believed that 'propaganda alone would result in the realisation of socialism'. Propaganda alone was deemed an 'inadequate' means of realising socialism and anyone who considered it *adequate* was 'utopian'.

Does this mean, therefore, that when one talks of Marx's antiutopianism one is talking merely of an opposition to propaganda as a means of realising socialist visions of the future? Levitas herself casts doubt on this when she suggests that 'Marx rejected as utopian all those plans for the future which are not realisable because they are not rooted in a correct analysis of the present' (1979, p.20). For here it seems that the term 'utopian' *is* used by Marx to refer to the utopians' 'ends', i.e., their plans for the future. Utopias subsequently become those plans which, by virtue of not being 'rooted' in a correct analysis of the present, are unrealisable. Vincent Geoghegan also subscribes to this view, arguing that: 'What is under attack here is not anticipation as such, but rather the failure to root this anticipation in a theoretical framework cognizant of the essential dynamics of capitalism' (1987a, p.27). The implication here is that Marx *did not* reject as utopian those plans for the future which *were* rooted in a correct analysis of the present and *were* cognizant of the essential dynamics of capitalism. His dispute with the utopians thus becomes a dispute concerning the way in which their ends or goals were derived. Darko Suvin reiterates this point when he remarks that:

> What matters . . . is not the fact that the "utopian socialists" built a system from their head: Marx did so too. But he, as different from them, NOT ONLY used reason, his head, principles, etc., BUT ALSO took into account reality, facts, and historico-economical processes (1976, p.61).

It is suggested by each of these writers that Marx defined 'utopia' as a system built using 'reason, one's head, principles, etc.', and that Marx did not consider a system built using these things AND a correct analysis of the present based on 'reality, facts and historico-economical processes' to be a utopia. In short, it *was* the ends that the utopians sought — or at least the type of ends that they sought — that made them 'utopian' in the Marxist sense.

Nonetheless, when it comes to the question of what planning for the future using a theoretical framework that *is* cognizant of the essential dynamics of capitalism actually means, the answer is still formulated in terms of a means/ends dichotomy. Thus states Geoghegan:

> What emerges is that the utopian socialists are criticized by Marx and Engels for the highly abstract nature of their speculations — the lack, in other words, of any genuine connection between ends and means. Unaware of the real nature of society, overly subjective dreams are spun, detailed visions of other-worldly paradises constructed, but with no connection with any of the real tendencies at work in society. Under attack here is not anticipation of future conditions as such but rather the failure to ground this anticipation in a theory of effective political and social change (1987b, p.39).

The utopians' anticipations were highly abstract and overly subjective *because* they were not connected to any of the real tendencies at work in society and *therefore* lacked any genuine connection between means and ends. The abstract nature of the utopians' ends is thus explained in terms of the inadequacy of their means. It subsequently follows that establishing a genuine link between means and ends would rescue the ends themselves from the realm of abstraction. The key to avoiding utopian ends, in other words, lies in one's being able to find the genuine means to realise them.

When Geoghegan suggests that utopianism (in the Marxist sense) is a form of anticipation which lacks solid roots in a theoretical framework cognizant of the essential dynamics of capitalism, it is not, therefore, the anticipations themselves, i.e., the ends, that he is calling utopian. It is rather the fact that the ends, which Marx and Engels shared, were unrealisable, i.e., utopian, because the utopians had yet to discover the *means* by which they could be realised. This is also what Suvin means when he argues that Marx built a system using his head AND reality, facts, and historico-economical processes. For such a system is constructed at the point where 'utopia and knowledge meet' (Suvin, 1976, p.68), so that utopian ends meet a knowledge of reality which in turn produces a knowledge of the appropriate means by which the ends can be realised. Marx thus rescues his system from the clutches of utopianism by virtue of having discovered the means to realise it. For Suvin, then, as for the other proponents of the means/ends dichotomy argument, what distinguishes Marxism from utopian socialism is the fact that his project involved an adequate understanding of the means by which his ends were to be realised. As such, the 'differentia specifica' between Marxism and utopian socialism is described by Suvin as 'the basis, center, and purpose of Marxist socialism: it is *revolution*' (ibid.). Similarly, although Levitas fails to develop the idea that utopias were deemed by Marx to be plans which are unrealisable because they are not rooted in a correct analysis of the present, her general subscription to the means/ends argument would indicate that she means that utopias are plans that are unrealisable, *not* because as ends they can never be realised, but once again because the utopians' incorrect analysis of the present had yet to reveal the means by which they *could* be realised.

This complex relationship between 'utopian' ends and 'utopian' means is neatly captured by Keith Taylor when he argues that:

> Marx adopted the already established socialist view of the future as a stage when harmony, association, community and co-operation would be achieved; but he disagreed with his predecessors when it came to stating *how* this future

stage was to be reached. He knew that his strategy could not be reconciled with what he considered to be their naive (because it was unscientific) conviction that an intensification of the class struggle could be avoided. For him the class struggle was everything, and a realistic as opposed to utopian (in the sense of impracticable) strategy demanded that the proletariat must liberate themselves *through* the class struggle and not by merely wishing it away (Goodwin and Taylor, 1982, pp.166-167).

Marx adopted the utopians' *ends* as his own, disagreeing only when it came to the *means* by which these ends were to be realised. Because the utopians had failed to take into account reality, facts, and historico-economical processes when building their systems, they lacked a framework cognizant of the essential dynamics of capitalism and consequently believed that an intensification of the class struggle could be avoided. This led them to adopt a utopian (in the sense of impracticable) strategy. Marx, on the other hand, *was* cognizant of the essential dynamics of capitalism and realised that his system could be realised only *through* the class struggle. He was therefore anti-utopian in the sense that he adopted a realistic (in the sense of practicable) strategy for realising his system. Simply put, class struggle and revolution were considered 'realistic' means of achieving socialism whereas propaganda alone was dismissed as the 'utopian' alternative.

Some Problems with the Consensus

The most striking feature of the arguments contained within the means/ends dichotomy consensus is that they imply a complete misunderstanding of the term 'utopia' on Marx's part. In fact, if the commentators discussed above are to be believed then it would appear that Marx redefined 'utopia' to such an extent — from a description of certain ends that people advocate to a notion almost entirely divorced from any consideration of ends — that one must seriously question why he chose to use the term in the first place.

This is, in fact, what many writers have done in the past. Rather than examine Marx's critique of 'utopian socialism' in any great depth, they merely dismiss it as unhelpful nonsense founded on a misguided notion of what utopianism is all about. Marie Berneri, for example, argues that prior to the intervention of Marx and Engels 'utopia was considered as an imaginary ideal commonwealth whose realisation was impossible or difficult', but that subsequently it 'included all social schemes which did not recognise the division of society into classes, the inevitability of the class struggle and of the social revolution' (1971, p.207). As a result, she argues, one should ignore Marx and Engels in any discussion of utopianism.

Martin Buber offers an extended version of the redefinition ascribed to Marx by Berneri:

> Originally Marx and Engels called those people Utopians whose thinking had preceded the critical development of industry, the proletariat and the class war, and who therefore could not take this development into account; subsequently the term was levelled indiscriminately at all those who, in the estimation of Marx and Engels, did not in fact take account of it; and of these the late comers either did not understand how to do so or were unwilling or both. The epithet "Utopian" thereafter became the most potent missile in the fight of Marxism against non-Marxian socialism (1988, p.5).

'Utopians', then, were either those people who preceded the class struggle or those who ignored it. Because she too believes that this is what Marx meant by the term 'utopian', Judith Shklar 'wishes that Marx and Engels might have chosen another epithet. Certainly many useless verbal wrangles over the "true" meaning of the adjective "utopian" might have been avoided' (1973, p.103).

The question raised by all of this is how Marx came to have such a bizarre conception of what the epithet 'utopian' actually meant. Why, in other words, would he have gone to such great pains to construct an elaborate critique of a group of thinkers whom he had studied in depth, only to undermine his own critique by branding them with a completely inappropriate label? In response to this question it is common to suggest (as Buber does above) that Marx simply used the term as a political missile. For ever since the publication of Louis Reybaud's *Etude sur les réformateurs, ou socialistes modernes* in 1840, it had become popular within intellectual circles to dismiss utopianism as a pointless and childlike game. Moreover, Reybaud it was who first grouped Fourier, Saint-Simon and Owen together under the banner 'utopian socialism'. What some writers suggest, therefore, is that Marx merely jumped on the contemporary bandwagon and appropriated a familiar term of opprobrium when criticising rival political movements. This is the kind of argument that Bertell Ollman has in mind when he states that:

> Marx's objection to discussing communist society was more of a strategic than of a principled sort. More specifically, and particularly in his earliest works, Marx was concerned to distinguish himself from other socialists for whom prescriptions for the future were the main stock-in-trade (1977, p.8).

Barbara Goodwin also argues that 'the critique of utopian socialism appeared largely in the early works of Marx, written while disciples of the utopians were still active . . . while the later Marx quotes More approvingly in *Capital*. There is therefore no reason to think that Marx saw himself as offering a universal analysis or indictment of utopianism' (Goodwin and Taylor, 1982, p.73). Both Goodwin and Ollman point to the fact that Marx's anti-utopianism was more pronounced in his 'early' works, when utopian socialism still attracted popular support. From this they conclude that Marx's anti-utopianism was part of a strategic attack upon his political rivals. When the popularity of these waned, so too did Marx's objection to them, indicating that this objection was 'more of a strategic than of a principled sort'. In sum, when Marx criticised the 'utopians' he was not at all rejecting utopianism as a mode of thought. Instead, he was deploying a familiar term to deride those who failed to recognise the importance of the class struggle and the need for revolution.

I find it extremely difficult to believe any of this. First of all because the 'strategic' determination argument is based upon a very feeble kind of logic. For we can conclude now, before having looked at a single word that Marx ever wrote, that *of course* his anti-utopianism took on a more vitriolic guise during the periods in which utopian socialism was a serious political rival — there was quite simply a more pressing need to stress the flaws in the utopian approach. This does not mean, however, that at other times Marx was *not* a 'principled' anti-utopian. It simply means that the need to stress this principle had diminished. In general, people who object to certain political movements on principle tend to voice their objections more strongly when the movements in question are seen to be gaining popular support. This is an obvious point which also applies to those who object to utopianism on principle.

More importantly, if Marx really did use the term 'utopian' to describe those people who failed to recognise the necessity of revolution, then not only does this imply that Marx abused the term 'utopian', it also implies that he completely misunderstood the 'utopians' themselves. For whilst some of them *were* anti-revolutionary (Fourier, Saint-Simon, Owen), just as many were not (Proudhon, Weitling, and after the 1831 Lyons uprising, all of Saint-Simon's 'disciples'). Indeed, Keith Taylor hints at this when he phrases the standard means/ends argument thus:

> What he [Marx] objected to in their [the utopians'] work was not so much their ultimate vision of social harmony, but their characteristic reliance (apart from the occasional exception like Weitling) on gradual reform and non-revolutionary methods of achieving this harmony (Goodwin and Taylor,

1982, p.166).

What this does not explain, however, is why Marx would use the term 'utopian' to describe someone like Weitling. For as is well known, Weitling displayed a degree of revolutionary commitment that scared almost everyone around him. If, therefore, Marx used the term 'utopian' to describe those who placed their faith in propaganda alone as a means of realising socialism, then not only was this a misuse but it was also an incorrectly applied misuse of the term. Now, once again, perhaps Marx *was* mistaken in his understanding of some of the 'utopians', and perhaps he *did* use completely the wrong term to articulate a critique based on a complete misunderstanding of the thinkers he was using the wrong term to criticise. One descends into the realms of farce here, however, and the means/ends interpretation begins to lose credibility as a result.[1]

One could, of course, extend the argument discussed above and claim that Marx referred to all of his opponents as 'utopian', irrespective of their views on propaganda, revolution and the class struggle. This simply is not true, however, for Marx quite rightly refused to label as 'utopian' people such as Max Stirner or the 'true socialists' (who were also his political rivals during the 1840s). And Marx chose not to refer to these thinkers as 'utopian' because they were not in fact utopians. Marx understood full well what the adjective 'utopian' meant and he only used it in relation to those people to whom it actually applied. For if one asks Marx the two questions posed at the beginning of this chapter, namely, why he used the term 'utopian' to describe the 'utopian socialists' and why he criticised the utopianism so defined, then one finds a succinct reply in the letter he wrote to Sorge in October 1877:

Utopian socialism especially which for decades we have been clearing out of the German workers' heads with so much effort and labour — their freedom from it having made them theoretically (and therefore also practically) superior to the French and English — *utopian* socialism, playing with fantastic pictures of the future structure of society, is again spreading like wildfire . . . It is natural that utopianism, which *before* the era of materialistically critical socialism concealed the latter within itself in embryo, can, now, coming belatedly, only be silly, stale, and reactionary from the roots up (Marx and Engels, 1969, p.376).

It is clear from this letter that Marx used the adjective 'utopian' to describe socialists who 'play with fantastic pictures of the future structure of society'. Now, simplistic and unrefined this definition of utopianism may be, but a *re*definition it is not. Moreover, if one reads 'description' for 'picture', 'imaginary' for 'fantastic', and 'a state or society' for 'the future structure of society', then its resemblance to the definition offered by J. Max Patrick becomes clear. More importantly still, I find it impossible to conclude from this statement that Marx's understanding of utopianism was divorced from the question of 'the ends that the utopian socialists sought' or from 'images of the socialist society to be attained'. For it seems to me that Marx defined 'utopian socialism' *solely* in terms of the ends sought and the images constructed by the 'utopian socialists' — the term 'utopian' referred to the pictures themselves, not the means proposed to realise them (which did not even get a mention).

As to why utopianism so defined was considered worthy of critique, Marx provides the answer here too: utopianism was 'silly, stale and reactionary' because it had now been superseded by 'materialistically critical socialism' (the meaning of this enigmatic term will be explored in chapter 4). In other words, the 'utopian socialists' were not utopian (in some muddled and obscurely redefined sense) because they were reactionary, anti-revolutionary or failed to understand the class struggle; instead, they were reactionary *because* they were utopian (in the traditional sense by which Marx quite clearly understood the term). The utopians were utopian because they played with fantastic pictures of the future structure of society and they were criticised because they were *still* playing with these pictures *now*.

Because selective quotation is the first analytical tool that any Marxologist acquires, rejecting a position forwarded by a number of writers on the basis of a single passage from Marx is always rather dubious. For this reason, I will spend a large part of the following discussion arguing for the consistency of Marx's anti-utopianism. Before I do that, however, I think it necessary to spend some time looking at the 'utopian socialists' themselves.

The 'Utopian Socialists'

I want to make two main points here. The first is that the 'utopian socialists' did not regard themselves as in any way 'utopian'. Quite the contrary, in fact — as far as they were concerned, their views constituted the very pinnacle of scientific achievement. Fourier, for example, distances himself completely from the utopian tradition when he asks:

> What is Utopia? It is the dream of well-being without the means of

execution, without an effective method. Thus all philosophical sciences are Utopias, for they have always led peoples to the very opposite of the state of well-being they promised them (cited in Spencer, 1981, p.126).

Utopia, for Fourier, was an unrealisable dream. His vision of an alternative reality, on the other hand, was eminently realisable because it was based upon the precise mathematical science of passionate attraction. Fourier claimed to have discovered the existence of twelve passions, each of which is distributed differently in each of the 810 different types of man and woman that he had also discovered exist. He then claimed to have discovered how each of these passions is linked to the rest of the world — to colours, shapes, minerals, everything — and to have calculated the optimal combination of these colours, shapes, passions and people. Because, therefore, he had discovered a science of society, and with it 'the truth', Fourier's vision of Harmony, founded upon this scientific truth, was not (as far as Fourier himself was concerned) a 'utopia'.

The same applies to Robert Owen. His alternative reality, i.e., a collective happiness induced by a rationally reorganised society based around the principles of sexual restraint, temperance, frugality and obedience to the Christian dictum 'do unto others', was no mere whim or imaginative fancy. These were rather 'uniformly consistent principles, derived from the unvarying facts of the creation; principles, the truth of which no sane man will attempt to deny' (Owen, 1963, pp.46-47). Indeed, Owen directly contrasts his empirical science to others' imaginative abstraction:

> In this inquiry [into the nature of the 'good society'], men have hitherto been directed by their inventive faculties and have almost entirely disregarded the only guide that can lead to true knowledge on any subject — experience. They have been governed, in the most important concerns of life, by mere illusions of the imagination, in direct opposition to existing facts (ibid., p.94).

With regards to Owen's own particular 'Good Society', however, 'as it is a deduction from all the leading facts in the past history of the world, so it will be found, on the most extensive investigation, to be consistent with every fact which now exists' (ibid., p.70).

Saint-Simon was even more convinced than either Fourier or Owen that he had founded his 'utopia' upon scientific principles, proclaiming that:

> My object is to discover whether there is a form of government which is

intrinsically good, founded upon reliable, absolute and universal principles, valid for all times and places ... I will use the only two principles which can be relied upon to produce absolute proof: reason and experience (Saint-Simon, 1976, p.87).

He thus sought to *prove*, through the use of reason and experience, the intrinsic worth of his industrial system. More than this, in fact, he sought to scientifically prove that his system *was* the future. Nor did he see this as a difficult task, convinced as he was that:

The future consists of the last items of a series of which the first composed the past. When one has properly examined the first terms of a series, it is easy to postulate those following. Thus, from the past, deeply observed, one can with ease deduce the future (cited in Durkheim, 1959, p.102).

The first point, then, is that each of the 'utopian socialists' categorically denied, and this repeatedly, that their societies of the future were derived from imaginative abstraction. Each of them emphasised instead that their visions of the good life had been derived from only the most rigorous of scientific methods.

The second point I would like to make is that the 'utopian socialists' were pompous, patronising and elitist theorists who each believed themselves to be some form of messiah. As Manuel and Manuel rightly remark:

With utter faith in their election, they stepped into the age-old roles of saviours and messiahs. They sometimes imagined that in their persons the Messiah himself had already arrived. Saint-Simon thought he was the reincarnation of Socrates and Charlemagne; the disciples evoked the analogy with Jesus; Fourier, though not given to historical learning, demonstrated from Scripture that his appearance had been foretold; Owen identified himself with both Jesus and Columbus (1979, p.583).

Each of the three 'utopian socialists' repeatedly proclaimed that only they had accessed 'the truth' and that the general population, indeed the intellectuals and *philosophes* as well, had singularly failed to work out where their emancipation lay. Each of them also argued that the emancipation of humanity depended upon the realisation of their own particular system. Conversely, each of them declared that if their own particular system was *not* realised then humanity would descend into chaos and universal ruin.

Saint-Simon, for example, saw it as his own personal task to complete the French Revolution by providing the industrialists with the plans that the *philosophes* and Jacobins had failed to supply. For he believed that:

> The principal occupation of philosophers consists of conceiving of the best system of organization for the epoch in which they live, of ensuring its acceptance by the governors and the governed, of perfecting this system insofar as it is possible, thereafter of overthrowing it when it has reached the extreme limits of its perfection, in order to construct a new one with materials gathered everywhere by men devoted to specialized intellectual pursuits (cited in Manuel, 1956, p.216).

The new Industrial System — not only the best system of organisation for Saint-Simon's epoch but also the best system of organisation full stop — had been *conceivable* since the latter part of the eighteenth century. The *philosophes*, however, had become too embroiled in abstractions to contemplate the best system of organisation and had been too busy disabusing the world of theology to petition the governors and the governed. Whilst, therefore, they had succeeded in creating a critical framework within which a conscious need for change had developed, they had singularly failed to shed any light on the organisational structure of the society that was to follow the change. This, for Saint-Simon, had been the root cause of the Terror — the Terror was the inevitable outcome of a revolution effected by lawyers armed with meaningless abstractions rather than concrete plans for the future.

Thankfully, however, Saint-Simon was at hand, equipped with the scientific knowledge that his vision of a new society was 'intrinsically good'. Saint-Simon alone had been able to free himself of all metaphysical baggage and actually conceptualise the best system of organisation for his epoch. And Saint-Simon — like all the other utopians around him — also believed that only the realisation of his system could stave off the otherwise inevitable descent into anarchy. As he often told the industrialists he was attempting to woo:

> The laws in the hands of the property-holders are instruments which allow them to manipulate the inferior class. If they do not know how to modify the action of these instruments or to simplify them or to recast them in order to make them flow into new moulds, they will expose themselves to revolutions, that is to say, to the men without property (cited in ibid., pp.72-73).

Saint-Simon was fond of pointing out that 'we want only to facilitate and illuminate the inevitable progress of events' (Saint-Simon, 1976, p.105). He thus warned the class in whose hands the destiny of history lay, i.e., the property-holders or industrialists, that if they did not know how to recast society into the new moulds demanded by historical development then the men without property would recast society themselves. Delaying the inevitable (realisation of his system) was tantamount to pronouncing a death sentence on the world. To ignore the wise words of the new Socrates was to openly embrace chaos, anarchy and despotism. In this way, Saint-Simon sold himself as a saviour; a man whose vision would ward off the evils of revolution and lead the industrialists into a new land of Harmony. It was not without reason that his last work proudly announced itself as *The New Christianity*.

Owen too possessed a messianic conviction that his vision of the good society represented humanity's only salvation. Indeed, like a true Messiah, only Owen had been granted the ability to 'see'. For whilst he never tired of hammering home his one 'great and universal principle', namely, that individual characters are determined entirely by their environment, neither did he fail to marvel at the fact that this did not apply to him: 'Causes over which I could have no control, removed in my early days the bandage which covered my mental sight' (Owen, 1963, p.108). As such, Owen had been granted the privileged position of being able to divine 'the whole' (ibid.).

As a self-proclaimed visionary, Owen was not afraid to adopt the appropriate language. He could thus contrast present cataclysm — 'Past history exhibits no combination of circumstances which bears any analogy to the present crisis' (ibid., p.133) — to future redemption: 'the past ages of the world present the history of human irrationality only, . . . and we are but now advancing towards the dawn of reason, and to a period when the mind of man shall be born again' (ibid., p.155). He could even equate this rebirth with the new millennium itself:

> The time is . . . arrived when the foretold millennium is about to commence, when the slave and the prisoner, the bond-man and the bond-woman, the child and the servant, shall be set free forever, and oppression of body and mind shall be known no more (cited in Tsuzuki, 1971, p.36).

Into this millennial context steps Owen, who was convinced that 'the mission of my life appears to be, to prepare the population of the world to understand the vast importance of the second creation of humanity' (cited in Oliver, 1971, p.181). As a Messiah, of course, Owen also recognised that his role as saviour would not be complete without an element of martyrdom:

> Should I be content and rest satisfied with the suffering which has fallen to my lot, while you remain in your ignorance and misery? Or shall I sacrifice every private consideration for the benefit of you and our fellow-men? (Owen, 1963, p.117).

Unable to tolerate the ignorance and misery everywhere around him, Owen sacrificed all private considerations in his quest to redeem humanity and prepare it for the foretold millennium. With the bandage covering his mental sight having been removed by mysterious forces at an early age, Owen travelled far and wide propagating his vision of the harmonious whole.

Owen's messianism pales into insignificance when compared to Fourier's, however. For it was not at all unusual to find Fourier declaring things such as this:

> Wretched nations, you are very close to the great metamorphosis which seemed to be announced by a great upheaval. Today the present is indeed pregnant with the future, and excessive suffering must be leading towards the moment of salvation. From the continual sequence of vast political tremors it looks as if nature is straining to shake off an oppressive burden . . . all the earth offers today is hideous political chaos which demands the strength of a new Hercules to purge it of the social monstrosities which defigure it . . . This new Hercules is here . . . he it is who shall raise universal harmony on the ruins of barbarism and Civilisation. Breathe again, forget your former sorrows (Fourier, 1996, pp.104-105).

In similar fashion to Saint-Simon, Fourier ascribed the current state of hideous political chaos to the ineptitude of the *philosophes*, and in particular to their reluctance to think the future. Fourier goes one step further than Saint-Simon, however, in suggesting that 'the persistence of so many scourges could be attributed to the absence of some form of organisation intended by god but unknown to our scholars' (ibid., p.7). He then goes one step further still and pronounces that he in fact *has* gained knowledge of the form of organisation intended by god: 'Now at last that day has come, and mortals will share with god a foreknowledge of future events' (ibid., p.102).

Fourier had gained access to God's divine wishes, so that the realisation of his own vision was not so much an act of faith as an act of Faith. Fourier was doing God's own bidding, and as he modestly pointed out, 'this is not the first time that God has made use of the humble to put down the proud and mighty, nor the first time that he has chosen the obscurest man to bring the most important message to the world' (ibid., p.105).

The scientistic and messianic foundations of 'utopian socialism' tend to be given far less coverage than the precise details of the utopians' plans for the future or arguments to the effect that the utopians pre-empted Marx in this, that or the other way. I think it extremely important to emphasise these foundations, however, as doing so allows us to gain a fuller understanding of Marx's critique.

Demonstrating the 'Utopianism' of the 'Utopian Socialists'

Marx's critique of 'utopian socialism' begins at the beginning — it begins, that is, by pointing out that the utopians were in fact 'utopian'. Shlomo Avineri rightly remarks here that:

> To Marx the main trouble with the utopians is ultimately epistemological. It is not that their schemes are unrealizable, impractical, or rooted in never-never land. It is because the utopians concoct systems at all that they are wrong (1973, pp.323-324).

The utopians were wrong first and foremost because they constructed fantastic systems and then denied that these systems were derived from imaginative abstraction. Marx criticised them, therefore, because he disagreed with their assessment of what science could do — for the 'utopians', science enabled one to know the form that the future will take, whereas for Marx it did not. No particular epistemology needs to be ascribed to Marx here, for the idea that one can scientifically ground a vision of the future can be criticised on the basis of virtually any theory of knowledge. All that needs to be said is that, for Marx, because one cannot know the form that the future will take, the 'scientific' derivation of it by the utopians was not scientific at all but 'utopian'. This is why, in the *Manifesto* (1848), Marx and Engels take pains to emphasise that the utopians' 'new social science' was nothing more than 'an organization of society specially contrived by these inventors' (Marx and Engels, 1967, p.115); this is why, in *The Poverty of Philosophy* (1847), Marx emphasises that the utopians 'seek science in their minds' (Marx, 1976b, p.177); this is why, in his obituary to Proudhon (1865), Marx tells us that 'the utopians are hunting for a so-called "science" by which a formula for the "solution of the social question" is to be excogitated *a priori*' (Marx and Engels, 1969, p.188); this is why, in 'Political Indifferentism' (1873), Marx refers to utopian systems as 'idealistic fantasies' concocted by 'doctors in *social science*' (Marx, 1974d, p.329); and so on and so forth.

Most tellingly of all, it is this conclusion which lies behind the most famous of Marx's anti-utopian soundbites, namely, his assertion that he does not write 'recipes for the cookshops of the future'. For the full quotation — from the preface to the second German edition of *Capital* (1873) — has Marx telling us that he is 'confining [him]self merely to the critical analysis of actual facts, instead of writing recipes (Comtist ones?) for the cook-shops of the future' (Marx, 1976a, p.99). And one of the reasons why Marx does not write 'Comtist' recipes (in addition to the fact that he was responding to a Comtist critic) is that Comte was precisely the type of person who disguised his utopianism beneath the cloak of science. For Comte all too often said things like this:

> it is quite in accordance with the nature of the human mind that observation of the past should unveil the future in politics, as it does in astronomy, chemistry and physiology. The determination of the future must even be regarded as the direct aim of political science, as in the case of the other positive sciences. Indeed, it is clear that knowledge of what social system the elite of mankind is called to by the progress of civilization — knowledge forming the true practical object of positive science — involves a general determination of the next social future as it results from the past (cited in Kumar, 1986, pp.23-24).

Statements such as this are exactly the kind of statements that Marx took exception to. Comte, like Saint-Simon, Fourier and Owen, claimed to be able to *know* what the society of the future will look like, and he claimed to base this knowledge upon scientific principles. For Marx, on the other hand, one cannot know what the society of the future will look like and *any* vision of it must therefore be 'utopian', i.e., simply conjured by the imagination.

It is in this context that one can best understand Engels' notorious critique of the utopians in *Anti-Dühring* (1878) and *Socialism: Utopian and Scientific* (1880). For in these works, Engels says of Saint-Simon, Fourier, Owen and Weitling that: 'To all these socialism is the expression of absolute truth, reason and justice and has only to be discovered to conquer all the world by virtue of its own power' (Engels, 1978, pp.28-29; 1968c, p.404). Engels recognises, in other words, that the utopians each regarded their systems as the scientific expression of 'the truth'. He adds, however, that:

> The solution to the social problem, which as yet lay hidden in undeveloped economic conditions, the utopians attempted to evolve out of the human brain

> . . . These new social systems were foredoomed as utopian; the more completely they were worked out in detail, the more they could not avoid drifting into pure phantasies (1978, p.311; 1968c, p.398).

In contrast to the utopians' own claims, therefore, their systems are derided as utopian. They represented, not the discovery of the truth, but fantasies of the human brain. Like Marx, then, the term 'utopian' was used pejoratively by Engels because he was trying to point out that, despite their 'scientific' claims, the 'utopian socialists' were in fact 'utopian'. The term did not need to be redefined in order to become an insult because its traditional meaning was insulting enough — describing the nature of socialism was 'utopian', and this meant that a group of socialists who prided themselves on their 'science' became, no doubt to their utter dismay, nothing more than 'utopians'.

Engels, in fact, compounds this critique by mocking the ahistorical nature of the utopians' systems thus:

> If pure reason and justice have not, hitherto, ruled the world, this has been the case only because men have not rightly understood them. What was wanted was the individual man of genius, who has now arisen and who understands the truth. That he has now arisen, that the truth has now been clearly understood, is not an inevitable event, following of necessity in the chain of historical development, but a mere happy accident. He might just as well have been born 500 years earlier, and might then have spared humanity 500 years of error, strife, and suffering (1978, p.28; 1968c, p.398).

The utopians are caricatured here as individuals who simply do not understand that concrete theory needs to work *with* history rather than above it in the supra-historical ether of the detached human brain. Marx says much the same thing in 'The *Débat Social* of February 6 on the Democratic Association' (1848). For there he argues that 'German communism is the most determined opponent of all utopianism, and far from excluding historical development in fact bases itself upon it' (Marx, 1976d, p.538). The distinction is therefore clear — utopians exclude historical development whereas Marx bases his brand of communism upon it.

Superficially at least, this lends support to the argument forwarded by Suvin in which the utopians are criticised by Marx for building systems using ONLY their heads whilst Marx builds his using this AND a knowledge of reality, facts and historico-economical processes. Such support is, however, only superficial. For in basing their communism upon historical development, what Marx and Engels were attempting to do was *avoid the need to construct systems altogether.* In order to understand that this is what they were attempting to do, one needs to be aware of their 'political' critique of utopianism.

Why Utopianism is now Silly, Stale and Reactionary

Utopian Socialism as Political Anachronism

Marx's critique of the doctors of social science had two broad aims: the first was to demonstrate that the self-professed scientists were actually utopian (the epistemological critique of concocting systems); the second was to demonstrate that they were also, by virtue of being utopian, *politically dangerous* (the subsequent political critique). Behind this latter conviction lay Marx's belief that the progress of history had rendered utopianism redundant, and underlying this belief was the following premise, put forward in Volume 2 of *The German Ideology* (1846):

> All epoch-making systems have as their real content the needs of the time in which they arose. Each one of them is based on the whole of the antecedent development of a nation, on the historical growth of its class relations with their political, moral, philosophical and other consequences (Marx and Engels, 1976b, p.462).

When applied to the 'utopians' themselves, this premise gave rise to the conclusion that their 'systems' had as their real content the needs of an undeveloped proletariat:

> as to the systems themselves they nearly all appeared in the early days of the communist movement and had at that time propaganda value as popular novels, which corresponded perfectly to the still undeveloped consciousness of the proletarians, who were just then beginning to play an active part (ibid., p.461).

One finds exactly the same point being made in the *Manifesto*. Because, in the early stages of capitalism, the proletariat remained 'a class without any historical initiative or any independent political movement' (Marx and Engels, 1967, p.115), this initiative had to be imported in the form of utopianism, the 'fantastic' and 'instinctive' nature of which adequately represented the 'fantastic' and 'instinctive' nature of the proletariat's own undeveloped consciousness:

> Such fantastic pictures of future society, painted at a time when the proletariat is still in a very undeveloped state and has but a fantastic conception of its own position, corresponded with the first instinctive yearnings of that class for a general reconstruction of society (ibid., p.116).

In both *The German Ideology* and the *Manifesto*, therefore, Marx and Engels argue that 'utopian socialism' was relevant to, because it was a product of, the early stages of capitalism; a period during which capitalism itself, the class struggle and proletarian class consciousness were each in their formative stages. In both works again, however, they argue that 'utopian socialism' had no relevance to the 1840's, i.e., to a period in which each of these things were maturing:

> In proportion as the modern class struggle develops and takes definite shape, this fantastic standing apart from the contest, these fantastic attacks on it, lose all practical value and all theoretical justification (Marx and Engels, 1967, p.117).

> As the party develops, these systems lose all importance and are at best retained purely nominally as catchwords (Marx and Engels, 1976b, p.461).

One should note here that it is the utopians' 'systems', i.e., their ends, that lose all importance, practical value and theoretical justification as history progresses. One should note also that whilst Marx allows them to retain the status of 'catchwords', he is by no means either endorsing them or suggesting that they are wrong merely because they lack a genuine link with some appropriate means. On the contrary, he is suggesting that utopian system-building has lost all importance and theoretical justification because, quite simply, the proletariat no longer needs such systems.

Marx is clearly referring here to Utopia's *source*. As a political phenomenon, utopianism found its source in 'the first instinctive yearnings of the proletariat for a general reconstruction of society'. It was thus tied to a certain historical period (the early stages of capitalism) and 'corresponded' to the needs of a certain class (the nascent proletariat). In 'Political Indifferentism' Marx makes this link very clear:

> The first socialists (Fourier, Saint-Simon, etc.), since social conditions were not sufficiently developed to allow the working class to constitute itself as a militant class, were necessarily obliged to limit themselves to dreams about the *model society* of the future (Marx, 1974d, p.329).

A 'utopia' is thus defined as 'a dream about the model society of the future' and 'utopian socialism' as a political movement — i.e., as a movement of socialists who dream about such model societies — is said to have found its source in social conditions which, by virtue of their insufficient development, prevented the proletariat from constituting itself as a militant class. The implication here, of course, is that social conditions which *allow* the proletariat to constitute itself as a militant class also enable it to supersede the need for socialists to dream about the model society of the future on its behalf. Because Marx believed that such conditions *were* now in existence, he was also convinced that contemporary utopianism was devoid of any positive function.

Utopian Socialism as Reactionary Prophetism

Marx was in no doubt that utopianism had *once* served a positive function: utopias had had 'propaganda value as popular novels, which corresponded perfectly to the still undeveloped consciousness of the proletarians'. Marx was in no doubt either, however, that contemporary utopianism no longer served such a positive function — utopias were now '*at best*' mere catchwords because they had lost all importance, practical value and theoretical justification. There were, I believe, three reasons why Marx considered contemporary utopianism devoid of any positive function.

The first Marx announces in his letter to Domela-Nieuwenhuis of February 1881. There he suggests that: 'The doctrinaire and necessarily fantastic anticipation of the programme of action for a revolution of the future only diverts one from the struggle of the present' (Marx and Engels, 1969, p.410). Utopias, as necessarily fantastic anticipations of the future, are classified here as nothing more than irrelevant diversions. What Marx means by this is that socialists could all too easily get bogged down in discussions concerning the relative merits of various utopian proposals (arguing passionately about every detail of Cabet's vision of Icaria, a day in the life of a *phalanstère*, or whatever) and that such discussions would more than likely descend into obscurantism and thus prove utterly fruitless.

The second links utopianism's contemporary function to its historical source. In other words, because utopian socialism had emerged as the result of the proletariat's inability to emancipate itself, the idea that the proletariat *is* unable to emancipate itself formed an integral part of the utopian mindset. It is worthwhile emphasising here just how important the notion of proletarian self-emancipation was to Marx. For not only was the principle that 'the emancipation of the working classes must be conquered by the working classes themselves' the first of the 'Provisional Rules' of the First International drawn up by Marx in 1864 (Marx, 1974a, p.82), it was also a principle that Marx and Engels were willing to alienate themselves from the leadership of the German Social-Democratic Workers' Party in order to defend. Thus, in their 'Circular Letter to Bebel, Liebknecht, Bracke, *et al.*' (1879), they declared:

> When the International was formed, we expressly formulated the battle-cry: the emancipation of the working class must be the work of the working class itself. We cannot ally ourselves, therefore, with people who openly declare that the workers are too uneducated to free themselves and must first be liberated from above by philanthropic big bourgeois and petty bourgeois. If the new party organ assumes a position which corresponds to the opinions of those gentlemen, which is bourgeois and not proletarian, then nothing remains, much though we should regret it, but to declare publicly our opposition to it and to abandon the solidarity with which we have hitherto represented the German party abroad (Marx and Engels, 1974b, p.375).

What irritated Marx about the utopians was their messianic conviction that the emancipation of humanity depended entirely upon the realisation of their own particular visions. For this quite clearly implied a process of liberation 'from above' and just as clearly implied that the workers were unable to liberate themselves. Of course, the messianism which accompanied the original utopians' 'systems' was understandable — because the proletariat lacked any initiative of its own it did indeed need visions of a new Jerusalem to inspire it. What was beyond comprehension, however, was that such messianic utopianism continued to thrive *now*, at a time when the proletariat was able to emancipate itself without the aid of Messiahs. For thrive it did; so much so in fact that Bazard and Enfantin, Saint-Simon's 'disciples', turned Saint-Simonism into a formal Church, replete with a hierarchy of Priests and a spiritual leader, the 'General Priest', whose appointment was mysteriously 'revealed' by Divine intervention; so much so that Cabet turned his hand to writing tracts preaching 'The True Christianity According to Jesus Christ', and so much so that Weitling inherited the mantle of Messiah incarnate, a role he cherished and played with true conviction ('Wilhelm Weitling had long advocated a messianic dictatorship with him as the messiah, and in 1848 he openly advocated a dictatorship with a "single head"', says Hal Draper, 1987, p.15).

Is it any wonder then that Marx found utopianism somewhat antithetical to the spirit of proletarian self-emancipation? For all the utopians, both original and contemporary, saw themselves as evangelical missionaries destined to save the world by virtue of a vision granted them by divine fiat. When Marx met Weitling at a meeting in the spring of 1846, one can well understand the hostile welcome he gave the utopian. According to Paul Annenkov:

> The gist of his sarcastic speech was that to arouse the population without giving it firm and thoroughly reasoned out bases for its actions meant simply to deceive it. The stimulation of fantastic hopes that had just been mentioned — Marx observed further on — led only to the ultimate ruin, and not the salvation, of the oppressed. Especially in Germany, to appeal to the workers without a rigorous scientific idea and without a positive doctrine had the same value as an empty and dishonest game at playing preacher, with someone supposed to be an inspired prophet on the one side and only asses listening to him with mouths agape allowed on the other (1968, p.169).

The stimulation of fantastic hopes by means of fantastic visions was for Marx the essence of utopianism. This took the form of 'an empty and dishonest game', with the utopian playing the inspired prophet and the oppressed masses assuming the role of gaping asses. The game was empty and dishonest because the prophet's vision could never be anything more than a fantasy grounded in abstract speculation. One cannot know the form that the society of the future will take and those who claim to possess such knowledge are deceiving the population with their empty and dishonest visions, arousing fantastic hopes devoid of any reasoned content. More importantly still, the utopian-prophet occupies his exalted position by virtue of the existence of only 'asses' beneath him. Utopians such as Weitling assume the masses to be nothing more than ineffectual vacuums, gawping into space with mouths agape, waiting for redemption to arrive in the form of a utopian Messiah whose vision of Jerusalem will act as the cattle-prod which rouses them into action.

Given Marx's deep-seated faith in the ability of the proletariat to emancipate itself, and given also his conviction that the emancipation of the proletariat could *only* be effected by the proletariat itself, one can quite clearly see why utopianism of this kind disturbed him. One can also see that it was because the utopians were prophets-cum-philanthropists who assumed that the masses were too uneducated to emancipate themselves that they were 'silly, stale and reactionary from the roots up'.

Those who forward the means/ends dichotomy argument could, however, still defend their position here. For if one phrases Marx and Engels' critique of utopianism as Edmund Wilson does when he suggests that 'they saw that the mistake of the utopian socialists had been to imagine that socialism was to be imposed upon society from above by disinterested members of the upper classes' (1972, p.170), then a distinction between means and ends could still apply — the utopians were correct in their description of socialism's 'ends' but failed to recognise that these ends could only be realised by the proletariat itself. Gareth Stedman Jones and Ian Patterson make a similar point when they argue that utopian socialism was 'faulted for its failure to understand the active and revolutionary part to be played by the proletariat in its own emancipation' (1996, p.x), but not for its conception of what socialism will look like.

As we have already seen, however, Marx and Engels went to great lengths to criticise the utopians' *ends*, which were said to have lost *all* importance, *all* practical value and *all* theoretical justification. Whilst, therefore, Marx did fault utopian socialism for its failure to understand the active and revolutionary part to be played by the proletariat in its own emancipation, this is not all it was faulted for. Indeed, what I have been arguing here is that Marx's attack upon utopianism was nothing less than an attack upon 'the utopian mindset' as a whole. The utopians were not criticised, that is, because of the inadequacy of the means they proposed to achieve their ends, nor were they criticised because their visions were not rooted in a correct analysis of the present; they were criticised because utopianism *as a whole* operated on a set of assumptions which had become reactionary. Because the utopians proclaimed that the emancipation of humanity lay in the realisation of their utopias — or 'the cerebrations of the individual pedant' as Marx elsewhere describes them (Marx, 1979, p.123) — they were deceiving the masses at the same time as they were heralding themselves as prophets. And such prophetic messianism was simply, as far as Marx was concerned, reactionary.

The key to understanding the reactionary nature of the utopian mindset can, in fact, be found in Marx's rejection of the means/ends dualism itself. For in *The Class Struggles in France* (1850) he condemns the 'party of *Anarchy*' for

> proclaiming itself the *means of emancipating the proletariat* and the emancipation of the latter as its *object*. Deliberate deception on the part of some; self-deception on the part of others, who give out the world transformed according to their own needs as the best world for all, as the realisation of all revolutionary claims and the elimination of all revolutionary collisions (ibid., p.122).

Marx thus rejects in its entirety the dualistic approach which posits an *end* towards which one seeks the appropriate *means*. For in formulating a system which corresponds to one's object, one is prophetically claiming for one's own pedantic cerebrations the status of 'the best world for all'.

This picture becomes clearer still if we closely examine the text most often used in *support* of the means/ends argument — the 'First Draft of *The Civil War in France*' (1871). For in response to claims that the Commune had not been socialist because it had not tried 'to establish in Paris a *phalanstère* nor an *Icarie*' (Marx, 1974c, p.262), Marx begins by pointing out that:

> All the socialist founders of sects belong to a period in which the working classes themselves were neither sufficiently trained nor organized by the march of capitalist society itself to enter as historical agents upon the world's stage (ibid.).

Utopian socialism belongs, in other words, to the early stages of capitalism — to a period in which the proletariat lacked any political initiative of its own. Marx continues:

> The utopian founders of sects, while in their criticism of present society clearly describing the goal of the social movement, the supersession of the wages system with all its economical conditions of class rule, found neither in society itself the material conditions of its transformation, nor in the working class the organized power and the conscience of the movement. They tried to compensate for the historical conditions of the movement by fantastic pictures and plans of a new society in whose propaganda they saw the true means of salvation (ibid.).

The utopians, *in their criticism of society* rather than in their utopias, described the goal of the social movement, which was the supersession of the wages system. The undeveloped state of both society and the proletariat, however, meant that this goal could not as yet be realised. In order to compensate for this, the utopians then devised fantastic pictures of a new world in which the wages system *had* been superseded. In spite of the fact that the wages system could not as yet be superseded, they then attempted to realise their fantasies by means of propaganda. Now comes the important part:

> From the moment the working men's class movement became real, the fantastic utopias evanesced, not because the working class had given up the end aimed at by these utopians, but because they had found the real means to realize them, and in their place came a real insight into the historic conditions of the movement and a more and more gathering force of the militant organization of the working class (ibid.).

What Marx is saying here is *not* that the working class had found the appropriate means of realising the utopians' utopias, but rather that they had found the appropriate means of realising the goal *aimed at* by the utopians, which was the supersession of the wages system. What the working class had discovered once it had constituted itself as a militant class was that a *real* insight into the movement of society, rather than a fantastic one, together with their own growing militancy, had become the appropriate means of superseding the wages system. And what this meant in turn was that the need for utopias had evanesced now that the proletariat had found something better to put '*in their place*'. Marx goes on:

> But the last two ends of the movement proclaimed by the utopians are the last ends proclaimed by the Paris revolution and by the International. Only the means are different, and the real conditions of the movement are no longer clouded in utopian fables (ibid.).

The last two ends to which Marx refers had earlier been described as 'the emancipation of labour, and the transformation of society' (ibid., p.261), so that once again when he argues that the means towards these ends are now different he is not referring to the utopians' *utopias*, which were merely fantastic descriptions of these general ends. What he is saying is that the means toward the emancipation of labour and the transformation of society have now been found in the real conditions of the movement *of* society, so that this movement no longer needs fantastic fables to hurry it along.

In fact, the whole point of this section of the draft had been to indicate that socialism was no longer synonymous with establishing utopias. In response to those who had argued that the Commune had not attempted to establish an *Icarie* and was therefore not 'socialist', Marx was emphasising the fact that establishing *Icaries* was no longer what socialism was about. Indeed, what Marx was arguing had nothing at all to do with what the means/ends dichotomy consensus has him arguing. For rather than propaganda being the 'utopian' means of realising socialist utopias, Marx was indicating that the socialist 'utopias' themselves, together with their propagation, were the 'utopian' *means* of realising the emancipation of labour. The pictures of a new society, far from being the 'ends' aimed at by the proletariat or the International, had been the *means* deployed in order to compensate for the lack of sufficiently developed material conditions. Once these conditions had developed, however, the appropriate means had become discernible, and an increasingly militant proletariat armed with a real insight into society took the place of utopias as a means of realising the emancipation of labour.

Speaking of those who still believed that socialism meant establishing *Icaries*, Marx concludes this section of the draft by remarking that:

> It is not the fault of the Paris proletariat, if for them the utopian creations of the prophets of the working men's movement are still the 'social revolution', that is to say, if the social revolution is for them still 'utopian' (ibid., pp.262-263).

This remark is instructive, for Marx quite clearly defines here what he means by the epithet 'utopian' — an understanding of the social revolution is utopian if it bases itself upon the utopian creations of prophets. Not only, therefore, does Marx specifically use the term 'prophets' to deride the utopians, thus supporting the argument to that effect being forwarded here, but he also uses the term 'utopian' to refer to their creations, i.e., their utopias, failing altogether to mention anything about the means proposed to realise them.

The whole discussion in the First Draft is nonetheless saturated by references to 'means' and 'ends', and one might therefore be tempted to argue that, whatever the conclusions reached by Marx, he reached them by embracing a means/ends dualism. Such temptations should, however, be firmly resisted. For what Marx is saying is that 'a real insight' into the conditions of the working class movement reveals that the means *are* the ends; that the two exist in a dialectical unity tied to the movement itself. The ends to which Marx refers, the emancipation of labour and the transformation of society, are to be realised *through* the transformation of the material conditions of society and *through* the self-emancipation of labour made possible by such a transformation. Marx is not suggesting that historical development has allowed him to grasp a genuine link between the utopians' descriptions of socialism and the real tendencies at work in society, thus rendering the descriptions non-utopian and shedding light on the means required to realise them; he is suggesting that a real insight into the tendencies at work in society has allowed him to grasp how and why society will be transformed and labour emancipated *without the aid* of descriptions of socialism — the ends are *contained within* the means and simply do not need (and cannot be) described.

In Marx's critique of utopian socialism one therefore finds a critique of both the utopians' means *and* their ends. This having been said, however, one can perhaps understand why it has been misconstrued as a critique solely of their means. For it just so happens that many of the utopians whom Marx criticised were openly anti-revolutionary, and it just so happens that their anti-revolutionary strategies were founded, at least as far as Marx was concerned, on theoretical frameworks lacking cognizance of the essential dynamics of capitalism. As a consequence, Marx often criticised them for forwarding anti-revolutionary strategies and for failing to understand the essential dynamics of capitalism. This was not, however, why Marx criticised them for being 'utopian'. Marx criticised them for being utopian because they constructed utopias and because the entire utopian approach was premised on a means/ends dualism that was *in and of itself* reactionary. It was the whole process of constructing an end — any end — towards the realisation of which one proposed some means — any means — that Marx was criticising. For in the very construction of their 'pictures and plans of a new society' the utopians were proclaiming themselves the prophets of the working class movement, blessed with a visionary gift denied to the masses. In constructing pictures of a world in which all revolutionary collisions are eliminated, the utopians were deceiving both themselves and everyone else into believing that this was the best world for all, when, in fact, it was nothing more than the world transformed according to their own needs and by their own pedantic cerebrations. Now, some of the utopians were so naïve as to believe that their world could be realised by peaceful persuasion, and Marx criticised them for their naiveté. Others, however, believed that their visions could only be realised by means of a revolutionary cataclysm, and yet Marx *still* criticised them for their naiveté. For in continuing to present their visions as the best world for all, these utopians had yet to understand that visions of the best world had now become irrelevant. As fantasies compensating for the fact that the material conditions for the emancipation of labour had yet to exist, the need for utopias evanesced as soon as these material conditions had come into existence. As far as the needs of the socialist movement were concerned, therefore, pictures and plans of the society of the future were evanescent, ephemeral, transitory things which, by definition, evanesced, i.e., vanished, once their time had passed.

Final confirmation of Marx's trenchant rejection of utopianism comes in *Herr Vogt* (1860). *Herr Vogt* is a text which is seldom referred to. This is a shame because in it Marx defends himself against his bourgeois denigrators and offers a personal historiography in which he explains exactly what he was trying to do at certain times and in certain texts. With regards to his involvement in the Communist League, Marx begins by explaining that 'we argued in popular form that it was not a matter of putting some utopian system into effect' (Marx, 1981, p.79). Note here that Marx was *not* arguing that it was a matter of putting utopian systems into effect by means that were somehow 'adequate' to the task — it was simply a matter of not putting such systems into effect full stop. In response to a criticism made by a certain Herr Techow, in which Marx is accused of creating his own system, Marx then draws his critic's attention to 'the *Manifesto* which criticises and, if he likes, "ridicules" socialist and critical utopianism of every kind' (ibid., p.90). If this message were not clear enough, Marx goes on to state that 'I rejected systems of *every* kind' (ibid.). Marx rejected systems of *every* kind. The emphasis is Marx's own and it indicates the passionate disbelief with which he greets the claim that he himself is a system-builder: has not Techow read the *Manifesto*, does he not realise that I rejected systems of *every* kind? Faced with Marx's response to such a claim, I find it difficult to agree with Levitas, Geoghegan and Suvin when they suggest that Marx criticised the utopians because they built their systems using ONLY reason and their heads instead of using these AND a correct analysis of the present. For Marx rejected systems of every kind, irrespective of what they were built with.

For Marx, the utopian process looked like this: one builds a system, declares oneself a prophet and then proclaims that the emancipation of humanity depends upon the realisation of one's system. It matters not whether the realisation of one's system is to be effected by peaceful or revolutionary means, for either way one's basic assumptions are 'silly, stale and reactionary from the roots up'. In arguing that the emancipation of humanity depends upon one's system being realised at all — and Fourier, Owen, Saint-Simon, the Saint-Simonians, Cabet and Weitling each argued this — one is implicitly assuming that the oppressed masses cannot devise their own emancipatory strategy and therefore need a prophetic system to guide them. Marx, on the other hand, 'ridicules' utopianism of *every* kind and rejects systems of *every* kind. Holding no truck with either the utopians' means or their ends, for they are each a part of the same problem, Marx rejects them both outright. For Marx, proletarian self-emancipation is both the means and the ends and this is a concept which utopian system-builders of every kind fail to understand; it is not a part of their language or mindset. Such is the second element of Marx's critique of utopianism.

The third element is, by comparison, quite straightforward. For given that the creation of the emancipated society is to be the work of the proletariat, the task of defining it will also be the work of that class. Thus remarks Engels in *The Origin of the Family, Private Property and the State* (1884):

> What we can conjecture at present about [what will take place] after the impending effacement of capitalist production is, in the main, of a negative character, limited mostly to what will vanish. But what will be added? That

will be settled after a new generation has grown up . . . Once such people appear, they will not care a rap about what we today think they should do. They will establish their own practice and their own public opinion, conformable therewith, on the practice of each individual — and that's the end of it (Engels, 1968d, p.508).

Neither Marx nor Engels could lay claim to a knowledge of the form that the future would take. Nor were they even going to conjecture on the subject for the form that the future will take will, as it should, be decided by the individuals who inhabit that future. This element of Marx's critique attracts the sympathy of both Lawrence Crocker and Vincent Geoghegan:

> The chief and best reason that Marx had such a low opinion of utopianism was his deep-seated belief that the task of designing and constructing the socialist society belongs properly to those who will create and live in it (Crocker, 1981, p.34).

> One of Marx and Engels' principal objections to utopianism was precisely that it would foreclose the future by substituting past and present obsessions for the creative novelty of the proletariat (Geoghegan, 1990, p.64).

'The creative novelty of the proletariat' is a nice phrase and it serves to underline Marx's critique of utopianism as a whole. For it was precisely because the proletariat now possessed a creative novelty of its own that it no longer required utopian prophets to inspire it, and it was precisely because it possessed such a creative novelty that it could determine for itself the shape of the society that it would both construct and inhabit.

Conclusion

In popular mythology, Marx the utopian humanist has often been pitted against Marx the scientific anti-utopian. What I have been arguing here, however, is that Marx's anti-utopianism was actually founded on two thoroughly *humanist* principles — the principles of proletarian self-emancipation and self-determination. Contrary to those who forward the means/ends dichotomy argument, Marx did not focus his critical attention on the means by which the utopians sought to realise their visions; he focused his attention instead on the utopian process itself. For Marx, political utopianism implied a process of prophetic messianism based on deceit which foreclosed the future and denied the proletariat the right to form its own self-determining emancipatory strategy. It was therefore in and of itself silly, stale and reactionary.

Moreover, Marx's critique was entirely accurate. He did not misrepresent or distort the ideas of the 'utopian socialists', for each of them *did* construct imaginary visions of an alternative state or society; each of them *did* claim that their respective visions were 'true'; each of them *did* assume the role of messiah and each of them *did* argue that the emancipation of humanity depended entirely upon the realisation of their own particular vision. Summarising Marx's position as a whole now, I offer the following five propositions:

i) that Marx understood the utopian socialists to be utopian in the sense that they painted fantastic pictures of the future structure of society or dreamed about the model society of the future.

ii) that in spite of their scientific claims, the utopians were utopian because all pictures of the future structure of society are fantastic and all descriptions of the model society of the future are dream-like. One simply cannot know the form that the society of the future will take and descriptions of it are therefore always utopian.

iii) that utopian socialism as a movement corresponded to the early stages of capitalism, i.e., to a period during which the proletariat lacked any initiative of its own. Because the proletariat could not constitute itself as a militant class, the early socialist movement sought to reconstruct society 'from above'. Thus emerged a group of utopian prophets whose fantastic pictures reflected the proletariat's own fantastic conception of itself.

iv) that utopian socialism as a movement became a political anachronism once the proletariat *had* gained an initiative of its own and *could* constitute itself as a militant class. More than this, in fact, utopian socialism became silly, stale and reactionary in proportion as the class struggle developed.

v) that utopian socialism was silly and stale because playing with fantastic pictures, precisely because they are fantastic, only diverts one from the struggle of the present. Those who continued to paint these fantastic pictures did so from within a utopian framework which claimed for the utopian the exalted role of prophet and claimed for his or her pictures the status of humanity's only hope of salvation. Such naïve political elitism ignored the fact that humanity's salvation, or what amounts to the same thing, the emancipation of the proletariat, rested solely in the hands of the proletariat itself. Such elitism was therefore reactionary. Furthermore, by suggesting that the emancipation of humanity depended upon the realisation of such and such a fantastic picture, the utopians were foreclosing the future and depriving the proletariat of the right to determine for itself what the future holds. This too was reactionary.

Such was Marx's critique of utopian socialism, a critique directed neither at the means proposed by the utopians nor at the manner in which they constructed their systems, but rather at the activity of constructing systems altogether. This, then, is the first element of Marx's 'anti-utopian utopianism'. It is time now to discuss the second — his 'utopianism'.

Note

1   John Torrance offers a more sophisticated version of the means/ends argument. For whilst he accepts that Marx's critique is centred around the utopianism (in the traditional sense) of the utopians' ends (1995, p.270), he suggests that this critique itself should be understood in light of Marx's absorption of the Jacobin 'myth of proletarian revolution', a myth which the utopians consciously rejected (ibid., pp.406-407). Again, however, this fails to account for someone like Weitling, who had absorbed the myth of proletarian revolution like a sponge but whom Marx nonetheless described as a 'utopian socialist'.

2 Marx's Description of the Lower Phase of Communism

Introduction

Was Marx a 'utopian'? Did he describe, in a variety of aspects and with some consistency, an imaginary state or society which he regarded as better, in some respects at least, than the one in which he lived? In the following two chapters I explore this question at length. Given that Marx himself divides the communist future into two halves or 'phases', I will divide my own discussion into two halves, with this chapter focusing on the dictatorship of the proletariat and the following chapter focusing on full communism.

With regards to how I differentiate between the two, it will be assumed here that whenever Marx talks about communism or socialism he is referring to its higher stage, unless, that is, he *specifically* states that he is referring to its lower stage. This is because Marx himself never made a distinction between communism and socialism as historical 'stages' — the idea that 'socialism' refers to the lower stage and 'communism' the higher post-dates Marx and is generally attributed to Lenin. By assuming that Marx used the terms communism and socialism to refer to the same stage of historical development, unless he specifically stated otherwise, one can avoid the difficulties which arise from reading Lenin's distinction back into Marx. Stanley Moore provides a good indication of what these difficulties are when he agonises over the content of *Capital* thus:

> Nowhere does Marx clearly separate the transition to socialism from the transition to communism. The passage predicting expropriation of the expropriators — in the section entitled "Historical Tendency of Capitalist Accumulation" — is his nearest approach to predicting a transition from capitalism to socialism. Yet the language of that passage is so vague that it can be read as predicting transition to either socialism or communism. The passage predicting disappearance of commodity fetishism — in the section entitled "The Fetishism of Commodities and Its Secret" — is his nearest approach to predicting a transition to communism. Yet the context of that passage indicates that this prediction could be fulfilled by either communism

or socialism (1980, p.52).

Unlike Moore I do not see a conundrum here. For there is no good reason to believe that when Marx talks about the transition to socialism or communism in *Capital* he is talking about anything other than the transition to full communism. This goes for all of Marx's other works as well, except those in which he tells us that he is not talking about the transition to full communism.

Having made this distinction, what I argue here is that Marx's description of the lower phase cannot really be seen as a part of that which is referred to as his 'utopia'. This in turn is part of the wider argument — to be continued in chapter 3 — which suggests that the term 'utopia' can only really be applied to a limited number of specific concepts in Marx's thought.

The Lower Phase and the Theory of Permanent Revolution

Marx specifically referred to the lower phase of communism in four of his works — the *Manifesto*, *The Class Struggles in France*, *The Civil War in France* and the *Critique of the Gotha Programme*.[1] This in itself seems rather odd. For if Marx always thought that a transitional lower phase was a necessary precondition for the development of 'full communism', then why did he mention it in only four of his works? Why, in other words, did he not mention it in all of the works in which he talked about the transition to communism? The answer to be forwarded here is that Marx *did not* always believe that a transitional phase was necessary because the model of a transitional phase was only ever utilised in the context of his theory of 'permanent revolution'.

Although this theory remained nameless until the 'Address of the Central Committee to the Communist League' of March 1850 — talking of the German workers, Marx and Engels ended the Address by proclaiming that: 'Their battle-cry must be: The Permanent Revolution' (Marx and Engels, 1973, p.330) — its substance can be traced back to the *Manifesto*.[2] The substance of the theory itself is now so familiar that it seems rather simplistic: applied to societies which have yet to complete their bourgeois phase of revolution, the theory states that when the bourgeoisie have completed this phase and want to stop the revolutionary process in its tracks, the proletariat must take the helm and ensure that the revolution continues to proceed as far as socialism. As Marx and Engels remark in their Address of March 1850:

> While the democratic petty bourgeois want to bring the revolution to an end as quickly as possible, achieving at most the aims already mentioned ('welfare measures' and 'an extension of state employment'), it is our interest and our task to make the revolution permanent until all the more or less propertied classes have been driven from their ruling positions, until the proletariat has conquered state power and until . . . the decisive forces of production are concentrated in the hands of the workers (ibid., pp.323-324).

The theory of permanent revolution was specifically designed to deal with imperfect revolutionary situations — situations in which Marx had to explain the transition to communism in a society which had yet to complete its bourgeois phase of development. What I argue here is that the 'dictatorship of the proletariat' was also part of this theory; indeed an indispensable part. For it was by means of the dictatorship that the bourgeois phase of development was to be completed in those societies in which it was as yet incomplete, and the purpose of the dictatorship was *nothing other* than to complete this phase of development. As such, it was more a stage of capitalism than a stage of communism — a stage required *only* in societies lacking a developed capitalist framework and *precisely* in order to develop this framework. In what follows I attempt to defend this interpretation by examining in detail the four works in which Marx specifically talks about the lower phase of communism.

The Lower Phase in the *Manifesto* and *The Class Struggles in France*

In the *Manifesto* Marx and Engels tell us that 'the bourgeois revolution in Germany will be but the prelude to an immediately following proletarian revolution' (Marx and Engels, 1967, p.120). This, in a nutshell, is the theory of permanent revolution, a theory founded on the following claim:

> The bourgeoisie finds itself involved in a constant battle. At first with the aristocracy; later on, with those portions of the bourgeoisie itself, whose interests have become antagonistic to the progress of industry; at all times, with the bourgeoisie of foreign countries. In all these battles it sees itself compelled to appeal to the proletariat, to ask for its help, and thus, to drag it into the political arena (ibid., p.90).

The politicisation of the proletariat is both a consequence of the bourgeois revolution and a precondition for the 'immediately following' socialist one. For once they have developed political interests and have become a political force, the proletarians will be able to take 'the first step in the revolution by the working class', which is 'to raise' themselves 'to the position of ruling class, to win the battle of democracy' (ibid., p.104). This notion of 'the proletariat raised to the position of ruling class' is the first formulation of that which was to find a name in 'the dictatorship of the proletariat', and Hal Draper neatly explains its relationship to the theory of 'permanent revolution' in the following way:

> A German revolution would have to be pushed forward and still forward, from stage to stage, pressing leftward, until power could be taken by the extreme left, the revolutionary proletariat. This is the process which Marx summarized as 'permanent (that is, ongoing or continuous) revolution,' a revolution which does not come to a halt until the proletariat had taken power. It is this conclusion that introduced the question of proletarian power (or, same thing, proletarian 'dictatorship') into Marx's writings (Draper, 1990, p.294; 1987, p.17).

As Draper himself goes to great lengths to point out, in the nineteenth century the term 'dictatorship' meant nothing more than 'an emergency management of power, especially outside of normal legality' (1990, p.290). The process described in the *Manifesto*, therefore, sees the proletariat being dragged into the political arena during the course of the bourgeois revolution, and this revolution itself then being pressed continually leftward until the proletariat wins the battle of democracy and assumes dictatorial powers.

Once the proletariat had raised itself to the position of ruling class, it was to introduce a ten-point programme which the *Manifesto* famously describes thus:

> 1. Abolition of property in land and application of all rents of land to public purposes.
> 2. A heavy progressive or graduated income tax.
> 3. Abolition of all right of inheritance.
> 4. Confiscation of the property of all emigrants and rebels.
> 5. Centralisation of credit in the hands of the State, by means of a national bank with State capital and an exclusive monopoly.
> 6. Centralisation of the means of communication and transport in the hands of the State.
> 7. Extension of factories and instruments of production owned by the State; the bringing into cultivation of wastelands, and the improvement of the soil generally in accordance with a common plan.

> 8. Equal liability of all to labour. Establishment of industrial armies, especially for agriculture.
> 9. Combination of agriculture with manufacturing industries ...
> 10. Free education for all children in public schools . . . (Marx and Engels, 1967, pp.104-105).

In an excellent article, Wagner and Strauss point to the curious fact that 'the plan does not include several important socialist measures which were accepted — not least by the authors of the programme themselves — as essential to the completion of a socialist structure. The plan does not include the total socialization of the means of production. It does not demand or necessitate the abolition of hired labour or the elimination of the profit derived by the employer from its use. Finally, the plan does not include the nationalization of commerce' (1969, p.471). As is rightly emphasised here, the elimination of wage-labour and the profits derived by the capitalist from it were fundamental to Marx's conception of socialism. Indeed, the antagonism between capital and labour was seen as a very function of the system of wage-labour itself. Why, then, would a proletariat which had raised itself to the position of ruling class not aim to eliminate the source of its own exploitation?

It seems to me that the only possible answer to this question can be that Marx considered it practically unfeasible for the proletariat to do so (one can assume, that is, that if the supersession of the wages system had been deemed feasible then Marx would have advocated the measures required in order to facilitate it). If, however, the conditions were not yet ripe for the abolition of wage-labour or for the elimination of private production, then what was the function of the dictatorship going to be? Well, it seems fair to conclude on the basis of the outline provided by the famous ten-point programme that, once raised to the position of ruling class, the proletariat would strive to foster conditions that were ripe *for* the development of socialism. In other words, the *Manifesto*'s proposals did not define any socialist 'goal' but described instead, in circumstances where conditions were not yet ripe for the abolition of capitalism, the measures to be taken in order to render these conditions ripe.

Of particular importance is the fact that the dictatorship would ripen the conditions for socialism by facilitating the development of *capital*. As Wagner and Strauss rightly indicate, points 1, 5, 6, 7 and 8 of the *Manifesto*'s programme were each intended to rationalise capitalistic production rather than displace it (Wagner and Strauss, 1969, pp.471-472). Point 1, for example, still allowed for the private use of land and for the employment of wage-labour and the intention behind it seems to have been to stabilise the agricultural production process by eliminating the unpredictable forces generated by rentiers and speculators; point 6 had the railways specifically in mind, and their centralised ownership would put a stop to the perennial disruptions caused by the existing system of unequal transportation tariffs for competing firms; point 7 envisioned a public sector developing *alongside* the private sector, rather than in place of it, in order to extend the remit of productive capital; and point 8 sought to utilise the full labour force in order to facilitate increased production.

For Wagner and Strauss, however, the key to understanding the programme as a whole lies in point 5, behind which one finds the distinction made by Marx between the spheres of circulation and production and his emphatic belief that the former only hindered the development of the latter. Thus says Marx:

> The credit system, which has its focus in the so-called national banks and the big money-lenders and usurers surrounding them, constitutes enormous centralization, and gives to this class of parasites the fabulous power, not only to periodically despoil industrial capitalists, but also to interfere in actual production in a most dangerous manner — and this gang knows nothing about production and has nothing to do with it (Marx, 1959, p.532).

Citing this passage, Wagner and Strauss indicate that point 5 was designed to remove the credit system from the hands of 'this gang' in order to prevent them from interfering in production. Indeed, they go on to argue that the aim of the programme *as a whole* was to reform the sphere of circulation by placing it under state control whilst leaving the sphere of production well alone. They thus conclude by saying that 'the removal of the circulation mechanisms from private ownership and their transfer into the hands of society will not only not harm productive capital but is even calculated to help it' (Wagner and Strauss, 1969, p.478).

What needs to be emphasised here, then, is that the proletariat raised to the position of ruling class would rule over a system that was still in essence capitalistic. Moreover, whilst points 2 and 3 sought to rid the present system of its most grotesque inequalities, the *Manifesto*'s programme as a whole was designed to rationalise capitalism and render its productive sphere more efficient. The purpose behind this, as has already been indicated, was to foster conditions that were ripe for the development of socialism in a country in which these conditions were not as yet ripe. F. L. Bender provides a neat summary of the underlying aim of the *Manifesto*'s programme when he suggests that:

> Marx was writing for the proletariat of economically under-developed Germany, so that many of the measures advocated in the *Manifesto* are supposed to bring the economy through industrialization stages similar to those already attained under bourgeois rule in the more developed countries (1990, p.364).

The *Manifesto*'s programme was written with economically underdeveloped Germany in mind, and rather than constituting a 'utopian' alternative world the first stage of communism here becomes a means of reproducing developments that have already taken place in the economically developed countries of the existing one. In the *Manifesto* itself, of course, Marx says that 'in the most advanced countries' the ten-point programme 'will be pretty generally applicable' (Marx and Engels, 1967, p.104). Given the context in which it was written, however (i.e., the reality of a bourgeois revolution), it would be reasonable to conclude that when Marx referred to 'the most advanced countries' he was talking of those that were themselves on the verge of a bourgeois revolution and whose bourgeois revolution could, like Germany's, be hijacked and rendered 'permanent'. He was not referring to 'advanced' countries like England or the Netherlands, whose bourgeois revolutions had taken place long ago, but rather advanced countries like France (as opposed to, say, India) who were now ready to undergo the process of 'permanent' revolution.

What I would suggest here, then, is that Marx only ever talked about the lower phase of communism in the context of countries which had yet to complete their bourgeois phase of development and whose economies were therefore relatively under-developed. The function of the lower phase in this context was then to develop the foundations of capitalism itself, as indeed the *Manifesto*'s ten-point programme was intended to do. From this I would further suggest that the *Manifesto*'s programme for the first stage of communism was designed to develop capitalism's productive forces and social relations, benefit the industrial bourgeoisie of economically underdeveloped Germany, and speed up the process of industrialisation so that German capitalism could reach the point at which, as was already the case in the more economically developed nations, the conditions for 'full' communism had been given sufficient scope to develop within it's womb. In other words, because the conditions for full communism only ripen and become discernible within a fully-developed capitalist framework, the purpose of the dictatorship was to ensure that the economically under-developed countries reached the stage of 'full' capitalism sooner rather than later.

This kind of approach allows one to understand the link established in the *Manifesto* between the lower and higher phases of communism. For Marx tells us that the ten measures in the *Manifesto*'s programme will, 'in the course of the movement, outstrip themselves, necessitate further inroads upon the old social order' (Marx and Engels, 1967, p.104). He then says that:

> When, in the course of development, class distinctions have disappeared, and all production has been concentrated in the hands of a vast association of the whole nation, the public power will lose its political character . . . In place of the old bourgeois society, with its classes and class antagonisms, we shall have an association, in which the free development of each is the condition for the free development of all (ibid., p.105).

What Marx is saying here is that there is a natural and *necessary* relationship between the ten-point programme and the characteristics of full communism he outlines. Unfortunately, however, he never attempts to demonstrate the existence of such a relationship. Instead, as Stanley Moore succinctly puts it: 'Pronouncement takes the place of reasoning' (1980, p.30). If one adopts the approach being forwarded here, however, then Marx's reasoning becomes quite clear. For if he believed that a fully developed capitalism creates the conditions which allow for the realisation of full communism, and if the function of the dictatorship of the proletariat was to facilitate the development of full capitalism, then the link between the two phases becomes so obvious that Marx need only pronounce it.

Such an understanding also sheds light on Marx's discussion of the dictatorship in *The Class Struggles in France*, in which he states that:

> Socialism is the *declaration of the permanence of the revolution*, the *class dictatorship* of the proletariat as the necessary transit point to the *abolition of class distinctions generally*, to the abolition of all the relations of production on which they rest, to the abolition of all the social relations that correspond to these relations of production, to the revolutionizing of all the ideas that result from these social relations (Marx, 1979, p.123).

The dictatorship does not *itself* abolish class distinctions; it does not *itself* abolish capitalist relations of production or their corresponding social relations; it does not *itself* revolutionise the ideas resulting from these social relations; it merely represents the *necessary transit point* to them. The dictatorship prepares the way for the abolition of capitalist forces and relations, and it prepares the way for a revolutionising of ideas, but it does not do any of the abolishing or revolutionising itself. Why not?

Well, as was the case with the *Manifesto*, Marx was writing for the proletariat of an economically under-developed nation — a nation whose economic foundations could not as yet support the development of full communism. As Engels candidly remarks in his 1895 Introduction to *The Class Struggles in France*, 'the state of economic development on the Continent at that time was not, by a long way, ripe for the elimination of capitalist production' (Engels, 1979, p.15). In that work, therefore, Marx had to concede that: 'The struggle against capital in its developed, modern form, in its decisive aspect, the struggle of the industrial wage-worker against the industrial bourgeois, is in France a partial phenomenon' (Marx, 1979, p.41). Because of this, it was now the proletariat's task 'to consolidate the shaky bourgeois relationships' (ibid., p.47) and to achieve communism by means of the dictatorship that would emerge from the permanence of the bourgeois revolution. To *consolidate* the shaky *bourgeois* relationships was what the dictatorship of the proletariat was going to do, and it was going to do this because the bourgeois relationships *had to be* consolidated if they were ever to become impregnated with the seeds of communism.

In both the *Manifesto* and *The Class Struggles in France*, then, Marx was talking about societies which had yet to complete their bourgeois phases of development and which could not, therefore, be expected to generate the conditions necessary for the realisation of full communism without a great deal of mediating help. This help Marx supplied in the form of the dictatorship of the proletariat, the function and purpose of which would be to develop the *capitalist* forces and the *bourgeois* relations of production. Only by means of such a dictatorship could full communism hope to gestate within the womb of an incomplete and immature capitalist framework.

The Lower Phase in *The Civil War in France*

Many commentators have detected a niggling ambiguity in Marx's attitude towards the Paris Commune. For on the one hand, in *The Civil War in France*, he specifically stated that:

> Yes, gentlemen, the Commune intended to abolish class-property which makes the labour of the many the wealth of the few. It aimed at the expropriation of the expropriators. It wanted to make individual property a truth by transforming the means of production, land and capital, now chiefly the means of enslaving and exploiting labour, into mere instruments of free

and associated labour — But this is Communism (Marx, 1968e, pp.290-291).

On the other hand, however, in the first draft of this Address, Marx claimed that: 'The principal measures taken by the Commune are taken for the salvation of the middle class' (Marx, 1974c, p.258). More ambiguous still is the fact that that Marx, in a letter written ten years after the event, remarked that 'the majority of the Commune was in no wise socialist, nor could it be' (Marx and Engels, 1969, p.410).

These ambiguities have been explained in various ways. Alistair Horne, for example, argues that Marx deliberately misrepresented the facts in *The Civil War in France* and thus 'distorted the Commune to create a myth portraying something it never was' (1981, p.352); Richard Adamiak suggests that Marx did not really support the Commune at all and was actually forced into singing its praises by the popularity it enjoyed within the Left as a whole (1970, p.11); Monty Johnstone claims that his talk of the Commune being communist but not socialist, proletarian but for the salvation of the middle-class, etc., was part and parcel of 'Marx's concept of proletarian hegemony', which sought to unite the workers, petty-bourgeoisie and peasantry in order to lay the foundation for the future construction of communism (1971, p.448); and Shlomo Avineri argues that, for Marx, the Commune 'as it actually was', '*in actu*', was in no wise socialist, but that '*in potentia*', 'as it could be', it was the harbinger of communism (1968, p.240).

Whilst each of these explanations has something to commend it (there is no doubt, for example, that Marx *had* to praise the Commune, whether he wanted to or not, and there is no doubt either that an element of mythologising crept into his account), Avineri's seems to me to be the most convincing. What is lacking in Avineri's account, however, is an explanation for the gulf which existed between the Commune *in actu* and the Commune *in potentia*, and for why, therefore, Marx felt the need to distinguish between the two. If, however, one interprets the Commune in terms of the concept of the dictatorship of the proletariat being forwarded here, then (hopefully at least) the reason for this gulf (and thus for the apparent ambiguities in Marx's analysis of the Commune) should become clear.

This interpretation begins by accepting that Marx equated the Paris Commune with the dictatorship of the proletariat. For although he did not specifically use this term in *The Civil War in France*, Engels, in his 1891 Introduction, did: 'Look at the Paris Commune. That was the Dictatorship of the Proletariat' (Engels, 1968b, p.259). More importantly, as Hal Draper helpfully points out, Engels, in making this remark, was merely repeating what Marx had said at the London meeting of the International in September 1871 (Draper, 1990, p.306; 1987, p.31). Now, given that the Commune, *qua* dictatorship, was the first stage of communism, it was obvious (to Marx at least) that its *aim* was full communism. Hence the famous remark to this effect noted above, and hence the language of this passage — the Commune *intended* to abolish class property, *aimed* at the expropriation of the expropriators, and so on. Given also, however, that the need for a dictatorship only arises in circumstances of economic underdevelopment, and that its purpose is to facilitate the development of *capitalism*, it almost goes without saying that the measures it effects will be to the advantage of the middle class. Given finally that a well-developed critical consciousness is unlikely to emerge from within the confines of undeveloped capitalism, it should come as no surprise to find that the majority of the Commune were 'in no wise socialist', or at least not in the sense by which Marx understood the term. In this way, one can make sense of those apparent ambiguities and render them, whilst maybe not completely unambiguous, certainly less so. Let us now look at Marx's analysis of the Commune and see if this interpretation can be supported.

Marx begins his analysis with the events of September 4th 1870, when Paris, in response to Louis Napoleon's surrender to Bismarck, declared itself a Republic. Now, whilst in *The Civil War in France* he considered the seeds of the Commune to have been sown by these events, the view of the Republic he had held *prior* to the existence of the Commune had not been so magnanimous. In fact, the Second Address to the General Council of the International, which he had given just five days after the Republic had been proclaimed, makes for rather depressing reading. When compared to *The Civil War in France*, moreover, it seems to confirm the existence of those ambiguities I am trying here to avoid confirming.

For in the Second Address he had described the Republic 'not as a social conquest, but as a national measure of defence' (Marx, 1968d, p.269), whereas in *The Civil War* he termed it 'the revolution of the 4th of September' (Marx, 1968e, p.279); in the Second Address, he had warned *against* an insurrection — 'Any attempt at upsetting the new Government in the present crisis, when the enemy is almost knocking at the doors of Paris, would be a desperate folly' (1968d, p.269) — whereas in *The Civil War* he heralded the 'glorious working men's Revolution of the 18th March' (1968e, p.280); in the Second Address, he preached gradualism to the workers — 'Let them calmly and resolutely improve the opportunities of Republican liberty, for the work of their own class organisation. It will gift them with fresh Herculean powers for the regeneration of France, and our common task – the emancipation of labour' (1968d, p.269) — whereas in *The Civil War*, he had seen the workers 'discover', *through* insurrection, 'the political form under which to work out the emancipation of labour' (1968e, p.290).

Examined in the light of *The Civil War in France*, then, it seems that Marx, in his Second Address, had been wrong about everything. Was this just a mistake on his part, or had he been forced to change his tune in response to the popular support the Commune had established? I think that neither is the case and would suggest instead that in the seven months which separate the two Addresses Marx had rediscovered the concept of the dictatorship of the proletariat, a concept which had lain abandoned since 1850.[3]

That the concept had lain abandoned is hardly surprising, for a lot of things had happened since 1850 to warrant exactly that. We may recall here that in *The Class Struggles in France* Marx had been advocating, nay predicting, a dictatorship to 'consolidate the shaky bourgeois relationships' that had been established by the unfinished bourgeois revolution of February 1848. By the end of 1851, however, his hopes had been shattered and he penned *The Eighteenth Brumaire of Louis Bonaparte*. Writing in the wake of Bonaparte (aka Louis Napoleon aka Napoleon III)'s coup d'état of December 2nd, Marx despairingly opined that:

> On December 2 the February Revolution is conjured away by a card sharper's trick, and what seems overthrown is no longer the monarchy but the liberal concessions that were wrung from it by centuries of struggle. Instead of *society* having conquered a new content for itself, it seems that the *state* only returned in its oldest form, to the shamelessly simple domination of the sabre and the cowl. This is the answer to the *coup de main* of February 1848, given by the *coup de tête* of December 1851. Easy come, easy go (Marx, 1968c, p.98).

Instead of proclaiming a dictatorship of the proletariat in order to complete the unfinished bourgeois revolution of 1848, the French workers had allowed society to regress. Rather than dispensing with the remnants of feudalism, they had resurrected them. 'Society now seems to have fallen back behind its point of departure', said Marx (ibid., p.99).

With the events of 1848 having told him that 'the German workers cannot come to power and achieve the realization of their class interests without passing through a protracted revolutionary development' (Marx and Engels, 1973, p.330); with the events of 1851 having dashed his faith in the French proletariat; with capitalism now entering an extended period of prosperous stability; with all the movements of the European Left in disarray as a result of this and their subsequent dwindling support; with all of this, is it any wonder that Marx abandoned the idea of the dictatorship of the proletariat and refused to entertain even the prospect of its appearance for the next twenty years?

Is it any wonder too that when Paris declared itself a Republic in 1870, Marx proceeded to examine it with caution? He had played with fire once, in 1850. Then he had predicted the permanence of the revolution of 1848 and the immanence of the class dictatorship of the proletariat. In 1851, however, his fingers had been well and truly burned by the victory of Louis Bonaparte and the Royalist counter-revolutionaries. In 1870, therefore, he regarded the new flame of the Paris Republic with suspicion: 'Is the Republic, by some of its middle-class managers, not intended to serve as a mere stopgap and bridge over an Orleanist Restoration?', he asked, wary of the fact that Restorations have a habit of following revolutions (Marx, 1968d, p.269). For this reason, he, unlike many on the Left, preached patience. Speaking of the German workers for whom the Republic signalled the end of Bonaparte's Second Empire, he said: 'Like them, we hail the advent of the Republic in France, but at the same time we labour under misgivings which we hope will prove groundless' (ibid.). These misgivings were that the hopes of 1870, like those of 1850, would be dashed against a counter-revolutionary coup.

These misgivings were, however, much to Marx's delight and probably even more to his surprise, to prove groundless. For on the 18th March 1871 the National Guard took control of the Government offices, and on the 28th the Commune was proclaimed. More than this, the Commune seemed to bear out Marx's theory of permanent revolution and truly represent the dictatorship of the proletariat he had spoken of twenty years earlier. It was 'the form at last discovered under which to work out the emancipation of labour' (Marx, 1968e, p.290). One can almost hear the sigh of relief as Marx wrote those words — 'the form *at last* discovered'. At last! This is what he had been waiting twenty years to see, and he could hardly believe his eyes.

With hindsight, Marx could now see that the Republic of September 1870 had been the first stage in the process of permanent revolution. He had not *changed his mind* since the Second Address. Instead, what he had *hoped* would happen, but dare not say for fear of burning his fingers once more, had happened. For the Republic, which *was* initially, as Marx had said, a purely defensive mechanism, mutated into a revolution as Thiers repeatedly demanded that Paris disarm itself. At first, the revolution was of a bourgeois nature — a revolution of 'kindly-minded liberals' as Alistair Horne has termed it (1981, p.97) — as can be evinced by the fact that

Trochu, the 'people's' choice for leader, would only accept the position on condition that the Republic aimed to uphold religion, property and the family, a condition with which most people were happy to comply. And the revolution remained essentially bourgeois in nature until January 28th 1871, when Fauvre signed the armistice with Prussia.

In contrast to 1848, however, the revolution did not end here. Quite the contrary: for a number of reasons — the humiliating terms of the armistice, dismay at the prospect of having to face these terms after the hunger, cold and heavy bombardment the Parisians had experienced over Christmas, and the fact that many of the bourgeois Republicans had fled Paris after the armistice — the Parisians voted in favour of the Republic, and against peace, in the forced elections of February 8th. When Thiers, in response to this, allowed the Prussians the benefit of a victory march through Paris, when he suppressed the powers and abolished the paid status of the National Guard, when he placed a reactionary puppet at its helm, and when he passed a death sentence on Blanqui and all the other potential leaders of subversion he could identify, the National Guard seized two hundred army cannons. When Thiers then attempted to suppress the Guard, they took over the government offices and ten days later proclaimed the Commune.

This brief historical digression reveals just how much Marx must have thought that the Commune had confirmed his ideas — the revolution of bourgeois liberals had become 'permanent' as the workers, personified in the National Guard (a democratic army of workers created by the bourgeoisie during the course of their own revolution), took command, won the battle of democracy, and raised themselves to the level of ruling class.

With regards to Marx's interpretation of the Commune itself, critics tend to pounce on two paragraphs in particular. The first we encountered at the beginning of this section, and in it Marx tells us that the Commune aimed at the abolition of class property and the socialisation of the means of production. The second, which immediately follows the first in Marx's text, reads thus:

> The working class . . . have no ready-made utopias to introduce *par décret du people.* They know that in order to work out their own emancipation, and along with it that higher form to which present society is irresistibly tending by its own economical agencies, they will have to pass through long struggles, through a series of historical processes, transforming circumstances and men. They have no ideals to realise, but to free the elements of the new society with which the old collapsing bourgeois society itself is pregnant (Marx, 1968e, p.291).

In both these paragraphs Marx is quite clearly talking about 'full' communism, and his critics tend to respond by pointing out that the Commune *did not* intend to abolish private property, nor was it aiming to free the elements of the new society with which the collapsing present one was pregnant. It was, instead, a petty bourgeois, Proudhonist ensemble whose radical achievements were noticeable only by their absence. Because Marx was seemingly oblivious to this fact, people such as Alistair Horne make it their business to claim that Marx 'distorted' the facts 'for his own dialectical ends' (1981, p.15).

We must distinguish here, however, between Marx's analysis of the immediate aims of the Commune and his long-term projections. For whereas the paragraphs in question represent the latter, the rest of *The Civil War in France* deals only with the former. Marx's critics are right, of course, to highlight an incongruity between the two, for there is no necessary relationship between what Marx describes as the Commune's *immediate* aims — the suppression of the standing army and the police, the reduction of all wages down to workmen's levels, the disestablishment of all churches, the provision of universal education, the use of universal suffrage and the abolition of nightwork for bakers (Marx, 1968e, pp.287-294) — and what he describes as its *ultimate* aim, namely, to abolish class property and usher in full communism. It is nonetheless unfair to accredit this incongruity to Marx's sinister dialectical distortions.

The incongruity only emerges, in fact, because Marx believed that the higher phase of communism would develop naturally as the processes initiated by the dictatorship 'outstripped themselves'. Whilst he was wrong to think this, the fact that Marx did think this should influence the way in which we look at his analysis of the Commune. For if Marx only ever talked about the lower phase in relation to economically under-developed countries and as a means of developing capitalism, then it implies that Marx *did not* think that the Commune itself was going to realise full communism — it implies instead that he considered it 'the necessary transit point to the abolition of class distinctions'. In the sense, therefore, that the long-term economic development resulting from the existence of the Commune would *lead* to a situation whereby class property could be abolished, Marx could talk about this being the Commune's intention. But because the Commune *itself* could not abolish class property, Marx quite sensibly declines from saying that this represented its *immediate* aim.

Indeed, Marx specifically described the purpose of the Commune *qua* dictatorship of the proletariat, and this purpose was *not* the realisation of full communism — it was 'the revolutionary overthrow of the political and social conditions that had engendered the Second Empire, and, under its fostering care, matured into utter rottenness' (Marx, 1968e, p.280). Its purpose was, in other words, to overthrow the remnants of the feudal relations that had been supporting the Second Empire since 1851, relations which had been ripe for overthrow in 1848 and which now, over two decades later, had become 'utterly rotten'. In this sense, the Commune differed from the ten-point programme outlined in the *Manifesto*. For that programme was designed to further the advance of full capitalism *directly*, by removing various obstacles to the optimal development of productive capital. The Commune, however, at least as Marx saw it, had neither the time nor the opportunity to effect any major economic changes. What it did do, however, was further the advance of full capitalism *indirectly* by striking at a number of broad social fetters; the church, army, police, electoral system and so on. This is why Marx later describes the Commune's purpose as the 'incubation of a new society' (ibid., p.296). Not the *realisation* of a new society, nor its *creation*, but its incubation. The Commune, in other words, was to free France of all the rotten feudal baggage that had been preventing the full development of communism's 'host', i.e., capitalism. Reverting to the metaphorical language of the womb so beloved by Marx, the Commune, as with all proletarian dictatorships, was to act as a surrogate mother, bearing the child that economically under-developed capitalism could not conceive. The Commune, that is, and again like all other proletarian dictatorships, resembled a capitalist mother far more than it did any communist child.

The Lower Phase in the 'Critique of the Gotha Programme'

In the 'Critique of the Gotha Programme' we find the final instalment of Marx's tale of communism's lower phase. Of it he says:

> What we have to deal with here is a communist society, not as it has *developed* on its own foundations, but, on the contrary, just as it *emerges* from capitalist society; which is thus in every respect, economically, morally and intellectually, still stamped with the birth marks of the old society from whose womb it emerges (Marx, 1968f, p.319).

What we have to deal with *where*? Well, what Marx was dealing with was the Lassallean-inspired programme for the Gotha Unity Congress. What he was dealing with in particular, however, was Lassalle's conception of socialism and more importantly still with how, in formulating it, Lassalle had 'falsified' the *Manifesto* 'so grossly' (ibid., p.322).

The first thing the Lassalleans had falsified was Marx's analysis of the bourgeoisie. For in the programme, this class, together with all other non-proletarians, had been described as 'one reactionary mass' (ibid.). In the 'Critique', therefore, Marx saw it as his duty to remind them that in the *Manifesto* the 'bourgeoisie is here conceived as a revolutionary class — as the bearer of large-scale industry' (ibid.). Engels expands upon this point in a letter to Bebel which also deals with the Gotha Programme:

> In the first place Lassalle's high-sounding but historically false phrase is accepted: in relation to the working class all other classes are only one reactionary mass. This proposition is true only in a few exceptional cases: for instance . . . in a country where not only the bourgeoisie has moulded state and society in its own image but where in its wake the democratic petty bourgeoisie, too, has already carried out this remoulding down to its final consequences. If in Germany, for instance, the democratic petty bourgeoisie belonged to this reactionary mass, how could the Social-Democratic Workers' Party have gone hand in hand with it — with the Peoples' Party — for years? (Marx and Engels, 1968, p.333).

Germany is here quite specifically *not* deemed to be a country in which bourgeois dominance had reached its 'final consequences' — these being that the productive forces of society had developed to such an extent that capitalism was ripe for overthrow. For this reason, the bourgeoisie was still considered a revolutionary class and a class with which the Workers' Party *should* be working hand in hand. That the Lassalleans were oblivious to this fact indicated that they had misunderstood and subsequently falsified the findings of the *Manifesto*.

The second falsification follows from this first. For the Lassalleans had failed to make a distinction between the lower and higher phases that communism would have to go through in Germany. In the *Manifesto*, Marx had argued for the existence of a lower phase in order to facilitate the gestation of communism within the capitalist womb. In the Gotha Programme, however, the Lassalleans were talking of a *direct* transition to a society based around 'equal right' and 'fair distribution', blissfully ignorant of the fact that 'defects are inevitable in the first phase of communist society', and that, therefore, '*equal right* here is still in principle — *bourgeois right*' (Marx, 1968f, p.320). When, therefore, Marx begins his famous proclamation with the words, 'what we are talking about here', what he is talking about is the practical impossibility of Germany witnessing a direct transition to anything other than the first stage of communism.

Incidentally, what he is *not* talking about is the practical impossibility of *any* bourgeois society witnessing a direct transition to 'full' communism. What he is talking about instead is the practical impossibility of *Germany* witnessing such a direct transition *now*. Because of the attention it has received from Marxologists over the years, it is easy to forget that the 'Critique' was a private letter addressed to five German socialists, which dealt specifically with one German programme drawn up by a group of Germans for a Conference which aimed to tackle specifically German problems. If one cares to remember that this is all the 'Critique' was, then its claims to universal validity seem somewhat dubious.

In order to highlight the practical impossibility of Germany directly witnessing the transition to full communism, Marx emphasised the preconditions required for this transition. In so doing, he produced that glorious passage concerning the 'higher phase' of communism:

> In a higher phase of communist society, after the enslaving subordination of the individual to the division of labour, and therewith also the antithesis between mental and physical labour, has vanished; after labour has become not only a means of life but life's prime want; after the productive forces have also increased with the all-round development of the individual, and all the springs of co-operative wealth flow more abundantly — only then can the narrow horizons of bourgeois right be crossed in its entirety and society inscribe on its banners: From each according to his ability, to each according to his needs! (ibid., pp.320-321).

This most famous of passages has sometimes been seen as a utopian flashback to Marx's 'early' days. It was, however, written with the serious intention of revealing all the preconditions required for full communism — when 'this', 'that' and 'the other' have taken place, *'only then'* can 'this' happen — in order to demonstrate that Germany was in no position at all to see its realisation.

For Marx, the Germany of 1875 had no more satisfied the preconditions required for the realisation of 'full communism' than had the Germany of 1848. In order to satisfy these conditions, a transitional phase would therefore be required. This lower phase would, indeed, be a protracted affair, for when it emerged from the womb of capitalism it would be virtually *all* birthmark — the proletariat will have won the battle of democracy and declared the dictatorship of the proletariat *in the course of* effecting the bourgeois revolution, so that communism's first stage will have been conceived the very minute that its capitalist mother had reached puberty. As a result, capitalism itself will hardly have had the chance to 'develop on its own foundations', leaving the dictatorship with a lot of work to do before the preconditions for 'full' communism could be met. The Lassalleans had simply no idea that this was the case, and this is why Marx went to such lengths to tell them.

With regards to the actual proposals outlined in the 'Critique', these are rather more esoteric than those proposed in the *Manifesto*, primarily because they are defined in relation to the Gotha Programme's statements and because they often involve tangential digressions concerning the theoretical ineptitudes underlying the latter. The similarities between the *Manifesto*'s programme and the Critique's proposals are nonetheless quite clear, especially when it comes to the relationship between the spheres of production and circulation. For once again, Marx nowhere defines the production process as a centralised activity confined solely to the organs of the state. Instead, he describes the ways in which the state will administer the circulation and distribution side of the economy with a view to increasing the capacity and the efficiency of productive capital. Hence the fact that each economic unit will have deducted from its output 'cover for replacement of the means of production used up' and an 'additional portion for expansion of production' (ibid., p.318). What Marx has in mind here is something akin to the idea put forward in the *Manifesto*, according to which private production would be supplemented by state production in order to facilitate the development of productive capital in general. It is true that deductions will also be made for the provision of schools and hospitals, and it is true also that no one will receive more than the equivalent of that which they have themselves produced. As was the case with the *Manifesto*, however, these measures were intended to rid capitalism of its more grotesque features, not to *replace* it. Indeed, the whole point being made by Marx was that capitalism was in no fit state to be superseded and that, therefore, a transitional phase was required during which capitalism would be rendered fit.

In addition to his ignorance concerning this issue, Lassalle's idea of 'full communism' was nothing like that set down in the *Manifesto*. For much to Marx's amusement and consternation, the programme announced that 'the German workers' party strives for "the free state"' (ibid., p.326). It is this idea which prompted another famous proclamation by Marx:

> Between capitalist and communist society lies the period of the revolutionary transformation of the one into the other. Corresponding to this is also a political transition period in which the state can be nothing but *the revolutionary dictatorship of the proletariat* (ibid., p.327).

The state, in other words, to the extent that it will exist at all in communism, will be by no means 'free'. So little, in fact, will the revolutionary state embody communism that it can be seen as *nothing but*, and nothing more than, the transition point to it. Marx had made this point almost three decades earlier and yet the Lassalleans had still failed to grasp it.

In a strong sense, then, the 'Critique' was a defence of the *Manifesto*. Its aim was to repeat the general schema elucidated there and to argue that the Lassallean programme was an inferior replacement. As Manuel and Manuel remark: 'Fundamentally, Marx in 1875 felt that a new party program was supererogatory; the *Manifesto*, cogent and lucid, had been around for popular consumption since 1848, and the publication of another statement of principles was likely to be obfuscatory' (1979, p.697). More than this, in fact, the principles stated were simply *wrong*, and they were wrong in one principal respect — they failed to realise that an economically under-developed country like Germany needed to go through a transitional phase before it could proceed to full communism. They failed to realise, that is, that the Germany of 1875 represented one of those instances where a dictatorship of the proletariat was required. And this is what the notion of the dictatorship of the proletariat as a whole meant for Marx and Engels: it was not a universal theory but a model which applied to *certain* situations, and the Germany of 1875, like the Germany of 1848 and the France of 1850 and 1871, was one of them.

Conclusion

Was Marx's description of the lower phase of communism — the dictatorship of the proletariat — a 'utopian' one? This is neither an easy question to answer nor, I would suggest, a particularly pertinent one. It is not easy because a utopia should describe in a variety of aspects and with some consistency an imaginary state or society which is regarded as better, in some respects at least, than the one in which its author lives. The first question one must ask, therefore, is whether or not Marx described the lower phase in a variety of aspects and with some consistency. I myself would argue that what Marx said about the lower phase was consistent but hardly described in a variety of aspects. Whether one agrees with this or not will ultimately depend upon whether one equates the ten-point programme outlined in the *Manifesto* with a varied description of a state or society. I do not view it as such but nor do I want to initiate some obscure discussion about what 'aspects' are and what 'varied' means. The second difficult question one needs to ask is whether or not the lower phase of communism truly represents an 'imaginary' state or society. Again, views on this will vary according to what one takes 'imaginary' to mean and again I do not want to debate the issue here. All I will say on the matter is that if one links the term 'imaginary' to the notion of *that which has never been experienced* then Marx's description does not fit into this category. For given that the function of the dictatorship was to reproduce economic developments that had already taken place elsewhere, it would seem rather strange to argue that the concept was founded solely in the imagination or that it referred to things which had never been experienced.

This is why I really want to argue that the question itself — was Marx's description of the lower phase a utopia? — is actually misplaced. For the lower phase was in no sense regarded by Marx as a desired 'end', nor was its description the result of cerebrations concerning the nature of alternative forms of society. Instead, it was the solution to a very specific problem, namely, how best to bring economically under-developed countries through industrialisation stages similar to those already attained under bourgeois rule in more developed ones. Confronted with this problem, Marx reasoned that the best solution would be for the proletariat in those countries which were presently undergoing their bourgeois phases of revolution to declare the permanence of these revolutions by raising themselves to the position of ruling class and by establishing a dictatorship. Once this had been achieved, the proletariat could speedily destroy the vestiges of feudalism and swiftly eliminate the fetters to productive capital, thus achieving a state of economic development that would otherwise have taken decades.

The lower phase of communism was thus the product of reasoned judgements concerning the best way to achieve rapid economic development in those countries still bound by feudal fetters. As such, it did not serve as an *alternative* model of society but was rather designed to facilitate the development of the *existing* one. The dictatorship would serve the interests of communism and constitute its 'lower stage' only in the sense that it would plant the seeds of communism within capitalism and thereby take control of the germination process. From this I would suggest that Marx's discussion of the lower phase of communism was completely unrelated to the process of 'utopian' description and I would therefore argue against the idea that the lower phase represents the first part, stage or element of Marx's 'utopia'.

Notes

1. Avineri (1968, pp.220-239; 1973, pp.327-329) argues that 'the stages of socialism' are also discussed in the *Economic and Philosophic Manuscripts*, where Marx distinguishes between 'crude communism' and 'communism as fully developed humanism'. What I think Marx is talking about here, however, is the progress of communism as an *idea*. For the language used in the *Manuscripts*, where Marx refers to 'crude communism' as 'the urge to reduce things to a common level', as mere 'levelling down' (Marx, 1977a, pp.88-89), is exactly the same as that used in the *Manifesto*, where Marx describes earlier socialist *theories* as 'social levelling in its crudest form' (Marx and Engels, 1967, p.155). Historical stages are nowhere even mentioned in the *Manuscripts* and for this reason it seems clear to me that Marx was not actually talking about them.

2. Although the theory is best known today as 'the theory of permanent revolution' (primarily because Trotsky later popularised it under this name), the phrase favoured by Marx and Engels was 'the revolution in permanence'. It was thus really Engels who first gave the theory its name, using this very phrase in his article on 'The Magyar Question' of January 1849 (Engels, 1973, p.213).

3. Marx did in fact use the concept in his famous letter to Weydemeyer of March 1852, in which he stated that:

What I did that was new was to prove 1) that the existence of classes is only bound up with particular historical phases in the development of production, 2) that the class struggle necessarily leads to the dictatorship of the proletariat, 3) that this dictatorship itself only constitutes the transition to the abolition of all classes and to a classless society (Marx and Engels, 1968, p.669).

There is, however, a very particular story behind its use here. For Weydemeyer had just written an article entitled 'The Dictatorship of the Proletariat', which sought to summarise the arguments of the *Manifesto*. Marx, in response to this, wrote the letter in question with the aim of clarifying those arguments which he felt Weydemeyer had misrepresented (see Draper, 1990, pp.303-304; 1987, pp.28-29).

3 Marx's Description of the Higher Phase of Communism

Introduction

If Marx was a utopian then he was utopian by virtue of his description of the higher phase of communism. This, I think, is something upon which everyone can be agreed. In the present chapter I follow R. N. Berki in distinguishing between the descriptions we are given of a 'mundane, heterogeneous, pedestrian communism' and those we are given of a 'visionary' and almost eschatological version of the same (1983, p.126). What I argue is that the term 'utopia' should only be used in connection with Marx's 'visionary' descriptions of communism because the descriptions he provides of its more 'mundane' aspects are so vague and nebulous that they hardly justify the term 'descriptions' at all. What I also suggest, however, is that even in relation to Marx's 'visionary' descriptions of full communism the term 'utopia' seems problematic. For as every Marxologist knows, these descriptions were never 'systematically' presented but were rather scattered about throughout Marx's writings. The fact that Marx's 'utopia' can only be assembled by collating a series of disparate remarks (together, of course, with the fact that Marx repeatedly told us that he was not in the business of contriving utopias) seems to indicate that there was more to Marx's 'utopianism' than the act of simply describing a utopia. I therefore conclude by suggesting that the existence of a utopia in Marx needs to be accounted for rather than merely demonstrated.

The Mundane Aspects of Full Communism

The Economic, Social and Political Structure of Full Communism

Four things can be said with absolute certainty about the mundane aspects of full communism as envisioned by Marx: that private property will have been abolished, that class distinctions will have disappeared, that the producers will have direct control over the means of production and that the individual will no longer be a slave to the division of labour. These four things effectively define the economic and social relations of production that will exist in full communism. What they also do, however, is represent *the sum total* of Marx's definition of the relations of production that will exist in full communism. For Marx never went beyond the level of general phrases and sweeping statements when it came to describing these relations and it is sometimes very difficult to imagine what they infer.

Take the abolition of private property as an example. In communism, says Marx, its place will have been taken by 'the possession in common of the land and of the means of production' (Marx, 1946, p.789). What, however, does this actually mean at the institutional and organisational level? Common ownership could be taken to mean a thousand and one things — and *has* been taken to mean a thousand and one things; just think of all the contrasting utopias to which the notion of common ownership has given rise — and yet Marx never outlines one of them. Nor does Marx specify the type of inter-personal relationships that will characterise a society devoid of classes. How will the fact that everyone occupies the same relation to the means of production affect the specific relations between these people? If no longer defined in terms of class, then what would these relations be defined in terms of? Marx supplies us with concepts such as community, co-operation and association, but unlike the 'utopian socialists' he never extrapolates any further than this. As Steven Lukes asks of the individuals who are to co-operate and associate under full communism:

> Do they come with attachments, commitments and loyalties, their identities shaped by local, regional, national, historical experiences and memories? Or are they the ultimate fruits of Enlightenment individualism: individuals who, once their class situation has withered away, are free of 'extraneous purposes', 'natural necessities' and 'social duties', with nothing existing 'independently of them'? (1984, p.166).

Consulting Marx for an answer to such questions will only lead to disappointment. Even Bertell Ollman, who scoured the works of Marx in search of everything he ever said about the future structure of communism, had to concede that the nature of post-class interpersonal ties and relations were left 'unnamed' (1977, p.22).

Similar things can be said with respect to Marx's concept of workers' control. For although the symbolic relevance of the notion is easy to grasp

— it symbolised both worker self-determination and their mastery over, rather than subservience to, the productive forces of society — the actual form that such symbolic self-determination would take remains a mystery. All that is certain is that the associated producers would 'regulate national production upon a common plan, thus taking it under their own control' (Marx, 1968e, p.291). What this plan would actually involve Marx does not say, how it would be drawn up Marx never specifies, how and by whom it would be implemented is anyone's guess. That there would be a plan is all we are told.[1]

Turning our attention now to the division of labour, whilst Marx does have a little more to say on this matter he probably does not have as much to say as one might think. For Marx was primarily concerned with the question of the abolition (not *Aufhebung* but abolition) of the division of labour and not with that of describing alternative modes of organising production within the factory. It would therefore be a mistake to describe the abolition of the division of labour as a 'Utopian' category, although it is often treated as such. In fact, the abolition of the division of labour had the same symbolic value for Marx as the concept of workers' control of the means of production: it was symbolic, that is, of a more fundamental aspect of communism — worker self-determination.

Underlying Marx's repeated attacks on the division of labour was the fact that it subjected individuals to an activity *forced* upon them. Marx thus refers to 'the subjection of the individual under the division of labour, under a definite activity forced upon him' (Marx and Engels, 1970, p.69) and argues that because 'each man has a particular, exclusive sphere of activity, which is forced upon him and from which he cannot escape' his own productive power 'enslaves him instead of being controlled by him' (ibid., p.54). This is why Marx repeatedly rails against the town/country and mental/manual labour distinctions (Marx and Engels, 1970, pp.68-72; Marx and Engels, 1967, pp.104-105; Marx, 1968f, p.320; Marx, 1946, p.513). For these distinctions, more than anything else, were deemed to illustrate the way in which exclusive spheres of activity are forced upon a worker and are then reinforced and rendered concrete by the division of labour. Similarly, underscoring Marx's famous claim that 'the life-long annexation of the workman to a detail function' transforms him into 'a living appendage of the machine' (Marx, 1946, p.363, p.489) was his fervent belief that the division of labour epitomised the labourer's 'complete subjection to capital' (ibid., p.350). When Marx described the preconditions for communism in the 'Critique of the Gotha Programme', it was thus 'the enslaving subordination of the individual to the division of labour' that would have to vanish (Marx, 1968f, p.320).

Now, with regards to what communism would look like once the subordination of the individual to the division of labour *had* actually vanished, we have, of course, the most ridiculed passage in the entire canon of Marxism. One hardly needs reminding that the passage reads as follows:

> in communist society, where nobody has one exclusive sphere of activity but each can become accomplished in any branch he wishes, society regulates the general production and thus makes it possible for me to do one thing today and another tomorrow, to hunt in the morning, fish in the afternoon, rear cattle in the evening, criticise after dinner, just as I have a mind, without ever becoming hunter, fisherman, herdsman or critic (Marx and Engels, 1970, p.54).

Fortunately, however, whilst this passage used to be seen as a 'utopian' embarrassment to be avoided by students of Marx, it can now be viewed as a celebration of Marx's humour and a testimony to his anti-utopianism. For as Terrell Carver has helpfully indicated, not only did Engels, rather than Marx, draft the passage in the first place, but Marx actually reprimanded Engels for so doing, adding the bits concerning after-dinner criticism 'in order to send it up' (Carver, 1988, p.135). As Carver therefore concludes:

> The famous passage on communist society from *The German Ideology* cannot now be read as one continuous train of thought. In fact it shows Marx sharply rebuking Engels for straying, perhaps momentarily, from the serious work of undercutting the fantasies of Utopian socialists (ibid.).

This subsequently raises problems for those who wish to emphasise Marx's implicit utopianism. For the hunter-fisherman-herdsman-critic passage can no longer be used in support of such a conclusion; other passages need to be found. When it comes to descriptions of how communism will function without the division of labour, however, there are no such passages. All Marx provides us with are proclamations concerning the need to abolish the division of labour and familiar (though still extremely general) remarks such as: 'In a communist society there are no painters but at most people who engage in painting among other activities' (Marx and Engels, 1970, p.109).

With regards to Marx's description of the economic and social relations of production that would exist in full communism, this much then should now be clear: that the term 'description' hardly applies to such vague and nebulous remarks. The same is also true of Marx's description of the political sphere. For although he tells us that there will be no parliaments in communism (Marx, 1960b, p.126) nor any soldiers, policemen, hangmen, legislators or judges (Marx, 1960a, p.52), and although we know for sure that when 'class rule has disappeared' there will be 'no state in the present political sense' (Marx, 1974e, p.336), what there *will* be is far less clear. All we have to go on is the notion of 'an aggregate body working merely for the satisfaction of the national wants' (Marx, 1959, p.830), within which 'the functions of government become purely administrative' (Marx and Engels, 1974a, p.314) and 'the public power will lose its political character' (Marx and Engels, 1967, p.105). What Marx actually means by a non-political aggregate public administrative non-state is never made explicit, however, and general phrases such as Engels' 'withering away of the state' are so general that a whole industry has been built around trying to decipher them.

If we turn our attention now to the few occasions in which the various strands of Marx's description are drawn together, we can see just how devoid of real content they are. In *Capital*, for example, Marx says:

> Let us now picture to ourselves, by way of change, a community of free individuals, carrying on their work with the means of production in common, in which the labour-power of all the different individuals is consciously applied as the combined labour-power of the community (Marx, 1946, p.50).

The point here is that picturing such a circumstance is extremely difficult. For one simply does not know what Marx means by 'the means of production in common' and one certainly does not know what he means by 'the community' or 'a community of free individuals'. These are phrases, not descriptions, and in a very real sense one could take them to mean almost anything one wanted them to. Similar considerations apply to Marx's claim that the Paris Commune

> wanted to make individual property a truth by transforming the means of production, land and capital, now chiefly the means of enslaving and exploiting labour, into mere instruments of free and associated labour — But this is Communism (Marx, 1968e, pp.290-291).

Perhaps it is, but what exactly does this tell us about the organisational *structure* of communism? What, in other words, does Marx mean by free and associated labour, what kind of instruments will the means of production, land and capital become and how will they be used? The only time, to my knowledge at least, that Marx ever expanded upon the concept of 'association' was in the *Manifesto*, when he told us that in it 'the free development of each is the condition for the free development of all' (Marx and Engels, 1967, p.105). This, however, is more of a riddle than a 'utopian' description — a mere phrase without content.

I would therefore summarise Marx's description of the economic, social and political structure of communism as nothing more than a selection of phrases devoid of content. The phrases themselves are familiar enough — common ownership, associated producers, a common plan, a community of free individuals, a non-political aggregate public administrative non-state — but nowhere does Marx actually tell us what any of these phrases mean.

The Influence of the Utopian Socialists

In spite of the paucity of detail provided by Marx, parallels are often drawn between his 'utopia' and those described by the 'utopian socialists'. It is important to note here, however, that the similarities between Marx and Engels' vision of communism and those of the utopians were generally confined to the elements of the present society that would *disappear* in the future. In the *Manifesto*, therefore, Marx and Engels say of the utopians that:

> They attack every principle of existing society. Hence they are full of the most valuable materials for the enlightenment of the working class. The practical measures proposed in them — such as the abolition of the distinction between town and country, of the family, of the carrying on of industries for the account of private individuals, and of the wage system, the proclamation of social harmony, the conversion of the functions of the State into a mere superintendence of production, all these proposals point solely to the disappearance of class antagonisms . . . (Marx and Engels, 1967, p.116).

It was these *negative* proposals which point to the disappearance of class antagonisms that Engels also had in mind when he declared that:

> German theoretical socialism will never forget that it rests on the shoulders of Saint-Simon, Fourier and Owen — three men who, in spite of all their fantastic notions and all their utopianism, stand among the most eminent

thinkers of all time and whose genius anticipated innumerable things the correctness of which is now being scientifically proven by us (Engels, 1968a, p.246).

Marx's 'science' was now proving that class antagonisms will disappear, so that the utopians' negative measures were correct *in spite of* the fantastic utopian alternatives they erected in their place.

With regards to the *positive* proposals apparently endorsed by Marx and Engels — most notably the Saint-Simonian idea concerning 'the conversion of the functions of the State into a mere superintendence of production' and the famous distributive principle of 'from each according to his abilities, to each according to his needs', first formulated by Cabet — there is no reason to believe that these were adopted as anything other than mere 'catchwords'. As we saw in chapter 1, 'catchwords' were all that the ideas of the utopian socialists amounted to in the era of materialistically critical socialism, and it is as catchwords that Marx's apparent adoption of some of their ideas should therefore be viewed.

To take one specific example, in fact, it is impossible to believe that Marx adopted Saint-Simon's notion of the government of people being transformed into the administration of things as anything *other* than a catchword. For as far as Saint-Simon was concerned, 'the administration of things' had to be based upon a strict and hierarchical division of power, and it was imperative that the scientists rule the most important, i.e., the 'spiritual', sphere of society. As he explains to the proletariat: 'A scientist, my friends, is a man who foresees; it is because science provides the means to predict that it is useful, and that scientists are superior to all other men' (Saint-Simon, 1976, p.76). The corollary of this, and equally as imperative, was the need for all power to be withheld from the proletariat. The reasoning behind this is explained to the proletariat thus:

> I must discuss with you something which angers you deeply. You say: *we are ten, twenty, a hundred times more numerous than the proprietors and yet they exercise a power over us very much greater than that which we wield over them.* I can understand, my friends, that you are aggrieved. But notice that the proprietors, although fewer in number, are more enlightened than you are and for the general good power should be distributed according to the degree of enlightenment (ibid., p.78).

Saint-Simon stressed the need for an élite minority to exercise political power, so that for him the 'government of people' would be transcended by the proletariat doffing their caps of their own volition. When Marx appropriated the phrase, one can therefore be sure that he did not appropriate the content of this 'utopian' idea: it was *just* a phrase and *just* a catchword.

Similarly, it is interesting to note that during the course of over four decades' work and who knows how many hundreds of thousands of words, Marx referred to Cabet's distributive principle only *once* — and only then in a pamphlet written for five of his friends and certainly not intended for publication. Elsewhere, indeed, Marx remained faithful to his anti-utopian proscriptions against foreclosing the future and specifically stated that 'the mode of distribution' within communism 'will vary with the productive organisation of the community' (Marx, 1946, p.50). Towards the end of *Capital* Volume II, of course, Marx tells us that money will no longer exist in communism, but this remark had nothing to do with any distributive theory of justice — the abolition of money was simply a natural consequence of the abolition of private property and the exchange relations engendered by it. Indeed, whilst his critics might regard this as one of the more 'utopian' (in the sense of naïve) elements of Marx's thought, Marx himself never attached a great deal of significance to the abolition of money. He certainly never mentioned it very often (more than just the once?) and just as certainly refused to specify the mode of distribution that would take its place.

So the fact that Marx referred to Cabet's distributive principle only once, in a private letter to his friends, must surely tell us something. Perhaps, indeed, it tells us that Marx was referring to some previous conversation that he had had with his friends or perhaps, as was the case with the hunter-fisherman passage, he was actually 'sending up' the views held by one or more of them. What it must tell us, however, is that Marx did not give the matter any detailed thought. For if Marx *really had* given the distributive principle in question his considered thought, and if it *really did* form an integral part of some clearly structured 'vision' of the future, then surely he would have referred to it again, at least in his private notebooks or correspondence. This, however, he did not do.

In fact, what Marx did do was appropriate a number of general phrases from the utopians. He did not subscribe to the content which lay behind these phrases, not did he attempt to fill them with a content specifically his own. Instead, he actually emptied the concepts of all specific content and utilised them as vague and deliberately ambiguous catchwords. This was, for Marx, all the ideas of the utopians amounted to.

The Nothingness behind Marx's Vague Comments

Browsing through Marx's correspondence, one will find that reference is never made to the future structure of communism. As Oscar J. Hammen remarks:

> The *Briefwechsel* contains nothing in the way of comment or speculation regarding the lot of humanity in the communist society to come — nothing to supplement the sparse, scattered and vague pronouncements that appear in the published critiques and other sources. Judging from the letters, the question of humanity and the form in which humanity would be realized occupied their thoughts very little, in contrast to matters of 'party' policy, proper tactics, the prospects of an economic crash, the privations of Marx's family, and the chances of revolution as such (1990, p.428).

In his private correspondence with Engels, Marx displays not the slightest bit of interest in the form that the society of the future will take. Nor did he display any interest in the matter during his after-dinner conversation, as Melvin Lasky informs us by way of a nice little anecdote concerning the diary of one of Marx's dining partners for the evening of January 31st 1879: Marx, said the man, was 'interesting and often, as I thought, showing very correct ideas, when he was conversing of the past or the present, but vague and unsatisfactory when he turned to the future' (Lasky, 1977, p.628n). Whilst such anecdotal evidence is relatively worthless on its own, it does suggest that Marx's description of communism was so meagre a) because Marx did not know what communism would look like and b) because he consciously avoided giving the matter any considered thought.

Indeed, this is the conclusion to which the whole of the preceding discussion gives rise. For as we have seen, Marx's description of full communism was generally phrased in the negative and concerned those things that would disappear in the future. Furthermore, when he did talk in terms of positives, these were either so vague as to defy understanding or were mere catchwords that lacked any content. Now, whilst one *could* attempt to contrive a 'utopia' out of this material (as Bertell Ollman, 1977, does), the question I would ask is why bother? For it seems to me that Marx's esoteric and ambiguous comments concerning the nature of communism were esoteric and ambiguous because Marx did not actually give them much thought. This really is the most rational explanation for the paucity of detail in Marx's supposed 'utopia'. Unfortunately, however, many commentators refuse to accept this explanation and search instead for hidden meanings behind Marx's nebulous phrases.

Radoslav Selucký, for example, manufactures some huge entity out of Marx's writings; an entity he refers to as 'a sort of religion or, at best . . . an ideological myth or utopia' (1979, p.82). According to Selucký:

> Whilst Marx's economic concept of socialism consists of a single social-wide factory based on vertical (hierarchical) relations of superiority and subordination, his political concept of socialism consists of a free association of self-managed work and social communities based on horizontal relations of equality. Whoever accepts in full Marx's first concept has to give up the latter, and vice versa: they are mutually exclusive (ibid., p.xi).

Selucký then proceeds to suggest that Soviet practice was informed by Marx's giant factory model of socialism whilst the Yugoslav experiment was founded on his self-managed community concept. More than this, however, Selucký traces the ultimate failure of both to intrinsic flaws in the original concepts upon which they were based — the giant factory economic model required a similarly hierarchical political structure to go alongside it, thus leading in the opposite direction of liberation, whilst the decentralised political framework simply could not be extended to the macroeconomic and macropolitical level, thus leading to a number of contradictions becoming incorporated into the Yugoslav Constitution (ibid., pp.91-116). Not only, therefore, is Marx held responsible for developing *two* utopian visions of the good life, but the inconsistencies within these two visions are then linked directly to the failure of socialism as a real and practical movement.

When one looks behind Selucký's bold claims, however, one finds that Marx did not, in fact, develop two utopian visions of the good life. More to the point, one finds that he did not even develop one. For in spite of the pivotal role that it plays in his critique of Marx, Selucký is forced to concede that 'it was only Kautsky and Lenin who deduced the one nation, one factory concept from Marx's implicit suggestions' and that 'Marx was not its explicit author' (ibid., pp.13-14). Similarly, whilst the concept of 'community' is supposed to form the focal point of Marx's self-managed association model of socialism, Selucký is again forced to concede that 'Marx has failed to define clearly what the term actually means' and is again forced to erect a critique around the feeble structure supplied by 'Marx's vague and unsystematic remarks concerning the 'genuine community'' (ibid., pp.82-83).

What Selucký does, therefore, is read Lenin and Kautsky back into Marx in order to criticise Marx himself and then read *his own* critique of Marx's vague comments concerning 'community' back into Marx in order to criticise Marx again. Selucký thus constructs two 'ideological utopias' out of material that simply is not there. Rather than conceding that Marx said nothing concrete about the future structure of communism, he insists on reading a series of hidden agendas into Marx's vague and ambiguous remarks. As he then proceeds to berate Marx for constructing the two mutually exclusive utopias that he did not construct, and as he furthermore goes on to trace the failures of actually existing socialism back to these utopian constructs, Selucký demonstrates quite clearly the dangers involved in reading too much into Marx.

In contrast to the kind of approach adopted by Selucký, what I would ask is this: that is it not reasonable to conclude that there was no hidden agenda behind Marx's vague remarks? Could it be the case, for example, that we do not know what Marx meant when he said that in communism 'there would be no state in the present political sense' because Marx did not know either? Could it also be possible that Marx did not really know what he meant because he had not actually thought beyond the level of general phrases? And could it be possible that Marx had not thought beyond the level of general phrases because he did not, in fact, think it useful or appropriate to do so? As he repeatedly told the utopians, one can never know the form that the future will take and attempting to contrive utopian pictures of it is just silly, stale and reactionary. General phrases apart, descriptions of communism had lost *all* importance, *all* theoretical justification and *all* practical value. Is it any wonder, then, that Marx did not offer us anything more than a collection of catchwords?

The Centrality of the Principle of Proletarian Self-Determination

One final thing needs to be said in relation to the 'utopianism' of Marx's description of the mundane aspects of full communism, and this concerns the centrality of the principle of proletarian self-determination. For this principle informed pretty much everything Marx ever said about the formal organisation of communism. More importantly perhaps, the same principle forced Marx to remain silent when it came to conceptualising the future far more often than it prompted him to describe it. Whilst, that is, the principle led him to proclaim that the proletariat would require a national plan to regulate production and thus bring it under their conscious control, it was also this principle which prevented him from saying anything about what this plan would actually involve. And whilst the principle led him to conclude that the division of labour would have to be abolished, it was also this principle which prevented him from describing how production would be organised in its absence. It was this principle, too, which prevented him from specifying the type of common ownership that would form the economic foundation of full communism, and it was this principle which prevented him from pre-empting the nature of the non-political framework that would emerge from within it. None of these things could be known in advance and utopian speculation was pointless: the proletarians would be more than capable of determining for themselves what communism would look like and they should be given the absolute freedom to do so.

Some may argue, of course, that saying things about the future on the basis of an ethical norm is tantamount to utopianism and that to suggest otherwise is to quibble pointlessly over semantics. I think that Marx should be treated with some degree of fairness here, however, for all too often he is declared utopian by virtue of having said *anything at all* about communism. It seems, in fact, that the normal rules governing what constitutes a 'utopia' are abandoned when it comes to anti-utopians such as Marx, so that the mere suggestion of a plan to regulate production within communism is seized upon as concrete evidence of utopian tendencies. Whilst it would therefore be churlish to deny that Marx argued for the superiority of communism over capitalism on the basis of a normative concept of self-determination, the question is whether or not Marx's arguments to this effect led him to contrive a 'utopia'. The normal rules do, in other words, apply to Marx, and one needs to judge his 'utopianism' accordingly.

Under normal rules, then, the issue is not about whether Marx judged capitalism and found it wanting (which he did), or about whether he said *some* things about the mundane aspects of full communism (which he also did); it is about whether or not the things that he said constitute a 'utopia'. In my view they do not, simply because the descriptions we are given are invariably vague and ambiguous and because their vague ambiguity stems from the fact that Marx did not give the descriptions any considered thought. With regards to the mundane aspects of full communism, I would therefore suggest that there are no hidden depths to be found in Marx's comments nor any 'utopia' to be retrieved from them.

Marx's 'Vision' of Full Communism

The Defining Concepts of Marx's Vision

It is common to suggest that Marx's vision of full communism extended beyond the realm of institutions, organisations and structures. What lay beyond this realm was 'a movement to humanise a world which currently confronts individuals as alien' (Sayer, 1990, p.684), 'the abolition of the estrangement between man and the world, the assimilation of the world by the human subject' (Kolakowski, 1978, I, pp.223-224) and 'a totally novel culture, with a new dominant philosophy, a new concept of reality and of human potentialities, new ways of incorporating the individual biography into societal history' (Bauman, 1976, p.75). That Marx described the mundane aspects of communism with such vague ambiguity should therefore come as no surprise — he was far more concerned with what communism would mean for the human subject. The question then arises: What *would* communism mean for the human subject?

Well, in answering this question, few people have missed the opportunity to quote the most famous passage from the *Economic and Philosophic Manuscripts*. In this passage Marx describes:

> *Communism* as the *positive* transcendence of *private property* as *human self-estrangement*, and therefore as the real *appropriation* of the *human* essence by and for man; communism therefore as the complete return of man to himself as a *social* (i.e., human) being — a return accomplished consciously and embracing the entire wealth of previous development. This communism, as fully developed naturalism, equals humanism, and as fully developed humanism equals naturalism; it is the *genuine* resolution of the conflict between man and nature and between man and man — the true resolution of the strife between existence and essence, between objectification and self-confirmation, between freedom and necessity, between the individual and the species. Communism is the riddle of history solved, and it knows itself to be this solution (Marx, 1977a, p.90).

I noted earlier that Marx never specified the type of inter-human relationships that would characterise a classless society. The type of co-operation and association that he envisaged (if he envisaged any particular type at all) remained unstated, as did the kinds of attachments, commitments and loyalties that individuals would bring with them. From the passage quoted here it seems that Marx focused his attention on something far more fundamental, namely, the new form that humanity itself would take under communism. Rather than describing how individuals as we perceive them now would unite and interact following the positive transcendence of private property, Marx presented us with a vision of the different way of *being* that would follow it. According to this vision, 'being' would be reconciled with everything that had once faced it in antithesis. Embodied within the communistic individual would be, and existence within communism could only be defined as, the resolution of the antitheses between humanity and Nature, the individual and the species, existence and essence, etc. Not only would communism be a classless society, it would be a society devoid of any fragmentation and separation: within it one would be 'whole'. Following Ernst Fischer I will term this aspect of Marx's vision 'The Dream of the Whole Man' (1970, p.15) — a dream so at odds with humanity as it presently stands that Kumar is forced to say of it that: 'Such a dazzling vision of universal harmony is hardly to be found anywhere else in the serious utopian literature' (1987, p.62).

In addition to this new way of being, communism would also involve 'the development of the all-round individual'. Marx gives a good indication of what this means when he approvingly quotes a Frenchman on his return from San-Francisco:

> Once in the midst of this world of adventurers, who change their occupation as often as they do their shirt, egad, I did as the others. As mining did not turn out remunerative enough, I left it for the town, where in succession I became typographer, slater, plumber, &c. In consequence of thus finding out that I am fit for any sort of work, I feel less of a mollusk and more of a man (Marx, 1946, p.493n).

In objectifying a whole host of one's individual powers through a diverse range of labour activities one becomes 'more of a man'. This is because 'it is the vocation, the destination of each man to develop himself in many different ways, to realize all his dispositions' (Marx and Engels, 1965, p.316). 'The *rich* human being is simultaneously the human being *in need of* a totality of human manifestations of life' (Marx, 1977a, p.99) because human beings need to 'be brought into practical connection with the material and intellectual production of the whole world' (Marx and Engels, 1970, p.55). In order to be rich, therefore, to reach their destination, people *need* to experience the totality of life activities.

This aspect of communism is something more than a positive

extrapolation from the abolition of the division of labour. For whilst the latter would release individuals from their enslaving subordination to activities forced upon them, thereby providing them with free scope to develop their individualities, Marx presents the development of the all-round individual as an imperative rather than an opportunity. Not only will individuals be free to experience the totality of human manifestations of life, Marx also states that in order to be 'rich' they will *need* to experience these manifestations. In short, whilst the abolition of the division of labour was a demand informed by the principle of proletarian self-determination, the development of the all-round individual looks more like an argument from human destiny.

Existence within communism would also be founded on and driven by 'the ontological necessity of labour'. In Marx's own terms, this would mean that in communism 'labour has become not only a means of life but life's prime want' (Marx, 1968f, p.320). People need to see themselves in a world *they* have created, and because of this, 'production for its own sake means nothing but the development of human productive forces, in other words the development of the richness of human nature as an end in itself'(Marx, 1971a, pp.247-248). In communism, therefore, labour becomes 'but a means to widen, to enrich, to promote the existence of the labourer' (Marx and Engels, 1967, p.77). Labour has become life's prime want because the individual 'can only express his life in real, sensuous objects' (Marx, 1977a, p.136). To 'be' in communism is to physically create, and such life-affirming creativity represents nothing less than 'the individual's self-realization' (Marx, 1973a, p.611).

It has often been claimed that the key to understanding Marx's conception of the human subject within communism lies in the extension of free-time rather than the need for labour. As Kumar points out, however: 'This suggests a persisting duality or dichotomy quite at variance with Marx's general concept of future society. In communal production, both socially necessary work and free creative activity will find their synthesis' (1987, p.57). In *Grundrisse*, for example, Marx quite specifically states that 'Free time — which is both idle time and time for higher activity — has naturally transformed its possessor into a different subject, and he then enters into the production process as this different subject' (Marx, 1973a, p.712). In other words, free-time creates 'room for the development of the individual's full productive forces' (ibid., p.708), and once developed the individual in possession of these productive forces will be able to realise him or herself *in* and *through* the labour process (rather than being dominated by it).

Similarly, I find it difficult to read a persisting duality into the notorious realm of freedom/realm of necessity passage at the end of *Capital* Volume III. For in this passage Marx states:

> In fact, the realm of freedom actually begins only where labour which is determined by necessity and mundane considerations ceases; thus in the very nature of things it lies beyond the sphere of actual material production. Just as the savage must wrestle with Nature to satisfy his wants, to maintain and reproduce life, so must civilized man, and he must do so in all social formations and under all possible modes of production. With his development this realm of physical necessity expands as a result of his wants; but, at the same time, the forces of production which satisfy these wants also increase. Freedom in this field can only consist in socialized man, the associated producers, rationally regulating their interchange with Nature, bringing it under their common control, instead of being ruled by it as by the blind forces of Nature; and achieving this with the least expenditure of energy and under conditions most favourable to, and worthy of, their human nature. But it nonetheless still remains a realm of necessity. Beyond it begins that development of human energy which is an end in itself, the true realm of freedom, which, however, can blossom forth only with this realm of necessity as its basis (Marx, 1959, pp.799-800).

Whilst this has been taken to imply that Marx saw labour as an inherently alienating process rather than the embodiment of ontological freedom (Marcuse, 1973; Walliman, 1981; Rattansi, 1982), he does explicitly state that the individual can achieve freedom *in* the realm of necessity. As far as I can see, therefore, this merely supports the claim that in communism labour would become *not only* a means of life *but also* life's prime want. As Avner Cohen rightly points out:

> What characterizes labour is its status as an activity whose goal is not contained within it. Marx, on the other hand, was able to describe a society which supplied its own subsistence needs through an activity which contained its own goal (1995, p.45).

When Marx refers to 'labour' becoming life's prime want, he is not referring to labour as 'that activity which produces capital'; he is referring instead to 'the human activity in which man transforms nature, develops his potentialities, and strives to create a human-social world after his own image' (Kellner, 1973, p.7). Rather than standing in antithetical contrast to free-time, it is on the basis of the productive forces developed by individuals *during* their free-time that labour in communism facilitates 'the fulfilment of the personality' (Mandel, 1977, p.144).

The Dream of the Whole Man, the development of the all-round individual and the ontological necessity of labour: these three concepts define what full communism would mean for the human subject. These three concepts also define Marx's vision as his own. For unlike the concepts deployed by Marx when describing the mundane aspects of full communism, which were both devoid of content and yet familiar ground, Marx's vision of the human subject stands out as something different, something powerful, and something specifically formulated by Marx himself — one might even say Marx's own contribution to the utopian tradition.

The 'Utopianism' of Marx's Vision

Those who emphasise the human dimension to Marx's vision of full communism are quite correct to do so. For it seems that the higher phase of communism does indeed involve a new concept of human potentialities, does indeed involve the development of individual capacities, and does indeed involve the assimilation of the world by the human subject. From this one could further conclude that Marx did indeed describe in a variety of aspects and with some consistency the nature of *the individuals* that would inhabit the imaginary state or society which he regarded as better than the one in which he lived but which he described only vaguely. Marx, in other words, can be said to have presented us with a 'humanist' utopia.

Whilst this is a legitimate conclusion to reach, there is also a sense in which it is far too simplistic. If we look at the opening paragraphs that everyone feels obliged to write before they discuss Marx's 'utopia' then this should become quite clear. Take the following as examples:

> Marx . . . never offers a systematic account of the communist society. Furthermore, he frequently criticises those socialist writers who do as foolish, ineffective and even reactionary. There are also remarks which suggest that one cannot describe communism because it is forever in the process of becoming . . . Yet, as even the casual readers of Marx know, descriptions of the future society are scattered throughout Marx's writings (Ollman, 1977, p.8).

> [Marx] and Engels had little to say about the nature of the society which would succeed the transitional period of the 'dictatorship of the proletariat'.

Indeed, on occasion they evinced a certain distaste for the activity of drawing up blue-prints for the new society; nevertheless in broad outline, certain things may be said with some degree of confidence about communist society as it was envisaged by Marx and Engels (Sanderson, 1969, p.98).

It should be noticed that Marx said comparatively little about the shape of the society he envisaged. This is not surprising; like his master, Hegel, he was extremely chary of predicting the future and often castigated more "utopian" socialists for their idealistic forecasts. For if all ideas were a product of contemporary social reality, then a detailed projection of these ideas into a distant future was bound to result in idealism — ideas that were completely imaginary since lacking an empirical reference. Nevertheless, the broad outlines of Marx's picture are clear enough (McLellan, 1969, pp.459-460).

Observant readers may have noted the similarity between these opening paragraphs and my own. This stems from the need to highlight from the outset the incongruity between Marx's trenchant critique of utopianism and the idea that he himself was a utopian. The point is, however, that whilst each of the writers quoted above acknowledges that Marx never offered a systematic account of the communist society, they each proceed to discuss it as if he had. Whilst, therefore, such discussions invariably conclude by arguing that Marx's descriptions constitute a 'utopia', in so doing they tend to bypass a whole series of questions to which their opening remarks give rise: Why, if Marx was simply a 'utopian', did he never offer a systematic account of the communist society? Why, instead, does one have to scurry around pasting various disparate remarks together in order to assemble Marx's humanist 'vision'? Is not ascribing the term 'utopia' to such scattered and disparate remarks just a way of reading into Marx something that was not really there? And if Marx was really trying to present us with a humanist utopia then why did he never once tell us that this is what he was doing?

Ollman, Sanderson and McLellan each choose to avoid these questions by inserting the words 'nevertheless' or 'yet' into their discussions: Marx refused to construct a utopia and criticised those who did; *nevertheless* Marx did construct a utopia. What this seems to indicate, however, is that Marx's 'utopianism' had far more complex origins than these writers are willing to concede (or at least discuss). For it is not just a case of compiling a catalogue of comments and then declaring with joy that one has discovered a 'utopia', it is also a case of explaining why one has had to spend a great deal of time compiling a catalogue in the first place and why one has discovered a 'utopia' that Marx never once admitted to writing. Whilst one could reply here — as Ollman himself does, for example — that 'strategic' considerations prevented Marx from admitting to his own utopianism, this will not do because, as we have already seen, in his personal correspondence with Engels Marx never once showed the slightest bit of interest in the form that humanity would take in the future. To argue that Marx's humanist vision was the product of a consciously articulated utopianism would therefore be to argue that it was the product of a consciously articulated utopianism that he not only hid from his political rivals but also from himself.

In any case, if Marx really did attempt to conceptualise a humanist utopia, then what becomes of his vehement anti-utopianism? Are we expected to believe that Marx simply contradicted himself? Are we expected to believe that Marx systematically avoided any concrete suggestions concerning the nature of the mundane aspects of communism only to shoot himself in the foot by describing the nature of the individuals that would inhabit it? Or should we subscribe to the 'nevertheless' argument which observes that Marx *did* describe communism and that is just the way it is? Both options appear to me to be entirely unsatisfactory. I do not, that is, think that Marx set about constructing a humanist utopia in spite of his proscriptions against so doing, nor do I believe that his descriptions of full communism were just 'there', waiting to be observed or explained by a shrug of the shoulders and the word 'nevertheless'. Instead, what I would suggest is this: that whilst Marx did provide us with a series of scattered and unsystematic descriptions of the nature of the human subjects that would inhabit communism, these descriptions were not the product of a consciously articulated utopianism. Whilst, that is, these scattered descriptions could, if assembled together, be taken to constitute a 'utopia', they were not the result of any attempt on Marx's part to describe, in a variety of aspects and with some consistency, an imaginary state or society which he regarded as better, in some respects at least, than the one in which he lived. In short, if Marx did present us with a utopia then it was not his intention, either overtly or covertly, to do so.

Conclusion

The defining features of full communism as envisioned by Marx are well-known. Levitas identifies four: the abolition of the division of labour (requiring the abolition of private property); the development of individual potential; the transformation of work; and material abundance (1990, pp.40-45). Ollman expands upon this list by adding that people will have gained absolute control over the forces of nature; that their activities will no longer be organised by external forces; and that divisions among the human species will have ceased to exist (1977, pp.21-22). Others tend to prioritise one or more of the above, with Lukes, for example, emphasising 'freedom from extraneous purposes' (1984, p.163) and McLellan (1969; 1980) viewing 'Marx's concept of work' as the key factor.

What I have tried to argue here is that the term 'utopia' can only be used in relation to Marx's vision of the human subject within communism. His descriptions of the more mundane aspects of communism's higher phase were vague to say the very least; a symptom, in my view, of the fact that Marx did not give the subject any detailed or considered thought. His descriptions of the human subject, on the other hand, were much more colourful and, indeed, 'utopian'. By means of three central categories — The Dream of the Whole Man, the development of the all-round individual and the ontological necessity of labour — Marx presented us with a varied and consistent picture of what human existence in the higher phase of communism would involve. It is this picture which E. K. Hunt describes as 'the grandest and noblest vision in human history' and which Kumar refers to as being 'more dazzling in its utopianism than that of even the most utopian of utopian socialists'.

Nonetheless, whilst it is widely recognised that Marx was more concerned with what communism would mean for the human subject than he was with its more mundane institutional aspects, there is a sense in which the writers who recognise this go too far. For in noting the existence of a humanist 'utopia' within Marx's writings they tend to imply that whilst he was reluctant to describe communism's structure he was more than happy to present us with a utopian picture of its inhabitants. This is, however, a rather dubious conclusion to reach. For given his critique of utopian socialism, the fact that Marx described the nature of communism at all seems surprising. Even more surprising is the fact that Marx described the nature of the individuals that will inhabit it. For was not the nature of communism unknowable, and was it not the task of *the proletariat* to define it once they had victoriously overthrown the society of the present? Was it not, furthermore, both dangerous and deceptive to describe that which cannot be known? Was it not, indeed, the epitome of paternalistic elitism to announce in prophetic tones that one has discovered what the emancipation of humanity looks like? For Marx, as we saw in chapter 1, it was indeed. For this very reason I think that we should hesitate before labelling Marx's vision of communism a 'utopia' proper. Rather than ascribe this vision to some utopian predisposition, that is, I think it wise to consider alternative accounts.

Note

1   The one and only thing that Marx had to say on the subject was this:

> all labour in which many individuals co-operate necessarily requires a commanding will to co-ordinate and unify the process, and functions which apply not to partial operations but to the total activity of the workshop, much as that of an orchestra conductor. This is a productive job, which must be performed in every combined mode of production (Marx, 1959, p.376).

As Radoslav Selucký points out, however, the notion of a production 'conductor' raises more questions than it answers; questions such as what would be played, how the orchestra would interpret the production symphonies, by which methods the conductor would be appointed and by whom (1979, pp.73-74). What is certain at least is that Marx never thought these questions through.

4 Materialistically Critical Socialism

Introduction

Utopianism in the era of materialistically critical socialism, said Marx in his letter to Sorge, can only be silly, stale and reactionary from the roots up. Utopianism should have evanesced, he argued in the First Draft of *The Civil War in France*, now that a real insight into the working class movement had become possible. Utopianism appealed to the workers without a rigorous scientific idea and without a positive doctrine, he added in his attack on Weitling. All of which indicates that Marx's critique of utopian socialism took place from the perspective of an alternative; an alternative founded on real insight, an alternative containing a rigorous scientific idea and a positive doctrine, and an alternative that was materialistically critical in nature. In the present chapter I offer a detailed examination of this alternative — which, following Marx, I refer to as materialistically critical socialism — as it was elucidated by Marx during his critique of the 'utopian socialists'. What I argue is that the framework established by this theory was intended by Marx to serve the same political function that utopianism had once done, imbuing the proletariat with the future optimism required in order to invoke the spirit of revolution, but that it was intended to do so in a manner consistent with the principles of proletarian self-emancipation and self-determination (i.e., the principles which utopianism undermined). What I also argue, however, is that materialistically critical socialism — or at least the simple version of it presented by Marx when directly contrasting his ideas to those of the utopians — failed to perform this function, as Marx himself well knew.

The Need to set People in Motion

The existence of an alternative to utopianism had been announced by Marx as early as 1843, when he told us that 'we do not anticipate the world with our dogmas, but instead attempt to discover the new world through the critique of the old' (Marx, 1975b, p.207). Like the utopians, then, Marx was attempting to discover the new world. Unlike they, however, he could do this without having to anticipate it in dogmatic (i.e., utopian) terms. Because his new method of discovery was based upon a mode of critique, Marx was able to distinguish between 'utopian communist systems' and his own 'critical communism' (Marx, 1976c, p.338). This critical communism, as its name suggests, was based solely on critique and not on dogmatic anticipation or system building. When talking of the part played by theory in the working class movement, George Lichtheim is therefore correct to suggest that: 'For Marx it was "criticism" — the analysis of the actual historical process' (1969, p.195). Lichtheim is also correct, however, to observe that: 'Criticism is powerless so long as it remains speculative. It becomes a material force when it sets men in motion' (ibid.). Given that utopianism had once been able to set people in motion (a fact never denied by Marx), but that its time had now passed, one needs to ask of Marx how his critique-driven alternative was able to do the same.

The answer to this question lies, of course, in the nature of the critique contained within critical communism, or rather in the 'rigorous scientific idea' embodied in such critique. Now, to argue that Marx contrasted his own 'science' to others' utopianism is to risk being accused of vulgarisation. Such a sharp dualism was alien to Marx, it is often argued, and is nothing more than a curse placed upon Marxism by Engels. This, however, is simply untrue. For Marx did quite deliberately contrast his own science to others' utopianism, and we know this because he told us so in his 'Conspectus of Bakunin's *Statism and Anarchy*' (1874). In this little notebook one finds Marx emphasising, in response to Bakunin's mention of '*scientific socialism*', that this 'was only used in opposition to utopian socialism, which wants to attach the people to new delusions, instead of limiting its science to the knowledge of the social movement made by the people itself' (Marx, 1974e, p.337). Scientific socialism, in other words, was a phrase *specifically* coined in order to contrast Marx's conception of socialism to that of the utopians.

That Marx did contrast his own science to others' utopianism does not, however, implicate him in some vulgar dualism. For Marx was convinced that utopianism had been made redundant by the progress of history and the working class movement. Socialist utopias and utopian socialism really had, therefore, had their day. When he criticises utopian socialism from the perspective of his own scientific socialism, he is consequently being neither vulgar nor 'undialectical' — he is merely criticising the old, superseded, form of socialism from the perspective of that which had superseded it. In this sense, Marx could quite legitimately claim that 'utopian socialism, in the era of materialistically critical socialism', was *wrong* (or some other such simplistic adjective) and yet still remain faithful to an anti-dualistic dialectical approach.

In the 'Conspectus of Bakunin's *Statism and Anarchy*', Marx claimed that utopian socialism was wrong (or some other such simplistic adjective) because it attaches people to delusions rather than limiting itself, as did Marx's scientific alternative, to a knowledge of the social movement. The question prompted by this claim, however, is how, by limiting one's science to a knowledge of the social movement made by the people itself, one is able to set these same people in motion.

Here the Content goes beyond the Phrase

For Marx, the key to setting people in motion without having to provide them with utopian descriptions of the future lay in comprehending the fundamental distinction between the revolutions of the seventeenth and eighteenth centuries and those of the nineteenth. The distinction in question, most succinctly expressed in *The Eighteenth Brumaire of Louis Bonaparte* (1852), was this: 'There the phrase went beyond the content; here the content goes beyond the phrase' (Marx, 1968c, p.98). What Marx meant by this was that the English and French Revolutions had required utopian 'phrases' in order to compensate for their lack of real 'content', whereas the content of the revolution of the nineteenth century was so real that no utopian phrase could do it justice. Put another way, the content of the English and French Revolutions could not inspire action without the aid of a deceptive and utopian language, whereas the content of the revolution of the nineteenth century rendered such language thankfully obsolete.

That the revolutions of the seventeenth and eighteenth centuries *did* require utopias Marx explains in terms of the economic limitations of the revolutions themselves. In fact, he explains the utopianism of the Puritans and Jacobins using the very same framework that he used to explain the utopianism of the utopian socialists. He thus begins by pointing out that:

In both revolutions [1648, 1789], the bourgeoisie was the class which was *genuinely* to be found at the head of the movement. The proletariat, and the other sections of the town population which did not form a part of the bourgeoisie, either had as yet no interests separate from those of the bourgeoisie, or they did not yet form independently developed classes or groups within classes (Marx, 1973b, p.192).

The English and French Revolutions had as their socio-economic background conditions which as yet precluded the development of an independent proletarian class. Though lacking independent initiative, the nascent proletariat nonetheless had its spokespersons in the form of Cromwell, the Levellers, Saint-Just, Robespierre, and so on. As was the case with the utopian socialists, however, these spokespersons could only articulate the needs of the proletariat-to-be in fantastic terms, given that the material conditions for its emancipation had yet to develop. In place of real insight into these conditions, therefore, the bourgeois representatives of the nascent proletariat saw the solution to its misery in terms of the application of reason. Thus says Marx:

> The classical period of political intelligence is the French Revolution. Far from seeing the source of social defects in the state, the heroes of the French Revolution see in social defects the source of political misfortunes. Thus Robespierre sees in extremes of poverty and riches only an impediment to pure democracy. So he wishes to establish a general Spartan frugality (Marx, 1977c, p.125).

The Golden Age utopia of Spartan frugality was conjured by Robespierre in order to compensate for his lack of understanding of the historical process (although Robespierre himself could not be blamed for failing to comprehend something which as yet defied comprehension). Marx then cites the Terror — 'the year 1794' to be exact — as an example of what happens when one attempts to impose a plebeian utopia on society when the economic conditions are simply not ripe for it. Essentially, all such attempts will end in Terror-like failure 'as long as in the course of history, in its "movement", the material conditions have not yet been created which make necessary the abolition of the bourgeois mode of production and therefore also the definitive overthrow of the political rule of the bourgeoisie' (Marx, 1976c, p.319).

In the *Manifesto*, Babeuf's attempt to impose his own plebeian utopia is interpreted by Marx in the same way:

> The first direct attempts of the proletariat to attain its own ends, made in terms of universal excitement, when feudal society was being overthrown, these attempts necessarily failed, owing to the then undeveloped state of the proletariat, as well as to the absence of the economic conditions for its emancipation, conditions that had as yet to be produced, and could be produced by the impending bourgeois epoch alone. The revolutionary literature that accompanied these first movements of the proletariat had necessarily a reactionary character. It inculcated universal asceticism and social levelling in its crudest form (Marx and Engels, 1967, pp.114-115).

In many respects, then, Marx's analysis of Robespierre and Babeuf was similar to his analysis of the utopian socialists: their systems were each the fantastic products of undeveloped economic conditions and each were doomed to failure. Shlomo Avineri is also correct to highlight the similarities between Marx's account of the Terror and that of Jacob Talmon, for whom the Terror was precisely the attempt to impose a crude utopia on a people who were neither prepared for nor desirous of it (Avineri, 1968, p.189).[1] Where, however, Marx differs from Talmon — and here my own interpretation differs from that of Avineri (ibid., pp.185-201) — is in his belief that the plebeian utopianism of Robespierre and Saint-Just was a *necessary* part of the revolutionary process. For when Marx argues that 'there the phrase went beyond the content', not only is he arguing that the utopian phrases could never be realised, he is also suggesting that there the phrase *had* to go beyond the content. Little else could make sense of the first few pages of *The Eighteenth Brumaire*, the key, in my opinion, to understanding how Marx considered himself able to overcome the need for utopianism.

Marx famously begins by bemoaning the fact that revolutionaries have always felt the need to disguise their actions in clothes borrowed from the past:

> Thus Luther donned the mask of Apostle Paul, the Revolution of 1789 to 1814 draped itself alternately as the Roman republic and the Roman empire, and the Revolution of 1848 knew nothing better to do than to parody, now 1789, now the revolutionary tradition of 1793 to 1795 (Marx, 1968c, p.96).

Marx then, however, proceeds to highlight the fundamental difference between the disguises of 1789-95 and those of 1848, the difference being that the disguises of the former were *necessary*:

unheroic as bourgeois society is, it nevertheless took heroism, sacrifice, terror, civil war and battles of peoples to bring it into being. And in the classically austere traditions of the Roman republic its gladiators found the ideals and the art forms, the self-deceptions that they needed in order to conceal from themselves the bourgeois limitations of the content of their struggles and to keep their enthusiasm on the high plane of the great historical tragedy (ibid., p.97).

The revolutionaries required heroic Roman 'phrases' in order to conceal from themselves the unheroic nature of the revolution's 'content'. The implication here is that without these phrases the revolutionaries' enthusiasm would have waned and the revolution itself would have collapsed. The same is true of the English Civil War, argues Marx, in which 'Cromwell and the English people had borrowed speech, passions and illusions from the Old Testament for their bourgeois revolution' (ibid.). As a consequence,

> the awakening of the dead in those revolutions served the purpose of glorifying the new struggles, not of parodying the old; of magnifying the given task in imagination, not of fleeing from its solution in reality; of finding once more the spirit of revolution, not of making its ghost walk about again (ibid.).

The disguises of 1848, on the other hand, had served only the negative functions mentioned above — parodying old struggles, fleeing from reality, etc. — because:

> The social revolution of the nineteenth century cannot draw its poetry from the past, but only from the future. It cannot begin with itself before it has stripped off all superstition in regard to the past. Earlier revolutions required recollections of past world history in order to drug themselves concerning their own content. In order to arrive at its own content, the revolution of the nineteenth century must let the dead bury their dead. There the phrase went beyond the content; here the content goes beyond the phrase (ibid., p.98).

In arguing that the revolution of the nineteenth century cannot draw its inspiration from the past, Marx is attacking those revolutionaries who, in 1848, had attempted to do exactly that, and who, as a consequence, had been 'fleeing from reality'. He was also criticising those who were *still* fleeing from reality and who were still, therefore, spouting 'utopian nonsense, to which an end must be put' (ibid., p.102). In addition, however, he was pointing out that it did not matter that the content of the future could not be phrased because, by virtue of being 'beyond' any phrases that could be conjured now, it would attract support without the aid of utopian drugs. The content of the revolution of the nineteenth century thus went beyond the phrase in two senses: firstly, in the sense that a knowledge of this content lay beyond anyone's epistemological reach; and secondly in the sense that the magnificence of the coming content itself defied representation in terms of the phrases available to one now — it was to be so qualitatively different that it lay beyond even our most imaginative attempts to phrase it.

The key to understanding the way in which Marx considered himself able to overcome the need for utopianism lies, therefore, in the way he perceived the 'content' of the revolution of the nineteenth century. It lies in his belief that this content would defy any expectations that could be phrased now and in his conviction that people would be set in motion by the promise of such a phrase-defying content. We must turn our attention now, therefore, to the question of *how* Marx knew that the content of the revolution of the nineteenth century would go beyond the phrase.

The Material Conditions for Emancipation

In Volume 1 of *The German Ideology*, Marx and Engels proclaim that:

> Communism is for us not a *state of affairs* which is to be established, an ideal to which reality [will] have to adjust itself. We call communism the *real* movement which abolishes the present state of things. The conditions of this movement result from the premises now in existence (Marx and Engels, 1970, pp.56-57).

Communism was a movement, the premises of which were *now* in existence, rather than an ideal 'end', the realisation of which would demand adjustments being made to reality by some independently conceived 'means'. For Marx, then, what distinguished his ideas from those of the utopians was that he had established a real and necessary link between the capitalist present and the communist future. Never before had this link been made, or, to put it another way, all previous attempts to make this link had been utopian ones — fantastic images of the classless society abstracted from the horrors of contemporary class divisions and heralded as 'oughts'. What

Marx *thought* he was doing that was new, then, (irrespective of whether this was *in fact* new), was superseding the fantastic abstractions and wishful thinking that typified utopianism by *grounding* the socialist future in the present.

It is interesting to note here that when directly contrasting his position to those of the utopians, it was always a deterministic version of historical development, with all its talk of 'necessity' and 'inevitability', that Marx employed. The essence of this position is well stated in *The Civil War in France*:

> The working class . . . have no ready-made utopias to introduce *par décret du people*. They know that in order to work out their own emancipation, and along with it that higher form to which present society is irresistibly tending by its own economical agencies, they will have to pass through long struggles, through a series of historical processes, transforming circumstances and men. They have no ideals to realise, but to free the elements of the new society with which the old collapsing bourgeois society itself is pregnant (Marx, 1968e, p.291).

Although, therefore, the future is many struggles and transformations away, this society *will be* an emancipatory one because the emancipated society is what the present bourgeois one is pregnant with — the present society is 'irresistibly tending by its own economical agencies' towards a 'higher form'. A knowledge of this enables the working-class to avoid the need for utopias.

The difference between the Marxist and the utopian positions is subsequently summarised by Engels in *The Housing Question* (1873):

> To be utopian does not mean to maintain that the emancipation of humanity from the chains which its historic past has forged will be complete only when the antithesis between town and country has been abolished; the utopia begins only when one ventures, 'from existing conditions', to prescribe the *form* in which this or any other antithesis of present-day society is to be resolved (Engels, 1962, p.628).

Marx and Engels did not have to describe 'the form' that communism would take in order to know that it will exist; their theoretical framework enabled them to read the future emancipation of humanity into the antitheses of present-day society and thus avoid utopianism.

In *The Poverty of Philosophy*, Marx explains how they were able to do this:

> Just as the *economists* are the scientific representatives of the bourgeois class, so the *socialists* and the *Communists* are the theoreticians of the proletarian class. So long as the proletariat is not yet sufficiently developed to constitute itself as a class, and consequently so long as the very struggle of the proletariat with the bourgeoisie has not yet assumed a political character, and the productive forces are not yet sufficiently developed in the bosom of the bourgeoisie itself to enable us to catch a glimpse of the material conditions necessary for the emancipation of the proletariat and for the formation of a new society, these theoreticians are merely utopians who, to meet the wants of the oppressed classes, improvise systems and go in search of a regenerating science. But in the measure that history moves forward, and with it the struggle of the proletariat assumes clearer outlines, they no longer need to seek science in their minds; they have only to take note of what is happening before their eyes and to become its mouthpiece. So long as they look for science and merely make systems, so long as they are at the beginning of the struggle, they see in poverty nothing but poverty, without seeing in it the revolutionary, subversive side, which will overthrow the old society. From this moment they see this side, science, which is produced by the historical movement and associating itself consciously with it, has ceased to be doctrinaire and has become revolutionary (Marx, 1976b, pp.177-178).

Here then, Marx once again contrasts his own position to those of the utopians. His basic position, so contrasted, was this: that utopianism had been symptomatic of an insufficiently developed capitalism and proletariat; that now, however, both had developed to such an extent that utopianism had been rendered obsolete; that the productive forces were now so sufficiently developed within the bosom of the bourgeoisie that revolutionary science need only 'take note of what is happening before its eyes'; that it need do no more than this, i.e., it need not improvise utopian systems, because the scientist can now 'catch a glimpse of the material conditions necessary for the emancipation of the proletariat'.

Marx provides a neat summary of this argument in his obituary to Proudhon. Here Marx tells us that 'the utopians are hunting for a so-called "science" by which a formula for the "solution of the social question" is to be excogitated *a priori*' (Marx and Engels, 1969, p.188). Immediately following this, however, and yet again contrasting his position to utopian *a priori* excogitation, he says that he derives *his* 'science from a critical knowledge of the historical movement, a movement which itself produces the *material conditions for emancipation*' (ibid.).

An important point to note is that both here and in *The Poverty of Philosophy* it is 'the material conditions *for*' the emancipated society that are grounded in the present and not the *nature* of that society itself. And the same phrase reappears during the *Manifesto*'s critique of the utopians:

> Since the development of class antagonism keeps even pace with the development of industry, the economic situation, as they find it, does not as yet offer to them the material conditions for the emancipation of the proletariat. They therefore search after a new social science, after new social laws, that are to create these conditions (Marx and Engels, 1967, p.115).

The phrase reappears once again in *Grundrisse*:

> if we do not find concealed in society as it is the material conditions of production and the corresponding relations of exchange prerequisite for a classless society, then all our attempts to explode it would be quixotic (Marx, 1973a, p.159).

Turning back a few pages, one might have noticed that Marx uses similar phrases in his critique of both the Jacobins and Babeuf. Turning back further still (to the first chapter in fact), one finds exactly the same phrase being used in the 'First Draft of *The Civil War in France*' (Marx, 1974c, p.262). From this I think it fair to conclude that the fundamental distinction between Marx's position and those of the utopians (as perceived by Marx himself) was that he had discovered 'the material conditions for the emancipation of the proletariat'. In his letter to Domela-Nieuwenhuis of 1881, Marx describes the material conditions in question thus:

> Scientific insight into the inevitable disintegration of the dominant order of society continually proceeding before our eyes and the ever-growing fury into which the masses are lashed by the old ghostly governments, while at the same time the positive development of the means of production advances with gigantic strides — all this is a sufficient guarantee that the moment a real proletarian revolution breaks out the conditions (though these are certain not to be idyllic) for its immediately next *modus operandi* will be in existence (Marx and Engels, 1969, p.411).

There are thus two 'material conditions for emancipation' or two elements to the 'sufficient guarantee' that the future lies in communism. The first is fairly straightforward — the masses are being lashed into an ever-growing fury, thus grounding the future existence of a revolutionary situation. The second — the fact that the means of production are advancing with gigantic strides — is slightly less straightforward because it is this element which guarantees that the revolution will usher in communism, as opposed to some other not-capitalism. Marx nonetheless means nothing more by this than what Engels had said in his *Principles of Communism* (1847), namely, that 'hitherto the productive forces had not yet been so far developed that enough could be produced for all', but that now 'large-scale industry and the unlimited expansion of production which it makes possible can bring into being a social order in which . . . all the necessities of life will be produced' (Engels, 1976, p.350, p.347).

'Materialistically critical socialism', as elucidated by Marx himself when specifically contrasting his position to utopianism, can therefore be summarised using the following categories: The 'increasing fury of the masses' and 'the possibility of the unlimited expansion of production', which represent 'the historically created material conditions for the emancipation of humanity', 'sufficiently guarantee' that when 'a real proletarian revolution' breaks out it will be the 'classless society' 'concealed within' these material conditions that will follow. Because, therefore, 'the present society is irresistibly tending by its own economic agencies towards a higher form', a 'science' based upon the 'critical knowledge' of these facts allows one to avoid the 'fantastic anticipations' and '*a priori* excogitations' which define the utopian methodology. If science 'takes note of what is happening before its eyes' it can also show why 'here the content goes beyond the phrase'.

When Marx contrasts his own 'rigorous scientific idea' to the utopians' *a priori* excogitations, he is therefore claiming no more than this: that theoreticians of the proletarian class such as himself take note of what is happening before their eyes and limit themselves to the knowledge of the social movement made by the people itself. They thus become the mouthpieces of 'science' in the sense that a) they consciously associate themselves with the historical movement which has made such 'science' possible and b) they recognise and can thus articulate the revolutionary nature of the science which the historical process has made possible. By means of an empirically-based analysis of, rather than *a priori* excogitations about, the historical movement, the theoreticians of the proletarian class are able to observe the present existence of the material conditions requisite for future human emancipation.

More than this, however, Marx believed that his own brand of critical communism enabled him to do all of the things that utopianism had once done but without falling into the traps that the utopians had fallen into. For the idea that the theoreticians of the proletarian class can discover 'the material conditions for emancipation' by merely taking note of what is happening before their eyes serves several distinct purposes for Marx: firstly, by establishing that the emancipation of the proletariat is grounded in the material conditions of the *present*, Marx's claims are kept safely within its epistemological confines; secondly, by establishing, through mere observation, that the emancipation of the proletariat is grounded in the material conditions of *its own existence*, Marx avoids the idea that these conditions have to be imported from outside and manages, therefore, to uphold the principle of proletarian self-emancipation denied by utopian philanthropists; thirdly, because it is the material conditions *for* the emancipated society, and not the *nature* of that society itself, which are grounded in the present, the future is not foreclosed and the principle of proletarian self-determination escapes unscathed; and finally, by emphasising that the material conditions for the emancipated society of the future *are* grounded in the present, the theoreticians are able to glorify and magnify the struggle *of* the present and thereby capture the spirit of revolution.

This is what Marx's critique of utopian socialism was all about — materialistically critical socialism could do everything that utopianism could do, but it could do so without foreclosing the future and without resorting to philanthropic paternalism or messianic elitism. As a consequence, utopian socialism, in the era of materialistically critical socialism, could only be silly, stale and reactionary from the roots up.

The Failings of Materialistically Critical Socialism

By taking note of what is happening before their eyes, the theoreticians of the proletarian class are able to identify the material conditions for the emancipation of humanity, i.e., the material conditions within which the classless society is concealed. The two principal 'material conditions' in question are the ever-growing fury of the masses and the simultaneous development of the means of production. According to Marx, these two factors between them ensure a) that society as it is will be destroyed and b) that a classless society will take its place. This, as we have just seen, is the essence of the 'materialistically critical socialism' which Marx directly counterposes to utopianism.

The merest glance at this schema reveals a problem, however. For how does Marx extrapolate from a) the productive forces of society are developing by means of gigantic strides to b) a proletarian revolution will usher forth a classless society? What, in other words, links the present development of the productive forces to the future existence of a classless society? In the lengthy passage taken from *The Poverty of Philosophy* Marx states that he is able to make this link because the productive forces are now 'sufficiently developed within the bosom of the bourgeoisie' to enable him to do so. He also argues that the theoreticians of the proletarian class no longer need to seek science in their minds because the struggle of the proletariat has now assumed clearer outlines. What these two remarks seem to indicate, therefore, is that the general claims made by Marx during his critique of the utopians were informed by two more specific ideas — one concerning the very nature of the development of the productive forces and one concerning the very nature of the proletarian struggle.

The Forces of Production, Historical Progress and the Classless Society

When Marx argues that the formation of a new society is grounded in the 'sufficient development' of the productive forces within the bosom of the bourgeoisie itself, what he is claiming is that the future existence of a classless society can be sufficiently guaranteed by an adequate understanding of the relationship between the forces and relations of production. What I want to do now, therefore, is take a look at the forces/relations model of historical development and assess the way in which it links the future development of a classless society to the present development of the productive forces.

Beginning with the way in which this model explains the development of a revolutionary consciousness within the proletariat, Marx says that 'this consciousness must be explained from the contradictions of material life, from the conflict existing between the social forces of production and the relations of production' (Marx, 1970, p.21). Here, revolutionary consciousness is explained in terms of the contradictions lying at the heart of the present and not in terms of the perspective granted by the conception of a utopian alternative. Indeed, this has to be the case, for: 'It is not the consciousness of men that determines their existence, but their social existence that determines their consciousness' (ibid.). On this basis, consciousness of a future set of social relations is denied access to everywhere except the imagination. This point is reinforced by the assertion that:

> In the social production of their existence, men inevitably enter into definite relations, which are independent of their will, namely relations of production appropriate to a given stage in the development of the forces of production (ibid., p.20).

In other words, one cannot become conscious of a set of social relations until one enters into them and one's entry into them is a matter beyond one's will, thus precluding the possibility of willing into existence an alternative set.

What Marx is offering here is both a realist-materialist epistemology (a subject/object dualism in which the object, i.e., the individuals' social existence, has explanatory primacy) and what M. Levin terms a 'topographical theory of consciousness' (how one interprets one's social existence is dependant upon one's economic position within it — see Levin, 1990, pp.298-299). The proletariat's social existence thus determines its consciousness but its economic position allows it to become conscious of the *contradictions* within this existence, ensuring that its consciousness becomes revolutionary. In this way, Marx avoids pure voluntarism (the proletariat's consciousness is actually *grounded in*, i.e., is something more than a mere response to, capitalism's structural weaknesses) and pure structuralism (it is the proletariat, and not capitalism itself, which constitutes the transformative force).

The model still leaves the future open, however, and fails to ground *socialism*, as opposed to *not-capitalism*, in the present. For the question is *how* the proletariat becomes aware of the structural contradiction between the forces and relations of production. According to Marx, one becomes aware of the fact that 'the productive forces of society [have] come into conflict with the existing relations of production' because one becomes aware that '[f]rom forms of development of the productive forces these relations [have] turn[ed] into their fetters' (Marx, 1970, p.21). This, however, begs another question, namely, how the proletariat (or anyone else for that matter) knows what the existing relations of production are acting as a fetter *on*.

In answer to this question, as we have already seen, Marx and Engels argued that the present was destroying itself a) because it was creating proletarian misery and b) because capitalism contained within itself the possibility of vastly increased production. From this we then saw them argue that c) the productive forces were now sufficiently developed to bring into being new relations that would satisfy everyone's needs, and d) that the abolition of the present relations of production would ensure that the free society would follow. But, as has already been suggested, to deduce c) and d) from a) and b) involves a giant leap of faith. For thus far Marx has merely stated that the productive forces of society could be developed more effectively than they are presently being allowed to and that by virtue of their economic position within capitalism the proletarians are able to discern that this is so. There is, however, nothing in these claims which even imply, let alone establish or demonstrate, that 'concealed within' the potential development of the productive forces is the actual development of a classless society — all that is implied is that the productive forces of society could be developed more effectively than they are presently being allowed to and that the proletarians are able to discern this. Marx seems to be deducing, therefore, that because the proletariat is able to discern some unrealised potential within the productive forces of society, these same proletarians are destined to introduce a classless society and thus emancipate the whole of humanity. To suggest that this was an optimistic conclusion to reach would be to understate the case a little.

Viewed in the light of the things that Marx tells us about the relations of production that will exist in full communism — i.e., that common ownership will have replaced private property, that classes will have disappeared, that the workers will control the means of production and that the division of labour will have been abolished — the problem faced by Marx can be reformulated as follows: how does he know that the present relations of production are fettering the development of *these* future relations of production? How, that is, does Marx know that these specific relations of production are 'appropriate' to the stage in the development of the productive forces that society will progress to once the current fetters have been destroyed? To suggest here that these proposals are merely negative extrapolations made from the capitalist relations of production they are supposedly going to supersede (the negation of the negation, as it were) will not do because, as Barbara Goodwin rightly points out:

> Although logical propositions have contradictions and contraries, there is no such thing as a contradictory institution: even inversion cannot achieve this unambiguously — the opposite of rule by men could be rule by women, children, monkeys or God . . . one might almost believe that *the* contrary to private property is collective ownership, or that the only alternative to the

nuclear family is the collective rearing of children, whereas these are drawn from a range of alternatives (Goodwin and Taylor, 1982, p.30).

If, therefore, the relations of production engendered by private property are indeed fettering the further development of the productive forces, this does not means that, once abolished, they will be replaced by common ownership of the means of production. For it may be the case that the productive forces of society develop better in response to a meritocratic ownership structure. Indeed, it could be the case that, as Saint-Simon believed, the development of the productive forces of society would best be served if control of them were placed in the hands of the 'scientists'. At any rate, what is certain is that common ownership is not the only possible negation of private property, nor is worker control of the means of production the only negation of control by capitalists.

Fortunately, however, Marx's vague pronouncements concerning the relations of production that would exist in full communism were not informed by the (false) belief that they represented the logical negation of the relations of production that exist in capitalism. As we saw in the previous chapter, they were informed instead by a belief that these relations would foster proletarian self-determination. What this seems to suggest, however, is that Marx's belief in the future existence of these relations was premised on nothing more than an ethical imperative: because the current relations of production hinder proletarian self-determination they should be abolished and because the ones he describes foster self-determination they should replace them. Not only, therefore, does this imply a norm-based voluntarism on Marx's part, it also undermines his basic claim that 'men inevitably enter into definite relations, *which are independent of their will*, namely relations of production appropriate to a given stage in the development of the forces of production'.[2]

One possible way of circumventing problems such as these would be to suggest that, for Marx, what *should* be *will* be. There is, in other words, a great coincidence between communism as an ethical norm and communism as an historical movement: people will enter the definite relations of communism independently of their will, but it just so happens that these relations will be the ones which Marx believes ought to exist. As far as the basic forces/relations model of historical development goes, however, this really would have to be a coincidence. For to argue that *because* certain aspects of the present relations of production hinder proletarian self-determination, the next relations of production will *therefore* facilitate this, is to confuse two separate and quite distinct issues. There is, at least as far as I can see, nothing to prevent the next relations of production from facilitating the development of the productive forces *without* a common plan, *without* the common ownership of the means of production or even *with* the increased subordination of the individual to the division of labour. Nothing other than a coincidence, that is.

Or a general theory of progress. For Marx did not treat the transition from capitalism to communism in isolation: he placed this transition in the context of all previous transitions, and the context established by these transitions was one of progressive historical development. On the subsequent basis of what may be tentatively termed his theory of 'progress', Marx considered himself able to deduce that the productive forces of the present, once released from their fetters, would generate a future set of social relations that would be considered 'emancipatory' when compared to those of the present because a series of precedents had established the inherently progressive nature of the historical process. With regards to the form taken by the inherently progressive nature of the historical process, Marx tells us in the Preface to *A Contribution to the Critique of Political Economy* that: 'In broad outline, the Asiatic, ancient, feudal and modern bourgeois modes of production may be designated as epochs marking progress in the economic development of society' (Marx, 1970, p.21). Progress is thus defined in terms of a series of radical transitions, from one mode of production to another. The radical transition from capitalism to communism is then referred to as the final mark of progress, confining all previous developments to the dustbin of 'prehistory' (ibid., p.22). A similar schema is put forward in *The German Ideology*, where Marx again divides history into four principal epochs: the tribal, ancient, feudal and capitalist (Marx and Engels, 1970, pp.43-48). Once again, then, progress is defined in terms of a series of radical transitions, and once again the transition to communism is seen as that which will mark the end of (pre)history. The central issue now, of course, is whether or not this context of progressive development allowed Marx to talk of the transition to communism without ultimately relying upon pure optimism.

The answer here is no, simply because Marx establishes this context so badly. In *The German Ideology*, for example, the four modes of production are merely described and no attempt is made to explain the transitions between them. Instead, the materialist conception of history is developed separately as a general theory and the reader is then left to apply this theory to the movement from one epoch to the next. In the Preface to *A*

Contribution to the Critique of Political Economy, moreover, the progressive development of the four modes of production is simply taken for granted and one is led to assume that Marx has established the progression elsewhere. Unfortunately, however, he had not, and the few attempts he did make invariably saw him becoming embroiled in a tangled mess of ideas. In *Grundrisse*, for example, Marx explains the transition made in Europe from the Asiatic (primitive communal or tribal) mode of production to the ancient – of which Rome was 'the most classic example' (Marx, 1973a, p.484) – in terms of competition for land, subsequent wars, the taking of slaves and the ultimate erection of an oligarchic empire (ibid., pp.471-494). When attempting to explain why this transition had not taken place in Asia itself, Marx first toys with the idea that the development of cities in Europe had something to do with it (ibid., pp.476-479) and then suggests that Europe transcended the Asiatic mode of production because the Asiatic mode of production never really existed in Europe — it was based instead on a specifically *Germanic* form of communal property which Marx directly contrasts to the Asiatic form. The first of these ideas leads Marx into murky waters, however, as he dismisses Asian cities as 'works of artifice' (ibid., p.479), whilst the second does no less than undermine his whole Asiatic-ancient-feudal-capitalist framework. Needless to say, Marx never satisfactorily resolves the matter.

More problematic still was the transition from the ancient or classical mode of production to that of feudalism. In fact, Marx never even *attempted* to explain this transition and one can well understand why. For as George Lichtheim remarks:

> One cannot deduce from a general law of social evolution the alleged necessity for one type of society to give birth to a more developed one — otherwise it would be incomprehensible why classical Antiquity regressed and made room for a primitive type of feudalism, instead of evolving to a higher level (1971, p.75).

Of the various transitions in question, the one which Marx *did* try his hardest to explain was the transition from feudalism to capitalism. Even here, however, his account is neither consistent nor entirely convincing. For in Volume III of *Capital* Marx acknowledges two possible modes of transition, a first in which 'The producer becomes merchant and capitalist' and a second in which 'the merchant establishes direct sway over production' (Marx, 1959, p.329). As Robert J. Holton rightly indicates, these two modes of transition emphasise completely different causal factors — the first explains the transition from feudalism to capitalism in terms of the growth of a 'wage-labour' force whilst the second does so by identifying 'the origins of mercantile activity and the growth of towns and trade' (1981, p.836). In Volume III of *Capital* itself, Marx describes the producer-merchant-capitalist route as 'the really revolutionizing path', whereas the merchant-industrialist route 'cannot', it is said, 'by itself contribute to the overthrow of the old mode of production' (Marx, 1959, p.329). In *The German Ideology*, however, Marx had quite clearly opted for the latter route and had explained the transition from feudalism to capitalism almost solely in terms of the development of towns and mercantile trade (Marx and Engels, 1970, p.74, p.80). The transition from feudalism to capitalism has subsequently formed the basis of various debates within the field of Marxist socio-economic history, and as Holton again points out, the sheer complexity and ferocity of these debates 'can probably be explained by the shifting and somewhat ambivalent character of Marx's comments on social change in general and the rather brief and unsystematic nature of his comments on the transition from feudalism to capitalism in particular' (1981, p.834).

In addition to the problems associated with Marx's account of the individual transitions contained within his historical schema, one also has to deal with the ambiguous legacy he bequeathed concerning its universal validity. For whilst in the Preface to *A Contribution to the Critique of Political Economy*, Marx seems to be arguing that societies in general progress by moving through the Asiatic-ancient-feudal-capitalist matrix, elsewhere he indicates that historical development is a multilinear process and that different societies may therefore progress in different ways and along different paths. The most famous example of this concerns Marx's discussion of Russia, the most pertinent aspects of which were set down in his notorious letter to Vera Sassoulitch. For in 1881 Sassoulitch had written to Marx asking him to confirm that, in his view, the mir (i.e., the traditional peasant commune) would have to disintegrate and give way to capitalism before Russia could expect to witness the realisation of communism. In response, Marx wrote with regards to the development of capitalism that 'the 'historical inevitability' of this movement is expressly limited to the countries of Western Europe' (Marx, 1977d, p.576), supplementing this with the claim that the peasant commune could act as 'the mainspring of Russia's social development' (ibid., pp.576-577). Indeed, in one of his draft letters, Marx added that 'the Russian 'rural commune' can . . . become a direct starting point for the economic system towards which modern society is tending. It can acquire a new skin without beginning by its suicide. It can obtain the fruits with which capitalist production has enriched humanity without passing through the capitalist regime' (ibid., pp.577-578).

Angus Walker accounts for the fact that Marx abandoned the Asiatic-ancient-feudal-capitalist model in the following terms:

> Disappointed by the failure of capitalism to give rise to the revolutionary movements on which he had pinned his hopes in Europe, his desire to encourage Russian radicals with economic ideas significantly different from his own, led him to betray the most powerful elements in his own theory (1978, p.200).

Whilst there is undoubtedly some truth to this, I would suggest in addition that Marx was willing to betray his own theory because he was prepared to accept that in certain circumstances it remained unconvincing. Marx had found it extremely difficult to explain the various transitions of which his theory was comprised and was therefore willing to accept that, in a country still stuck somewhere between the Asiatic and feudal modes of production, alternative transitional models may work better than his own. If, like Germany and France, Russia had been in the midst of a bourgeois revolution, then one would probably have found Marx advocating a revolutionary dictatorship as a means of consolidating its shaky bourgeois foundations. No such foundations existed in Russia, however, and Marx knew that he would have been unable to explain how these were to develop. As a consequence, he abandoned his general schema and opted instead for a specifically Russian one.

In terms of the present discussion, what this example reveals is that the context of historical progress within which the transition from capitalism to communism was supposedly set was itself resting on shaky foundations. What it also shows, however, is that Marx was aware of this. With regards to the forces/relations model of historical development, then, I feel more than safe in concluding a) that it failed in its attempt to ground the communist future in the capitalist present and b) that this failure undermined the basis upon which Marx's materialistically critical alternative to utopian socialism rested. Neither the progressive development of historical epochs in general nor the specific relationship between the forces and relations of production within capitalism could be used in support of the claim that a classless society was 'concealed within' the material conditions of the present. There was, that is, nothing inherently emancipatory about the development of the productive forces.

The Proletariat, Private Property and the Classless Society

Marx repeatedly criticised the utopians for their conception of the proletariat: 'Only from the point of view of being the most suffering class does the proletariat exist for them' (Marx and Engels, 1967, p.116). For Marx, on the other hand, the proletariat was not 'only' the most suffering class, it was also the historical guarantor of socialism. Not only, that is, did Marx believe that its economic position enabled the proletariat to become aware of the contradictions within capitalism, he also believed that its very nature as a class meant that it alone was able to resolve these contradictions and usher in communism as opposed to some other not-capitalism. Two analytically distinct models were employed by Marx in this respect, one which attempted to establish a direct link between the proletarian revolution and the transition to a classless society and another which attempted to link the proletarian revolution with the abolition of private property and thus, by logical implication, with the transition to a classless society.

The first of these models rests on two principal claims. The first is that each new class 'achieves its hegemony only on a broader basis than that of the class ruling previously', and the second is that 'the opposition of the non-ruling class against the new ruling class later develops all the more sharply and profoundly' (ibid.). The simplification of the class structure and the subsequent intensification of the class struggle, together with the 'broadness' of the base upon which the proletariat stands, ensures that a proletarian revolution will bring an end to 'class rule in general' (ibid.). Let us deal with each of these ideas in turn.

With regards to the simplification of the class structure, this is phrased in the *Manifesto* thus: 'Society as a whole is more and more splitting up into two great hostile camps, into two great classes facing each other: Bourgeoisie and Proletariat' (Marx and Engels, 1967, p.80). This is then placed in historical context. For: 'In the earlier epochs of history, we find almost everywhere a complicated arrangement of society into various orders, a manifold gradation of social rank' (ibid.). In these earlier epochs, Marx continues, the multitude of classes meant that the social ascendancy of one particular class could not possibly do away with class antagonisms altogether. Instead, remnants of old classes persisted into the new epoch, or they mutated into new classes, and thus brought with them 'new forms of struggle in place of the old ones' (ibid.). The 'distinctive feature' of 'the epoch of the bourgeoisie' is thus the sheer simplicity of its class structure; its division into 'two great classes' (ibid.).

Together with the splitting-up of society into two great classes comes the intensification of the struggle between them. This intensification is explained in terms of the increasing misery of the proletariat on the one (negative) hand and their expanding association on the (positive) other. As Marx proclaims in *Capital*:

> Along with the constantly diminishing number of the magnates of capital, who usurp and monopolise all advantages of this process of transformation, grows the mass of misery, oppression, slavery, degradation, exploitation; but with this too grows the revolt of the working-class, a class always increasing in numbers, and disciplined, united, organised by the very mechanism of the very process of capitalist production itself (Marx, 1946, pp.788-789).

In this passage one also encounters the notion that the proletariat is forever expanding and thus broadening its social base. The very nature of 'the epoch of the bourgeoisie' means, therefore, that once the day of its great face-off with the bourgeoisie arrives, the proletariat will encompass the vast majority of humanity. 'One capitalist always kills many', argues Marx, and the centralisation of capital brings with it the 'expropriation of many capitalists by few', consigning the victims of expropriation to the ranks of the proletariat (Marx, 1946, p.788). This, in turn, means that with the transition from capitalism to communism 'we have the expropriation of a few usurpers by the mass of the people' (ibid., p.789).

According to this first model, then, an end will be put to class rule in general because, with the victory of the proletariat in its coming confrontation with the bourgeoisie, history will quite simply have run out of classes. With society divided into two great classes, and with one of these comprising only 'a few usurpers', there would be no scope for the development of 'new classes, new conditions of oppression, new forms of struggle' once these usurpers had been expropriated (Marx and Engels, 1967, p.80). 'The proletarian movement' in this sense becomes 'the self-conscious, independent movement of the immense majority, in the interest of the immense majority' (ibid., p.92), and the inevitable victory of this movement represents the final disintegration of the proletariat and of classes in general.

Unsurprisingly perhaps, more than one writer has detected a

millenarian strain to this line of argument. Karl Löwith and Mircea Eliade each compare it to the Jewish-Christian belief in the final fight between Christ and Antichrist (Löwith, 1949, p.44; Eliade, 1987, p.207), D. Rudolf Bultmann compares it to 'the struggle between Good and Evil' (1957, p.69) and Reinhold Niebuhr suggests that it parallels the messianic belief in 'the final triumph over evil in history' (1949, p.210). Nor has the inadequacy of Marx's account of the simplification and intensification of the class struggle escaped the attention of subsequent commentators. As Oscar Berland remarks:

> When 'Marx' is refuted it is generally the concept of proletarian revolution resulting from the polarization of wealth on one side and poverty on the other that is toppled and re-toppled. It is an easy concept to criticize. Capitalist society has not polarized in the manner Marx anticipated; the proletarians of industrial nations have not become more revolutionary (1990, p.291).

The inadequacy of Marx's account of the simplification and intensification of the class struggle stems, in fact, from the inadequacy of his account of the nature of 'classes' in general. There is little doubt that Marx was conscious of this lacuna in his works, for he was still grappling with the subject on his deathbed (his death inconveniently interrupted the only systematic exploration of 'class' he ever attempted to offer, published by Engels as the final chapter of *Capital* Volume III). Of great importance, moreover, is the fact that when Marx did investigate the nature of 'class' he openly conceded that the matter was far more complex than his general pronouncements would have us believe. In Volume III of *Capital*, therefore, Marx remarks that: 'In England, modern society is indisputably most highly and classically developed in economic structure. Nevertheless, even here the stratification of classes does not appear in its pure form. Middle and intermediate strata even here obliterate lines of demarcation everywhere' (Marx, 1959, p.862). He then concedes that, according to his own criteria, the term 'class' can be applied to 'the infinite fragmentation of interest and rank into which the division of social labour splits labourers as well as capitalists and landowners' (ibid., p.863). Elsewhere, too, Marx clearly expresses the view that the bourgeois epoch was not splitting into two great camps. In the *Theories of Surplus Value*, in fact, the converse was true, for there Marx quite readily concedes that 'the middle class will increase in size and the working proletariat will make up a constantly diminishing proportion of the total population' (Marx, 1969, p.579). This, he then adds, is 'the tendency of bourgeois society' (ibid.). The debilitating effect of remarks such as these upon the first of Marx's models is quite obvious. For if the bourgeois epoch, like all those preceding it, was indeed typified by 'a complicated arrangement of society into various orders' then that epoch would cease to possess the 'distinctive feature' which enabled Marx to separate the interests of the proletariat from those of all the other classes which had hitherto existed. The bourgeois epoch becomes just another epoch and the proletariat just another class.

This, then, is where the second of Marx's models comes in. For here it is neither the numerical supremacy of the proletariat nor the simplification and intensification of its struggle with the bourgeoisie which guarantees its relation to communism, but rather the position it occupies in relation to private property. Unfortunately, however, many of the claims upon which this model is based pre-empt Lukács' attempts to 'out-Hegel Hegel'. Take the following passage from *The Holy Family* as an example:

> Private property as private property, as wealth, is compelled to maintain *itself*, and thereby its opposite, the proletariat, in *existence* . . . The proletariat, on the contrary, is compelled as proletariat to abolish itself and thereby its opposite, private property, which determines its existence, and which makes it proletariat . . . The proletariat executes the sentence that private property pronounces on itself by producing the proletariat . . . When the proletariat is victorious, it by no means becomes the absolute side of society, for it is victorious only by abolishing itself and its opposite. Then the proletariat disappears as well as the opposite which determines it, private property (Marx and Engels, 1980b, pp.46-47).

Here Marx argues that, by virtue of having produced the proletariat, private property pronounces its own death sentence. Why? Because the proletariat is *compelled* by dialectical logic to abolish that thing which created it. Simple! In his 'Towards a Critique of Hegel's *Philosophy of Right*: Introduction', Marx expands upon the nature of this compulsion when he describes the proletariat as

> a class with radical chains, a class in civil society that is not a class of civil society, of a social group that is the dissolution of all social groups, of a sphere that has a universal character because of its universal sufferings and lays claim to no particular right, because it is the object of no particular injustice but of injustice in general. This class can no longer lay claim to a

historical status, but only to a human one. It is, finally, a sphere that cannot emancipate itself without emancipating itself from all other spheres of society and thereby emancipating these other spheres themselves. In a word, it is the complete loss of humanity and thus can only recover itself by a complete redemption of humanity (Marx, 1977b, pp.72-73).

One finds here that humanity *will* recover itself because the proletariat, by virtue of its very existence, can *only* represent universal humanity. The proletarian revolution is guaranteed to 'emancipate humanity' because the emancipation of humanity is somehow contained *within* it. Here, I think it fair to say, dialectics descends into mysticism. More importantly, it was precisely this kind of mystical approach that Marx mocked the 'true socialists' for clinging onto. It was because they used 'an arbitrary connection with German philosophy' to 'fabricate some fantastic relationship' between the present and the future 'with the help of the "absolute" or some other ideological method' (Marx and Engels, 1970, p.119), i.e., it was precisely because the 'true socialists' *needed* to rely upon ideological concepts such as the 'Absolute' (the 'universal' subject) that Marx spent hundred of pages deriding them in *The German Ideology*.

What Marx's mysticism was trying to get at, of course, was the notion that 'The proletarians have nothing to lose but their chains' (Marx and Engels, 1967, pp.120-121). As Robin Blackburn remarks: 'Without any stake in capitalist private property, the proletariat's historical mission is to destroy it' (1990, p.241). In *Wage Labour and Capital*, Marx provides us with a non-mystic rendering of this theme when he talks of the 'free labourers' who are forced to sell themselves to the highest bidder at auction (Marx, 1968b, p.74). For the worker, argues Marx, 'whose sole source of livelihood is the sale of his labour power, cannot leave *the whole class of purchasers, that is, the capitalist class*, without renouncing his existence. He belongs not to this or that capitalist but to the *capitalist class*, and, moreover, it is his business to dispose of himself, that is, to find a purchaser within the capitalist class' (ibid., p.75). When Marx refers to the proletariat as the object of injustice in general, the complete loss of humanity, and so on, he is therefore referring to the fact that it belongs to a class that will allow it to starve unless the proletarians themselves continually prostitute themselves to it. From this Marx then deduces that the proletariat is destined to destroy the system which gives rise to such a complete loss of humanity.

The link made here between the proletariat and communism rests upon the claim that the proletariat as a class has no interests in the present system which, in a future system, will be foisted upon others. As Marx says in the *Manifesto*:

> All the preceding classes that got the upper hand sought to fortify their already acquired status by subjecting society at large to their conditions of appropriation. The proletariat cannot become masters of the productive forces of society, except by abolishing their own previous mode of appropriation, and thereby also every other previous mode of appropriation. They have nothing of their own to secure and fortify; their mission is to destroy all previous securities for, and insurances of, individual property (Marx and Engels, 1967, p.92).

Because the proletariat has nothing of its own to secure and fortify, the society it creates will not be subjected to its conditions of appropriation. The proletariat appropriates nothing and can therefore do nothing other than abolish all modes of appropriation. Hence the inevitability of its bringing forth a classless society.

There was one major flaw in this line of thought, however, as Marx himself was aware: the fact that the working class did not present itself as a unified class. Instead, it was bitterly divided and the various divisions did, in fact, believe that they had interests to secure and fortify. That Marx recognised this may come as a surprise, for his denigrators often criticise his failure to anticipate the proletariat's incorporation into capitalism and its inability to confront the system of private property as a unified force. Anticipate these things, however, he did. For even in the *Manifesto* Marx had complained that: 'This organization of the proletarians into a class, and consequently into a political party, is continually being upset again by the competition between the workers themselves' (Marx and Engels, 1967, p.90). Such upsets were, in turn, a necessary product of the proletarians' need to compete with each other on the labour market, thus rendering division, rather than unity, the end result of the proletarian's position within the system of private property. Indeed, in his 'Instructions for Delegates to the Geneva Congress' of the First International in 1866, Marx remarked that: 'The disunion of the workmen is created and perpetuated by their *unavoidable competition between themselves*' (Marx, 1974b, p.91). Compounding the effects of this competition within the working class was the fact that its representative organisations, i.e., the trade unions, were seeking to give it a stake in the very system which perpetuated its miserable existence. Whilst, therefore, Marx conceded that the fight for better wages, conditions and working hours was 'not only legitimate' but 'necessary', he also added that: 'Too exclusively bent upon the local and immediate struggles with capital, the trade unions have not yet fully understood their power of acting against the system of wage slavery itself' (ibid.).

The problem faced by Marx (and by all subsequent Marxists as well) was that the proletariat's objective existence as a class had yet to translate into a subjective awareness of its existence as a class. And yet it was precisely its subjective awareness of its class position that had enabled Marx to link the proletariat with a classless future. The future existence of a classless society had been extrapolated by Marx from the notion that the proletariat would recognise its existence as a class which had 'nothing of its own to secure and fortify'. If, however, the proletarians were divided by the *unavoidable* competition between themselves, and if this competition gave rise to competing organisations each of which attempted to further the interests that their members had in the system of private property, then what becomes of the proletariat's historical mission? How, that is, could Marx sufficiently guarantee that a proletarian revolution would give rise to a classless society when the proletariat itself was riven by an internal competition – itself the result of the proletariat's economic position within capitalism – aimed precisely at winning things to secure and fortify? The answer is, of course, that he could not (or at least not on the basis of any claims regarding the 'innate' character of the proletariat).

Having now examined the materialistically critical methodology that Marx directly counterposed to utopianism, I think we are in a position to conclude that it failed to perform the function asked of it. It did not, that is, provide a convincing reason for believing that the emancipation of humanity lay in the material conditions of the present. For each of the ideas developed by Marx in order to support the claim that it did perform this function were purely speculative in nature. Thus, even if one accepts the forces/relations model of historical change (and this is a big 'if' in itself), there is nothing in it which suggests that the next relations of production will embody the emancipation of humanity. All it suggests is that the present relations of production are acting as a fetter on something. And if one places this 'something' in the context of progressive historical development alluded to by Marx then one fares no better, firstly because Marx failed in his (meagre) attempts to explain the transitions between the previous epochs of history and secondly because this context provides not a shred of evidence to support the claim that the next epoch will mark the end of pre-history. Nor does Marx's talk of the proletariat's historical mission stand the test of scrutiny, for his cataclysmic notion of the final showdown between two great classes is undermined entirely by his own more reasoned analysis of the complex and manifold gradation of social classes within capitalism. His further attempts to characterise the proletariat as a class united in its antithetical relation to private property and thus destined to transcend it then fell at the hurdle of empirical observation and was, in fact, contradicted by Marx's own recognition that division rather than unity was the end result of the proletariat's economic position within capitalism. In short, when Marx specifically contrasted his own ideas to those of the utopians he emphasised the fact that he had discovered the future emancipation of humanity in the material conditions of the present. On further reflection, however, even Marx was forced to concede that his general pronouncements belied far more complex issues that he found difficult, to say the very least, to resolve.

Conclusion

When Marx specifically contrasted his own position to those of the utopians, he did so on the basis that he, unlike they, had established the necessity of communism. Nor was this a mere rhetorical flourish on Marx's part — it was the cornerstone of the theoretical framework that he was attempting to erect on the crumbling foundations of utopianism (the structure of which Marx had done so much himself to destroy). For Marx, historical materialism was (and had to be) more than just a theory of history (although it was of course such a theory and was used as such to trace the development of utopianism); it was (and had to be) a theory of history which served the same function as utopianism had done in the seventeenth and eighteenth centuries, setting people in motion by imbuing them with the future optimism required in order to invoke the spirit of revolution. By sufficiently grounding the existence of a future world of human emancipation in the material conditions of the present, Marx not only enabled the workers to conceptualise a better future, he also did this without undermining the idea that a) they would emancipate themselves and b) they would determine for themselves what the emancipated society was to look like.

I find it difficult to agree with Geoghegan, therefore, when he claims that 'Marx and Engels had not criticised the utopian socialists' 'search after a new social science, after new social laws', merely to put in its place a new tyrannical 'science'' (1987a, p.31). For the whole point of Marx's critique of the utopian socialists had been to demonstrate the tyrannical nature of their utopianism-masquerading-as-science. And Marx *did* put in its place a new science, precisely because this allowed the theoreticians of the proletarian class to *avoid* the tyranny of the utopian masquerade.

In the form outlined by Marx during his critique of the utopian socialists, however, his new science – that which has been referred to here as materialistically critical socialism – failed to perform the function asked of it. It provided no convincing reason to believe that a society embodying human emancipation was grounded in the real movement of the material conditions of the present. As a consequence, it formed a feeble basis upon which a radical hope in the liberatory promise of the future could be constructed. During his more sober analyses, Marx himself was even led to question some of the ideas underlying the model which, according to his own extravagent claims, had rendered utopianism obsolete.

This should perhaps come as no surprise. For I think it fair to suggest that when directly confronting the utopians Marx sought to emphasise the *fundamental* distinction between his ideas and theirs. When, that is, Marx directly challenged the utopian notion that the emancipation of humanity depended upon the realisation of this or that particular utopia, he wanted to stress his own belief that the emancipation of humanity was tied in with the movement of the present. And in order to emphasise this belief, Marx presented it in its starkest form. Hence the simple, vulgar and deterministic language employed by Marx during his critique of the utopians, and hence the vulgar and mystical nature of the ideas upon which Marx's critique was premised. Hence also, I would add, Marx's recognition of the flawed simplicity of this model.

The point is, however, that Marx considered it necessary to show how the emancipation of humanity was tied in with the movement of the present. He had not been saying this merely for the sake of it, nor had he been saying it as a means of distancing himself from his political rivals. He had been saying it because he really did object to utopian philanthropy and really did think it necessary to offer the proletariat hope in a form which avoided it. This was, in fact, Marx's *project*; his principal aim as a theoretician of the proletarian class. Outside his specific attacks upon the utopians, therefore, he attempted to develop and refine the basic model of materialistically critical socialism that he had outlined there by employing a variety of additional concepts and categories. As I shall argue next, however, it is these concepts and categories that are responsible for the development of his 'utopia'.

Notes

1. C. M. Sciabarra also draws convincing parallels between Marx's critique of utopianism and those presented by Hayek and Popper (see especially, Sciabarra, 1995, p.61).
2. G. A. Cohen's famous attempt to defend the forces/relations model of historical development (Cohen, 1978) falls down precisely because of his reliance upon a voluntarism which is alien to the model itself. According to Cohen, the emergence of new relations of production can be explained in terms of rational individuals recognising that the current relations of production are fettering the development of the forces of production and then deciding to replace them with alternative relations which, they have deduced by means of their intelligence and rationality, will promote the further development of the productive forces. Such 'rational-choice' Marxism does, however, rid the historical process of all its irritating complexities and does seem to imply that a) one's individual consciousness determines one's social existence and b) that entering into a set of social relations is entirely a matter of one's individual will. Ted Honderich (1982) offers an excellent critique of Cohen and all other attempts to mount a defence of historical materialism based on 'functional' explanations.

5 Marx the 'Accidental' Utopian

Introduction

Marx had to ground the future existence of communism in the movement of the present if he was to invoke the spirit of revolution in a manner consistent with the principles of proletarian self-emancipation and self-determination. The basic model of materialistically critical socialism outlined by Marx during his critique of the utopian socialists failed to do this convincingly, as Marx himself well knew. Elsewhere, then, he attempted to develop and refine materialistically critical socialism by employing a variety of additional concepts and categories — concepts and categories which Marx believed *would* convincingly ground the future existence of communism in the movement of the present. The discussion here focuses on these additional concepts and categories.

The way in which they are presented may appear rather schematic. For I treat the three principal concepts in question — Marx's teleological conception of history, his analysis of the structural transformation of capitalism and his pragmatic grounding of radical needs — as separate entities and discuss each of them in turn. This is not because I believe that Marx also treated them as separate entities and discussed each of them in turn, for he did not. It is merely because treating them in this way allows us to gain a clear sense of the relationship between the concept of socialism, the methodology of historical materialism and the three 'visionary' utopian concepts identified in chapter 3 — The Dream of the Whole Man, the development of the all-round individual and the ontological necessity of labour.

What I suggest is that the three explanatory concepts identified above (teleology, structural transformation and pragmatism) were each employed by Marx in an attempt to ground the socialist future in the capitalist present. What I also suggest, however, is that in each case the move to socialism involved a 'utopian leap', i.e., the leap from the present to some supposedly concrete future via a purely speculative category. These speculative categories were none other than the three defining elements of Marx's visionary conception of the higher phase of communism. What I argue, therefore, is that the speculative and utopian categories in question were each developed in order to 'fill the gaps' or 'plug the holes' in the materialist methodology that was supposed to supersede utopianism. As such, Marx was an 'Accidental Utopian' in the sense that the distinctive features of his utopia were devised, not as a conscious and deliberate attempt to think the future, but rather as an accidental by-product of his failure to establish the logical coherency of his (anti-utopian) historical framework.

The Utopian Leap into 'The Dream of the Whole Man'

One of the additional categories or explanatory concepts employed by Marx was teleology. This enigmatic concept has been the focus of much debate over the years, although the terms of this debate have tended to obscure things rather more than they have clarified them.[1] As it is to be used here, teleology refers to the belief that history has a purpose and that phenomena can be explained in terms of this purpose; in terms, that is, of their final as opposed to efficient cause. Understood in this sense, the concept is used by Marx in support of the claim that communism represents the end (*telos*), the 'final stage', of history — an end, moreover, which history itself is delivering. Phenomena are then explained *because* they lead towards, prepare the ground for or facilitate the realisation of communism. Historical movement is not seen in terms of accident, contingency or chance, but rather in terms of necessary, predetermined progression. With regards to historical materialism, Marx is able to say that capitalist relations of production are fettering the development of productive forces that will generate *communist* relations of production because communism is history's telos and capitalism its final preparatory stage.

Sometimes, of course, Marx denied possessing such a view of history. In *The Holy Family*, for example, he launches this famous tirade against the idea that history has some inherent 'meaning':

> *History* does *nothing*, it "possesses *no* immense wealth", it "wages *no* battles". It is *man*, real, living man who does all that, who possesses and fights; "history" is not, as it were, a person apart, using man as a means to achieve *its own* aims; history is *nothing but* the activity of man pursuing his aims (Marx and Engels, 1980b, p.116).

The fact that Marx sometimes denied possessing a teleological conception of history is not the point, however. The point is that at different times Marx employed different categories to do the job of grounding socialism in the movement of the present and that teleology was one of them. In *The Holy Family* itself, for example, Marx rejects the idea that 'history is the activity of man pursuing his aims' and replaces it with the idea that history *forces* people (in this case the proletariat) to pursue *its* aims, irrespective of what they consider *their* aims to be:

> It is not a question of what this or that proletarian, or even the whole proletariat, at the moment *regards* as its aim. It is a question of *what the proletariat is*, and what, in accordance with this *being*, it will historically be compelled to do (ibid., p.47).

What needs to be established here is not the existence of a teleological conception of history in Marx. This, I hope, is widely enough accepted to obviate the need for further discussion (see, for example, Kumar, 1987, p.53; Geoghegan, 1987a, p.29; and Longxi, 1995, p.66). What needs to be determined instead is the way in which Marx used this concept to ground the future existence of communism in the real movement of the present. To this end, therefore, we need to examine Marx's teleological conception of history in order to see what he thought it enabled him to do.

The Cunning of Reason and Mankind's Destiny

Marx bases his teleological reading of history on Hegel's concept of 'the cunning of reason': present conflicts and antagonisms are 'rational' because they are a necessary step towards the realisation of history's meaning. Indeed, he implicitly acknowledges his use of this concept during his Speech at the Anniversary of *The People's Paper* in 1856. For there he tells us that:

> Some parties may wail over it; others may wish to get rid of modern arts, in order to get rid of modern conflicts. Or they may imagine that so signal a progress in industry wants to be completed by as signal a regress in politics. On our part, we do not mistake the shape of the shrewd spirit (Hegel's 'cunning of reason') that continues to mark all these contradictions (Marx, 1980, p.656).

The shrewd spirit will resolve the contradictions of the present because, as Marx said in the Preface to *A Contribution to the Critique of Political Economy*:

> Mankind thus inevitably sets itself only such tasks as it is able to solve, since closer examination will always show that the problem itself only arises when the material conditions for its solution are already present (Marx, 1970, p.21).

One finds here that antagonisms and contradictions *only arise* when they are about to be solved and that, therefore, present conflicts are little more than (necessary) stepping stones toward some 'higher' end. This belief in the inherent rationality of the actual informs Marx's notorious approval of English imperialist atrocities:

> England, it is true, in causing a social revolution in Hindoustan, was activated only by the vilest interests, and was stupid in her manner of enforcing them. But that is not the question. The question is, can mankind fulfil its destiny without a fundamental revolution in the social state of Asia? If not, whatever may have been the crimes of England, she was the unconscious tool of history in bringing about that revolution (Marx, 1962, p.351).

Present evils, as evil as they may be, are 'rational' because history has created them in order to fulfil mankind's destiny.

For Marx, of course, mankind's destiny lay in communism. In arguing the point, however, he encountered a slight problem. For he was attempting to follow Hegel in reading history 'from the end back', interpreting the rationality of earlier events in light of their final development (i.e., communism, or mankind's 'destiny'). In this respect, it was only at the end of history that Marx, like Hegel, could understand history's meaning. Unlike Hegel, however, Marx did not believe that he *was* standing at the end of history. As a consequence, he (unlike Hegel again) was in no real position to identify the particularities of the present that would, in the future, be interpreted as 'rational' historical developments.

Put another way, if a teleological explanation of something accounts for phenomena in terms of the effects they have, then one needs to *know* the effects before one can offer an explanation. Hegel, of course, knew what these effects were — they had culminated in Wisdom and the modern State. He could therefore interpret earlier developments in terms of their final cause and could trace the movement of the cunning of reason as it guided Spirit on its way towards Wisdom. Marx, on the other hand, could not. For if he was to interpret past *and* present phenomena in terms of their final cause then he would have to assume what history's 'end' looked like. Nor could this problem be resolved by turning Hegel's dialectic 'right side up again' to 'discover the rational kernel within the mystical shell' (Marx,

1946, p.xxx). For Marx would still have to identify the negatives within which positives were waiting to reveal themselves, and in order to do this — in order to have the very concept of a positive at all — he would simply have to assume a final end to history.

In fact, Marx knew full well that his dialectical framework could not be used to *project* results. For his aim, as he wrote in a letter to Engels in 1858, was 'to bring a science by criticism to the point where it can be dialectically presented' (Marx and Engels, 1969, p.123). In order to establish the categories in which a science can be presented dialectically, however, Marx himself accepted that he would first need to accumulate a great deal of concrete empirical data (see Meikle, 1979). This is because:

> Man's reflections on the forms of social life, and consequently, also, his scientific analysis of those forms, take a course directly opposite to that of their actual historical development. He begins, post festum, with the results of the process of development ready to hand before him (Marx, 1946, pp.46-47).

Marx did not have the results of the process of historical development ready to hand before him, and could not, therefore, dialectically present its movement. His problem, then, was this: that within a teleological framework, 'The full development of what appears at the end brings to light what had appeared as subtle nuances in earlier formations' (Blanchette, 1990, p.37). Because Marx had not seen the full development of what appears at the end, he could not claim to have identified the subtle nuances in the present that were leading — dialectically or otherwise — towards this end (not without basing his claims on mere assumptions at any rate).

The Return to an Original State of Unity

This is undoubtedly why one finds an additional notion within Marx's work, namely, the idea of an historical *beginning*, an 'original', 'natural', unity to which communism will be the *return* on a 'higher' level. Marx, not having seen the end of history, thought he could convincingly argue that there was such an end, and that history was the dialectical movement towards it, if he could somehow establish the idea of an origin characterised by features that *will* characterise society again. This forces Marx into his first 'utopian leap', a leap into The Dream of the Whole Man.

Let us look once more at that famous passage from the *Economic and Philosophic Manuscripts*:

> *Communism* as the *positive* transcendence of *private property* as *human self-estrangement*, and therefore as the real *appropriation* of the *human* essence by and for man; communism therefore as the complete return of man to himself as a *social* (i.e., human) being — a return accomplished consciously and embracing the entire wealth of previous development. This communism, as fully developed naturalism, equals humanism, and as fully developed humanism equals naturalism; it is the *genuine* resolution of the conflict between man and nature and between man and man — the true resolution of the strife between existence and essence, between objectification and self-confirmation, between freedom and necessity, between the individual and the species. Communism is the riddle of history solved, and it knows itself to be this solution (Marx, 1977a, p.90).

As was noted earlier, Krishan Kumar says of this passage that: 'Such a dazzling vision of universal harmony is hardly to be found anywhere else in the serious utopian literature' (1987, p.62). The passage itself, however, does not belong to the field of 'serious utopian literature' — it belongs to the field of Marx's teleological conception of history, the purpose of which was to ground communism in the present and thus avoid the need for utopian literature of any kind. For the passage clearly talks of a '*return* of man to himself' and of this return solving the riddle of history. Communism knows itself to be the telos of human history because it knows itself to be the return to an original state of unity.[2]

There is no greater testimony to the importance attached by Marx to the notion of a return to an original state of unity than Engels' *The Origin of the Family, Private Property and the State*. For Engels tells us that his own book was based upon Marx's *Abstract of Morgan's 'Ancient Society'*, which Marx himself was intending to transform into a book highlighting Lewis Morgan's 'scientific' proof of historical materialism (Engels, 1968d, p.449). What is of primary interest in Engels' book, and in Marx's abstract which Engels quotes widely, is Engels' claim that Morgan was 'speaking of a future transformation of society in words which Karl Marx might have used' (ibid., p.460).

Two passages in Morgan's book, which both Marx and Engels quote with approval, are worthy of attention. The first appears when, talking of the Iroquois 'gens' (a sub-division of the native American tribe, based upon Mother Right), Morgan says:

> All the members of an Iroquois gens were personally free, and they were bound to defend each other's freedom; they were equal in privileges and in personal rights . . . and they were a brotherhood bound together by the ties of kin. Liberty, equality, and fraternity, though never formulated, were cardinal

principles of the gens (ibid., p.512).

The second appears when Morgan concludes his study in terms that must have brought a smile to Marx's face:

> Democracy in government, brotherhood in society, equality in rights and privileges, and universal education, foreshadow the next higher plane of society to which experience, intelligence and knowledge are steadily tending. *It will be a revival, in a higher form, of the liberty, equality and fraternity of the ancient gentes* (ibid., p.583).

Such was the excitement induced by Morgan's findings that Engels went as far as to qualify the opening remark of the *Manifesto* — 'The history of all hitherto existing society is the history of class struggles' (Marx and Engels, 1967, p.72) — with: 'That is, all *written* history' (ibid., p.72n).

What Engels' enthusiasm indicates, however, is not that Morgan had somehow 'proved' that history will witness the return to an original state of unity — Morgan's claims to this effect were based on unfounded speculation no less than were Marx's own — but rather the desperation which accompanied Marx's and Engels' *search* for such proof. For without it, Marx's original state of unity remained a mere assumption. Indeed, Marx attempted to divert attention away from the fact that it was a mere assumption by arguing that it did not require an explanation:

> It is not the *unity* of living and active humanity with the natural, inorganic conditions of their metabolic exchange with nature, and hence their appropriation of nature, which demands explanation, or is the result of a historical process, but rather their separation from these inorganic conditions of human existence and this active existence (Marx, 1973a, p.489).

By *assuming* such an origin, however, Marx makes the same mistake that he repeatedly castigated Hegel for making. For if Hegel abstracted from the divisions of bourgeois society and assumed these divisions to be universal in order to equip himself with an 'ideal subject' with which to begin his historical process, then Marx abstractly assumed that all present divisions were 'unnatural' in order to equip *himself* with an 'ideal subject' with which to begin *his* historical process. Indeed, empirical considerations would lend more weight to Hegel's ideal subject. For the division which Marx most frequently castigates Hegel for assuming to be universal, i.e., the division between mental and manual labour, seems to have been a defining feature of every mode of production, even the primitive communism described by Morgan.

Of course, even if Morgan *had* provided Marx's concept of the original state of unity with concrete support, he would have provided no logical grounds for supposing that its return could be guaranteed. That Marx, therefore, not only conceptualised such an original state of unity but also *did* suppose that its return could be guaranteed only serves to demonstrate that the concept itself was nothing more than a speculative assumption — indeed, what is more speculative than a concept of the future premised on the 'return' to an original state that did not itself actually exist? Commentators are therefore more than justified in referring to the vision of communism presented in the *Manuscripts* as 'utopian' — utopian in the sense of conjured by the imagination.

Marx's Accidental Utopianism (1)

Because it was founded on a purely speculative assumption, Habermas suggests that Marx's whole teleological schema was nothing more than a 'metaphysical heuristic' (1973, pp.251-252). Whilst Habermas is right to make the point, what we need to bear in mind here is the function ascribed by Marx to this metaphysical heuristic. For Marx's teleological framework was intended to show that humanity's historical destiny lay in the future realisation of communism. If he could somehow demonstrate that history possessed a 'meaning' and that this meaning was synonymous with communism, then he could also argue with persuasive authority that the emancipation of humanity was, as he had repeatedly been claiming, grounded in the real movement of the present.

More importantly, of course, if Marx could demonstrate this then the need for utopian *descriptions* of communism evanesced — Marx could present the broad, vague and ambiguous outlines of a world in which people are free to shape their own lives without having to provide all the gory utopian details. Paradoxically, then, Marx's teleological model, based as it was upon the notion of predetermined historical progression, was in fact designed to serve the interests of proletarian self-determination. The proletariat is historically compelled to abolish private property and break asunder the social relations of capitalism, but the shrewd spirit will resolve all the contradictions of the present and will usher in a world in which the notion of compulsion has no place. History thus becomes a riddle in the following sense — that its unconscious tools are compelled to create a society in which they are freed from the compulsive forces of history.

What I would suggest, therefore, is that when Marx appropriated the heuristic framework of unity-separation-reunification, this was due less to an overzealous endorsement of all things Hegelian and more to an attempt on Marx's part to capture the anti-utopian *spirit* of Hegel's schema and to harness this spirit for his own purposes. Hegel was, after all, the most emphatically anti-utopian of all anti-utopians and one can well see why his general historical framework might have appealed to Marx — it enabled him to ground the future existence of communism in the movement of the present and thus ignite the spirit of revolution without having to descend into the realms of messianic utopian invocations of the future form of society.

It is easy for us to see now that Marx's teleological framework failed miserably in this respect — compensating for the fact that he himself had yet to witness the teleological culmination of the historical process, Marx was forced to contrive the notion of an original state of unity to which communism would be the return on a higher level. That The Dream of the Whole Man was a contrived, 'hypothetical' and imaginary category is, however, less important than the reason why Marx imagined it in the first place. For he imagined it in order to provide his teleological conception of history with a logical starting point. His historical teleology, on the other hand, was itself designed to provide a concrete and decidedly non-utopian link between the capitalist present and the communist future. Drawing these strands together, I would conclude by suggesting that The Dream of the Whole Man — a concept which represents one of Marx's outstanding contributions to the utopian tradition — was also the foundation of an historical method designed to *overcome* the need for utopianism. In other words, Marx's utopia (or one element of it) was the direct result of the failure of his anti-utopian methodology (or one version of it).

The Utopian Leap into 'The All-Round Individual'

A second additional category employed by Marx was the structural transformation of capitalism. Here one finds that the proletarian revolution will issue forth communism as opposed to some other not-capitalism because the structural logic of capitalist production means that this is the *only* possible outcome. Underlying this approach is the 'womb' metaphor — the idea that socialism is somehow 'gestating' within capitalism. With regards to historical materialism, Marx is able to say that capitalist relations of production are fettering the development of productive forces that will generate *communist* relations of production because Marx has seen these communist relations of production as they gestate within capitalism.

The womb metaphor takes as its premise the claim that the transition from capitalism to communism has *already* taken place, *within* capitalism. As R. N. Berki puts it: 'Communism is the necessary outcome of capitalism, because communism is *already here*' (1983, p.90). Some writers have identified a certain problem with this claim, however. Angus Walker, for example, says of Marx that:

> On the one hand, he writes as if history and social change proceeded by way of a series of revolutions and disruptive jumps marked by violence and bloodshed. On the other hand, both descriptively and analytically, he often makes explicit allowance for transitions which clearly imply that the passage from one mode to another can be made without any discontinuity. This difficulty does not arise simply from special pleading or bad faith; it is connected with a real theoretical problem. Marx is concerned, in part, to explain and predict 'revolutions'. If revolution is conceived as a complete break in the process of social development, then the theoretical problem is that of specifying the conditions which will lead to the breakdown of a given system. But the 'completeness' of the break with the past makes it difficult to see on what basis it is possible to predict the new social system to which the revolution gives rise. On the other hand, if, in order to deal with this problem, revolution is conceived of as something less than a discontinuity, and the persistence of some determining factors in the old system is posited, then this position may be criticised on the grounds that it does not account for real revolutions, and here the term is being used simply to elevate into a social climacteric something which is better thought of, perhaps, as an accelerated but relatively continuous process of social adaptation (1978, p.191).

If communism is to represent a *revolutionary* departure from capitalism, it follows that its *nature* cannot be derived from an analysis of capitalism. Conversely, if one *can* derive the nature of communism from an analysis of capitalism then communism cannot be regarded as a *revolutionary* departure from it. This argument carries a certain weight. For as Adam Schaff says of the transition from capitalism to communism: 'Theoretically, both a peaceful and a violent change is possible: the important thing is that a qualitative change does take place at a certain moment' (1990, p.218). Marx faces two distinct problems here, then. For on the one hand he needs to be able to argue that communism is qualitatively different from capitalism in spite of its already existing within it, and on the other he needs to be able to derive the qualitative transition to communism from the quantitative changes taking place within capitalism (when one of the defining features of a qualitative change is that it cannot be derived from an analysis of quantitative changes).

With regards to the first of these problems, let us allow Marx the benefit of the doubt. Let us assume, that is, that the womb metaphor allows Marx to argue that the communist child, whilst gestating within capitalism, *could* represent a revolutionary departure from it. Putting the history of genetics to one side, let us accept that a child and its mother can take forms that are qualitatively different from each other. With regards to the second problem now, if Marx wants to argue that the qualitative change has *already* taken place — i.e., that the communist child is alive and kicking within its capitalist host — then he needs the socio-methodological equivalent of an ultra-sound. He needs to be able to distinguish between the things that belong solely to capitalism, the appearances produced by capitalism's pregnancy and the essential things that *will become* communism. David-Hillel Ruben claims that Marx possessed such equipment and argues that:

> For Marx and Engels, scientific socialism was distinguished from utopian socialism in just this way — the vision of the future was founded on the real (physical) possibilities inherent in the present (1979, p.58).

Marx's ultra-sound worked, therefore, by identifying the real (physical) possibilities inherent in the present. This, however, is not the same as describing what *will* happen:

> Since laws as they describe the nomic behaviour of individuals do not operate at the level of the actual, but rather at the level of the tendential, which may or may not become manifest, predictions cannot be immediately made from the statement of laws (ibid., p.71).

Describing what is possible can, however, act as a catalyst for its realisation. This is because,

> if what is physically necessary about the life history of a thing is only that it has a *tendency* to develop in certain ways, then one can see the relevance of revolutionary practice in using scientific results, *true ones*, to impede, block, or hasten and develop the actual manifestation of those physically necessary tendencies (ibid.).

What we are offered here, then, is a predictive model which rejects deduction in favour of an essentialism that is true even if it never manifests itself. Indeed, the realisation of a prediction depends less upon a correct observation of regularity than it does upon human action. This is the kind of self-fulfilling Marxism forwarded by Gramsci when he said that: 'In reality one can 'foresee' to the extent that one acts, to the extent that one applies a voluntary effort and therefore contributes concretely to creating the result 'foreseen'' (1971, p.438). Because Marx has identified that communism is gestating within capitalism and that, therefore, capitalism is *tending* towards communism, all one need do in order to realise communism is act upon these tendencies.

Although the tendential nature of the communist child does seem to rid the womb metaphor of its very coherency, we shall once again give Marx the benefit of the doubt. We shall assume, that is, that capitalism is pregnant with a qualitatively different child, although this child is only a real (physical) possibility, a tendency which may or may not become manifest depending on the actions taken by whatever midwives happen to be around at the time. Given such assumptions, then, what we need to do now is examine the tendencies towards communism identified by Marx.

The Tendencies toward Socialised Property and All-Round Development

Marx attempted to ground the future existence of communism in the structural tendencies of capitalism by means of two distinct arguments.[3] The first of these was based upon the claim that private property 'becomes a fetter upon the mode of production, which has sprung up and flourished along with, and under it' (Marx, 1946, p.789). The defining features of this 'new' mode of production are described as

> the co-operative form of the labour process, the conscious technical application of science, the methodological cultivation of the soil, the transformation of the instruments of labour into instruments of labour only usable in common, the economising of all means of production by their use as the means of production as combined, socialised labour, the entanglement of all peoples in the net of the world-market, and with this, the international character of the capitalist régime (ibid., p.788).

Due to the very nature of this mode of production Marx concludes that 'the transformation of capitalistic private property, already practically resting on socialised production, into socialised property' will inevitably ensue (ibid., p.789).

Unfortunately, however, Marx was not justified in reaching such a conclusion. For it was based upon the claim that socialised production and socialised property are inseparable, and whilst Marx spends a remarkable amount of time in *Capital* establishing that the laws of capitalist production tend inevitably towards socialisation, he spends very little time establishing that a tendency towards the socialisation of production implies a move towards socialised ownership. Indeed, to say that capitalism has a tendency towards 'socialised' production is merely to say that the laws of the concentration and centralisation of capital demand that all production becomes co-operative. Co-operative production, on the other hand, is defined thus: 'When numerous labourers work together side by side, whether in one and the same process, or in different but connected processes, they are said to co-operate, or to work in co-operation' (ibid., p.315). As such, it takes a feat of the imagination to establish a logical link between the development of co-operative production and the development of social ownership. It is probably for this reason that the Marx of *Capital Vol. III* does nothing short of embarrass himself by proclaiming that joint-stock companies actually *represent* socialised ownership.[4]

The second attempt made by Marx to ground the future existence of communism in the actual tendencies of capitalist production sees him take his second 'utopian leap', this time into the concept of the 'all-round individual'. Marx introduces the concept in the following way:

> Modern Industry, indeed, compels society, under penalty of death, to replace the detail worker of to-day, crippled by life-long repetition of one and the same trivial operation, and thus reduced to a mere fragment of a man, by the fully developed individual, fit for a variety of labours, ready to face any change of production, and to whom the different social functions he performs are but so many modes of giving free scope to his own natural and acquired powers (Marx, 1946, p.494).

Modern Industry is here said to possess a tendency, nay a compulsion, to produce the 'fully developed individual'. In this way, the second of the 'utopian' concepts developed by Marx and discussed in chapter 3 finds a concrete footing in, and becomes a real (physical) possibility created by, the logic of capitalism. Modern Industry possesses a tendency to produce the fully developed individual because:

> By means of machinery, chemical processes and other methods, it is continually causing changes not only in the technical basis of production, but also in the functions of the labourer, and in the social combinations of the labour-process. At the same time, it thereby also revolutionizes the division of labour within the society, and incessantly launches masses of capital and of workpeople from one branch of production to another (ibid., pp.492-493).

Because 'Modern Industry, by its very nature, therefore necessitates variation of labour, fluency of function, universal mobility of the labourer' (ibid., p.493), it also tears individuals away from one particular branch of production and demands that they become adept at a variety of tasks. However:

> At the same time, the capitalistic form of that industry reproduces the same division of labour in a still more monstrous shape; in the factory proper, by converting the workman into a living appendage of the machine (ibid., p.489).

Marx thus attempts to establish a link between the crippled detail-worker, that 'living appendage of the machine' who personifies the capitalistic form of Modern Industry, and the fully developed individual who personifies Modern Industry itself. This link he terms the 'absolute contradiction between the technical necessities of Modern Industry, and the social character inherent in its capitalistic form' (ibid., p.493). The living appendage of the machine is the negative side of Modern Industry and the fully developed individual the positive in the negative.

In making this link, however, Marx makes a fundamental conceptual error. For he naïvely confuses the mobility of labour with 'variation of work, consequently fitness of the labourer for varied work, consequently the greatest possible development of his varied aptitudes' (ibid., pp.493-494). This is a mistake because to say that workpeople are being launched from one branch of production to another is not at all to say that these same workpeople are *therefore* being given free scope to develop their powers. Indeed, the real contradiction of Modern Industry as identified by Marx is that people are being launched from one branch of production to another whilst at the same time 'the old division of labour with its ossified particularisations' is being continually reinforced within the factories in which these people land (ibid., p.493). What is happening, therefore, is that the labourers are being expected to perform a *greater* detail function within an expanding number of branches of production.

More importantly, of course, this is in fact what *was* happening. For five decades after the publication of *Capital*, Taylorism and Fordism had become the ruling production paradigms, and *their* development — i.e., the development towards an even greater degree of specialisation within the division of labour — can, as David Harvey points out, be traced back to the 1850's (1989, p.125). Empirical support for the tendency towards greater specialisation could therefore be churned out *ad nauseam* — one need only look at Durkheim's seminal study of the division of labour for evidence of this (Durkehim, 1960). Empirical support for the idea that the all-round individual emerges from within this dehumanising process is, however, tellingly lacking. Indeed, as any reader of *Capital* will know, when Marx talks of the tendencies for the rate of profit to fall, for the immiseration of the proletariat to increase, for the processes of the concentration and centralisation of capital to accelerate, etc., he supports his arguments with references to as many newspaper and periodical articles and as many parliamentary reports as he can possibly find. It is somewhat indicative, then, that all we get with regards to the development of the all-round individual is the passage we encountered in chapter 3 in which Marx quotes a Frenchman on his return from San Francisco.

What is most surprising about Marx's extravagant claims concerning the development of the all-round individual is that they are surrounded in *Capital* by discussions of the division of labour which point in the opposite direction. For example, in support of the claim that the division of labour 'increases the social productive power of labour, not only for the benefit of the capitalist instead of that of the labourer, but it does this by crippling the individual labourers' (Marx, 1946, p.359), he quotes Adam Smith's claim that, through the division of labour, the worker 'generally becomes as stupid and ignorant as it is possible for a human creature to become' and that it 'corrupts even the activity of his body and renders him incapable of exerting his strength with vigour and perseverance in any other employments than that to which he has been bred' (ibid., p.356). This hardly conforms to Marx's belief that the division of labour produces, or even has a tendency to produce, an individual fit for any task!

The examples in which Marx pre-empts the move towards Taylorism and Fordism are, in fact, too numerous to recount — it was a major factor underlying the creation and recreation of an Industrial Reserve Army for one thing (see ibid., p.656). And yet one finds deep in the very heart of *Capital* this unsubstantiated claim that the movement of workpeople 'imposes the necessity' of developing the full attributes possessed by each member of the workforce (ibid., p.493). One must really ask, therefore, why this is.

All-Round Development as a Precondition for Self-Determination

In *The German Ideology* Marx constructs an extremely important argument in which he tells us exactly why 'the development of the all-round individual' was considered an essential feature of the future form of humanity. He begins by arguing that:

> the abolition of a state of things in which relationships become independent of individuals, in which individuality is subservient to chance and the personal relationships of individuals are subordinated to general class relationships, etc. — the abolition of this state of things is determined in the final analysis by the abolition of the division of labour (Marx and Engels, 1970, p.117).

This we know already from chapter 3. Because the division of labour in the factory forces an activity upon the individual and thus enslaves this individual to the whims of chance, it undermines the principle of proletarian self-determination. For this reason, therefore, the division of labour has to be abolished. Marx then continues as follows:

> at the present time individuals *must* abolish private property, because the productive forces . . . have developed so far that, under the domination of private property, they have become destructive forces (ibid.).

This we know already from chapter 4. Because the relations of production supported by private property are now fettering the development of the productive forces, these relations, together with the whole concept of private property itself, must be abolished. What we also know from chapter 4, however, is that Marx could provide no satisfactory reason for supposing that, once the productive forces of society had been released from the fetters of private property, the next relations of production would represent the emancipation of humanity. It would be perfectly feasible to suppose, that is, that the next relations of production would promote the development of the forces of production by making full use of the division of labour in the factory. Undoubtedly aware of this, Marx then suggests that:

> private property can be abolished only on condition of an all-round development of individuals, because the existing character of intercourse and productive forces is an all-round one, and only individuals that are developing in an all-round fashion can appropriate them, i.e. can turn them into free manifestations of their lives (ibid.).

Before private property can be abolished, individuals need to be able to deal with the productive forces in a manner which precludes the need for the division of labour. Conversely, if private property is abolished and individuals are not in this position then some new despotic form of the division of labour would presumably ensue. A precondition, therefore, for the abolition of the division of labour is an individual who has developed in an all-round fashion and who can utilise the all-round productive forces without becoming subservient to them. If communism is to be a society in which individuals determine their own form of existence (and this is a belief which Marx held dear) then these individuals must have overcome the need for the division of labour and must, therefore, have developed in an all-round way. The all-round individual subsequently becomes a precondition for a future world of self-determination.

In *The German Ideology*, however, Marx does not establish that all-round development is inherent in the movement of the present — he merely asserts that it is the vocation of each 'man' to develop himself in an all-round way. In *Capital*, therefore, Marx attempts to demonstrate that the development of the all-round individual is implicit within the dynamic of Modern Industry itself. This is not to suggest that Marx used his 'scientific' method as a means of bolstering support for his 'utopian' ideal; as a means, that is, of revealing its historical inevitability (as Meisner, 1982, p.12 suggests, and Bahro, 1978, p.23 implies). It is rather to suggest that Marx used the concept of the structural transformation of capitalism as a means of demonstrating that a decidedly non-utopian world of self-determination was grounded in the movement of capitalism itself.

Marx's Accidental Utopianism (2)

According to the argument presented by Ruben, Marx sought to demonstrate, by means of his socio-methodological ultra-sound, that his vision of the future was founded on the real (physical) possibilities inherent within capitalism. In order to realise these possibilities, voluntary revolutionary action was required to hasten and develop their actual manifestation. What I have tried to argue here is that this was not quite the case. For by means of his analysis of the structural transformation of capitalism, Marx was not attempting to demonstrate that *his vision of the future* was founded on real (physical) possibilities inherent in the present. He was attempting to demonstrate that the conditions necessary for *a future world of self-determination* were inherent in the movement of the present. This in turn was part and parcel of Marx's wider attempt to discover the new world without having to anticipate its form.

In reality, of course, Marx failed to establish that a future world of self-determination was contained within the material conditions of the present. Private property was not tending towards its own transcendence and Modern Industry was not compelling society to produce the fully-developed individual. What I have tried to show here, however, is how, in arguing the case, Marx descended into the sort of utopianism that he was consciously seeking to avoid. Indeed, Marx's claims concerning the all-round development of the individual demonstrate quite clearly how his visionary 'utopian' concepts were linked to and emerged from within his wider anti-utopian project. For the all-round individual, i.e., the second element of Marx's utopia, was a concept devised by Marx, not as the result of some deliberate utopian speculation on the ideal form of the future, but rather as a means of guaranteeing that his anti-utopian methodology could sufficiently ground the non-utopian, self-determining socialist future in the movement of capitalism. Once again then, we can say that Marx dazzles us with the utopian foundation of his alternative to utopianism.

The Utopian Leap into 'The Ontological Necessity of Labour'

A third additional category employed by Marx was the pragmatic grounding of radical needs. Here, individuals do not confront the independent external world of which their thought is a mere reflection, but produce the external world in the course of satisfying their biological needs, creating new needs for themselves in the process. History thus becomes a process in which the subject continues to change the world and continues to create new needs for itself. With regards to historical materialism, Marx can say that capitalist relations of production are fettering the development of productive forces that will generate *communist* relations of production because humans, in the process of creating the world, have created the need for the development of these relations.[5]

Central to this model is a rejection of the subject/object dualism upon which 'pure' materialism is based:

> Men do not in any way begin by 'finding themselves in a theoretical relationship to the things of the external world'. Like every animal, they begin by *eating*, *drinking*, etc., that is, not by 'finding themselves' in a relationship, but by behaving actively, gaining possession of certain things in the external world by their actions, and thus satisfying their needs. (They thus begin by production) (Marx, 1977e, p.581).

As with the first of his *Theses on Feuerbach* (Marx, 1968a, p.28), Marx here criticises materialism for its failure to understand that the individual's perception *of* the objective world cannot be divorced from his or her practical activity *within* it. As George Plekhanov explains:

For [Marx] the gist of the matter was not the indisputable fact that sensation precedes thinking, but the fact that man is induced to think chiefly by the sensations he experiences in the process of his acting upon the world (1969, p.32).

This pragmatic concept of human activity has proven particularly attractive to contemporary writers, primarily because of the way in which it allows one to theorise the transition from capitalism to communism. Sean Sayers, for example, argues that:

Marx . . . portrays history as a progressive process in the sense that it involves the growth of human productive powers, and hence the development of human nature in all its aspects: needs and desires, powers and capacities, freedom and reason. This theory provides the basis on which he criticises capitalism and envisages socialism. It does not appeal to universal or transhistorical values . . . either of human nature or of morality and justice. Nor is it a teleological theory: it does not posit an ultimate end towards which history is tending (1994, pp.82-83).

Because human nature develops *in the process* of the individual's activity within the world, Marx can criticise capitalism and envisage socialism without having to appeal to universal theories of human nature or justice and without having to resort to a teleological conception of history. This is because:

When Marx criticizes capitalism for preventing the realization of human powers and potentialities, these are ones which have been developed within capitalism itself (ibid., p.74).

In his own terms, what Marx was emphasising here was 'the self-creation of man as a process' and the idea that 'objective man — true, because real man — [is] the outcome of man's *own labour*' (Marx, 1977a, p.132). And what he thought he had achieved by means of his pragmatic grounding of the human essence was the solution to a problem peculiar to his own theoretical system; namely, how workers come to transcend alienation from within it. According to Agnes Heller, his solution produces 'one of the most important paradoxes in Marx's theory' (1974, p.58):

on the one hand, capitalist society reduces to mere "having" and homogenises into "greed" the system of needs both of the dominant class and of the working class (though in different ways); on the other hand, it generates antagonistic "radical needs" which transcend capitalist society, and whose bearers are called upon to overthrow capitalism (ibid.).

In spite of the fact that capitalism reduces all needs to its own level, it also generates needs which transcend it. A paradox indeed. In telling us how he reached such a paradoxical conclusion, however, Marx makes his third utopian leap — this time into the ontological necessity of labour.[6]

The Self-Creation of an Ontological Need for Labour

Marx's discussion of the ontological need for labour had very little indeed to do with utopian speculation about the nature of the Good Life. Marx did not, in other words, develop an *a priori* 'model' of the human essence and then demand that society be restructured around it. Instead, the idea that labour becomes an 'essential' need as the result of the proletariat's own practical activity within capitalism represents the logical solution to a theoretical problem. The problem was that Marx had spent a great deal of time explaining the concept of alienation, i.e., the process by which the labourer, giving form to objects in order to survive, comes to regard these objects as mere things-in-themselves which are assimilated by Capital. So understood, the proletarians were unable to recognise their products as their own creations and were unable to relate to other workers as social creatures, i.e., as producers who produce for others and consume the products of others. The problem was, therefore, how a collection of alienated individuals could transform themselves into an association of self-determining producers consciously controlling the production process.

In response, Marx argues that the alienated labourer eventually comes to realise that the objects being given form are not things-in-themselves, but are, in fact, things for him/her. The labourer comes to be united with nature in the awareness that nature is not an external force but is there specifically for his or her use. As he says in *Capital*:

> Labour is, in the first place, a process in which both man and Nature participate, and in which man of his own accord starts, regulates, and controls the material reactions between himself and Nature. He opposes himself to Nature as one of her own forces, setting in motion arms and legs, head and hands, the natural forces of his body, in order to appropriate Nature's productions in a form adapted to his own wants. By thus acting on the external world and changing it, he at the same time changes his own nature. He develops his slumbering powers and compels them to act in obedience to his sway (Marx, 1946, pp.156-157).

The driving force behind this reconciliation with nature is coercion. The individual becomes united with nature only because he or she is forced by fear and necessity to consciously give form to objects. Submission to the dictates of another is a necessary precondition for self-realisation: 'The human being *had to be* reduced to this absolute poverty in order that he might yield his inner wealth to the outer world' (Marx, 1977a, p.94). By virtue of having nothing to gain from the labour process except the reproduction of a bare existence, the labourer is able to see labour for what it is — or rather for what it could be — rather than seeing in it the source of profit or whatever. The labourer thus *had to be* reduced to the status of alienated being in order to see in labour something other than alienation. This something other is the objectification of one's existence and the realisation of powers that were previously only latent. Through non-alienated labour, therefore,

> I would have objectified my *individuality*, its *specific character*, and therefore enjoyed not only an individual *manifestation of my life* during the activity, but also when looking at the object I would have the individual pleasure of knowing my personality to be *objective, visible to the senses* and hence a power *beyond all doubt* (Marx, 1975a, p.227).

The realisation that labour is an ontological necessity thus creates the *real* human being *within* capitalism and guarantees that true humanity will follow the abolition of private property:

> The abolition of private property is therefore the complete *emancipation* of all human senses and qualities, but it is this emancipation precisely because these senses and attributes have become, subjectively and objectively, *human* (Marx, 1977a, p.94).

The senses *have become* human *within* the system of private property because the system of private property demands that the labourer makes his or her personality visible to the senses. The labourer thus becomes human through the process of labour because he or she realises that to labour is to be human. This allows one to make sense of Marx's claim that 'its [communism's] *actual* act of genesis – the birth act of its empirical existence – is . . . the *comprehended* and *known* process of its *becoming*' (ibid., p.90). For to claim that communism exists empirically when its process of becoming is comprehended seems to imply that it exists before it exists. Marx simply means, however, that communism as *a potential way of being* exists within capitalism and that once the labourer comprehends this he or she will feel the need for communism *qua* the only form of society that can realise this way of being.

Heller was therefore correct to describe the emergence of radical needs within the proletariat as a paradox. For the radical needs which transcend the realm of alienation are generated by the very process of alienation itself — the labourer *had to be* subjected to alienation in order to see outside and beyond it. What is important here, however, is the way in which Marx develops his argument. For if the labour process was ever going to generate needs transcending the alienation it produced then it would have to be something *within* the labour process itself which triggered the development of these needs. It is no coincidence, therefore, that Marx linked the development of radical needs to the absolute poverty and degradation that the individual is subjected to within the labour process. Nor is it a coincidence that the needs themselves related to the labour process again — the recognition that labour is something other than the production of objects generates the need for this something other, i.e., the objectification of the personality and the manifestation of life.

Marx's ideas concerning the ontological necessity of labour were therefore inextricably linked to his attempt to ground the transcendence of alienation within the process of alienation itself. It was only by means of attributing some mystical properties to the labour process — and by arguing that these properties only became visible to those whose lives had been reduced to absolute poverty — that Marx could argue that capitalism creates the *need* for its own transcendence. When Marx talked about the ontological need for labour emerging within the proletariat and through the labour process, he was thus devising an ingenious resolution to a theoretical problem; namely, how to explain the transition to communism when he was dealing with subjects whose complete alienation he had himself so convincingly described.

Similar considerations apply to Marx's discussion of the ontology of labour in *Grundrisse*. *Grundrisse* is, of course, a horrible text to read and the few snappy quotations taken from it are generally divorced from the hundreds of pages of dense, tedious text surrounding them. From this one can sometimes gain the impression that *Grundrisse* is full of lively utopian passages describing the relative positions that labour and free-time will occupy within communism. The passages in question, however, are far from utopian, for they deal less with the status of labour in some future ideal end-state than they do with labour as a radical process operating in the midst of the present.

The bulk of the passages cited in the context of Marx's 'utopianism' are taken from three short sections in The Chapter on Capital (Marx, 1973a, pp.704-712). What Marx is doing in these sections is attempting to determine the radical role played by the labour process within capitalism now that capitalism relies less upon labour time and more upon the fixed capital produced during labour time. And whilst Marx certainly provides us with hints as to what communism will look like — for example, it is impossible to avoid the conclusion that people in communism will be given free scope to develop their individualities during their much increased free time — it is important to note that Marx makes no attempt here to actually *describe* communism.

Quite the opposite, in fact. For as always, Marx was attempting to show how the future existence of communism was grounded in the movement of the present whilst simultaneously avoiding having to say anything concrete about the form that communism will take. Hence the way in which Marx eulogises the extension of free time within capitalism and yet continually returns to the labour process as the real transformatory force. For the extension of free time does not, in and of itself, generate needs which transcend capitalism. Sure enough, free time transforms its possessor into a different subject, but this subject creates new needs for itself only through its activity in the production process. It is only by virtue of the labourer's *participation* in the labour process that he or she comes to realise that:

> Nature builds no machines, no locomotives, railways, electric telegraphs, self-acting mules etc. These are products of human industry; natural material transformed into organs of the human will over nature, or of human participation in nature. They are *organs of the human brain, created by the human hand*; the power of knowledge, objectified (Marx, 1973a, p.706).

This notion of labour as objectification does not enter Marx's thought as the result of utopian deliberations concerning the true or ideal form that humanity will take in a world constructed according to his own design. Instead, it represents an attempt to theorise the mechanisms by which self-created needs emerge within the proletariat, the realisation of which will usher in a future *non*-utopian world of freedom and self-determination. This is made clear by Marx when he criticises Adam Smith in the following terms:

> Certainly, labour obtains its measure from the outside, through the aim to be attained and the obstacles to be overcome in attaining it. But Smith has no inkling whatever that this overcoming of obstacles is in itself a liberating

activity – and that, further, the external aims become stripped of the semblance of merely external natural urgencies, and become posited as aims which the individual himself posits – hence as self-realization, objectification of the subject, hence real freedom, whose action is, precisely, labour (ibid., p.611).

Labour as objectification here becomes a subjective means toward self-liberation rather than an objective end towards which utopian energies should be directed. And consciousness of the fact that labour is objectification of the subject (a consciousness which only emerges within those who have been reduced to absolute poverty) constitutes the historical genesis of communism; that is, of a society in which self-creation, self-realisation and self-determination will be the guiding principles and in which 'Man makes his life activity itself the object of his will and of his consciousness' (Marx, 1977a, p.68).

Once again, therefore, the idea that labour represents the fulfilment of the personality and an ontological need so that in communism it would become life's prime want was not an idea derived from utopian speculation and *a priori* excogitation. It was yet another example of Marx's varied attempts to ground a future world of self-determination in the movement of the present. In this particular case, the self-creation of an ontological need for labour was also a theoretical conclusion (informed by a huge dose of optimism and Hope) deduced from the premises of Marx's description of alienation: Given alienation, by what possible mechanism could the need for its transcendence emerge from within it?

Marx's Accidental Utopianism (3)

Marx's pragmatic concept of historical development gives rise to the conclusion that 'capitalism as a social relation limits the enrichment of needs which are its own creation' (Heller, 1974, p.47). Heller quite rightly acknowledges, however, 'that in Marx's time these radical needs had not yet become actual' and 'that Marx therefore had to "invent" them' (ibid., p.86). More to the point perhaps, she concedes that 'the system of needs of united individuals are utopian' (ibid., p.130). I hope that we can all agree with Heller and recognise that the ontological need for labour was a utopian category invented by Marx.

Indeed, Marx himself would elsewhere have recognised the intrinsic utopianism of his own claims concerning the needs of the future. For in *The German Ideology*, when specifically referring to the fact that human needs and desires will be rather different within communism than they are at present, he says that 'which desires would be merely altered under a communist organization and which would be dissolved, can only be decided in a practical way, through the changing of real, practical desires' (Marx and Engels, 1965, p.282). And this, of course, is the only honest answer that Marx the anti-utopian could really have given.

All of which leads me to question the idea that Marx's discussion of the relationship between the labour process and the concept of 'species-being' was a purely philosophical exegesis. I do not think, that is, that Marx constructed a model of what it is to be human and then gradually built on it until he reached the level of 'truly human' needs. Nor do I think that Marx's concept of truly human needs formed the basis of any serious attempt at social and philosophical anthropology. Instead, what I have argued here is that the ontological need for labour was a need both invented and projected by Marx in order to establish a mechanism by which individuals become conscious of a self-created need, the satisfaction of which will guarantee a future world of self-determination.

Without this concept, Marx's pragmatic model is faced with both an empirical system of needs grounded firmly in (and continually reproducing) capitalism, and the apparent intransigence of this system of needs, i.e., the apparent impossibility of transcendent needs being created in the process of an individual's activity within the world. The ontological necessity of labour, which is the third element of Marx's utopia, was therefore forwarded as a means of guaranteeing the transcendence of capitalism and the simultaneous realisation of communism whilst remaining within a (supposedly) anti-utopian framework. The final stroke of Marx's utopian artwork is consequently forced by the failure of the last of his anti-utopian methodologies.

Conclusion

Marx was a theorist, a theoretician; a theoretician of the proletarian class no less. One can therefore be sure that when he theorised he did so for a purpose — he did not, in other words, theorise for theory's sake. So to suggest that a purpose lay behind the development of his various theoretical models, concepts and categories is merely to state the obvious. With regards to what this purpose was, I have argued that Marx considered it incumbent upon the theoreticians of the proletarian class to invoke the spirit of revolution in a manner consistent with the principles of proletarian self-emancipation and self-determination. To do so, therefore, was his own political imperative. The key to achieving this lay, in Marx's view, in his being able to ground the future existence of communism in the movement of the present. Indeed, when directly confronting the utopians, Marx repeatedly claimed that he had successfully done this and that, therefore, utopianism had been stripped of any positive functions that it had once possessed. Elsewhere, however, Marx continually struggled to develop a theory that would support his bold claims. When seeking to identify the nature of Marx's anti-utopianism, one should not, therefore, confine oneself to his specific attacks upon the utopians. One should instead regard his entire life's work as an attempt to supersede the need for utopianism and the philanthropic elitism which he considered integral to it.

This is important because when Marxologists deal with Marx's anti-utopianism they do tend to confine themselves to his specific attacks upon the utopians. In so doing, they are inclined to point out, and not without justification, that the position adopted by Marx in relation to the utopians was nothing other than a vulgar determinism. This is then contrasted to Marx's less deterministic ideas in order to demonstrate that Marx's vulgar opposition to utopianism was at odds with other elements of his thought and that it must, therefore, have been motivated by 'strategic' reasons. Once this has been established, commentators can then celebrate the 'utopian humanism' of the non-determinist Marx and can argue that, outside the realms of political in-fighting, Marx was not averse to utopianism after all. What I have tried to argue in this book, however, is that there were not 'two' Marxes, one a strategic anti-utopian and the other a more flexible and pragmatic man who was not *really*, in principle, opposed to the fanciful flights of the utopian imagination. Instead, there was just the one Marx who really was opposed to utopianism at all times. And whilst this one Marx did adopt a vulgar position when specifically confronting the utopians, the very same Marx developed other models when not specifically confronting them, and his aim in so doing was to support the claim that he had had found a way of superseding utopianism.

When Marx developed and experimented with his teleological, structural and pragmatic models of historical development, he was still, therefore, experimenting within the anti-utopian framework which guided all of his ideas. Indeed, these models testify to the efforts made by Marx to do what he had said he could do when he was criticising the utopians, namely, ground the future existence of communism in the movement of the present. So concerned was he to do this that he formulated various models, toyed with various ideas and adopted various positions, some of which were inconsistent with each other and some of which were more convincing than others. Each of these models, ideas and positions were, however, motivated by the same guiding principles and were part of the same project. The principles were those of proletarian self-emancipation and self-determination and the project was that of invoking the spirit of revolution in a manner consistent with them.

Now, it just so happens that none of the models in question succeeded in grounding the future existence of communism in the movement of the present. For underlying each was a speculative assumption claimed as empirical fact, and it is these speculative assumptions which together comprise Marx's 'utopia'. The teleological conception of history assumed an original and 'natural' state of unity so that it could interpret the present as an unnatural state of separation and the future as a 'natural' state of reunification. The Whole Man thus becomes less a utopian 'Dream' than an assumed starting point for Marx's teleological reading of history. The structuralist interpretation of capitalism, which sees communism tendentially gestating within it, attempted to demonstrate the empirical development of the all-round individual. It did so because only an individual who has developed in all-round way would be capable of utilising the productive forces in such a manner as to preclude the need for the division of labour. The all-round individual thus becomes less a utopian ideal than a precondition for the realisation of a future world of self-determination. The pragmatic conception of historical development, according to which individuals create and recreate their own needs in the process of acting upon the world, assumed that the ontological need for labour had already emerged within the proletariat so that it could explain the transcendence of alienation from within it. It too, then, was less the result of utopian speculation than theoretical need. Marx did not talk about labour becoming life's prime want in communism because he had constructed a utopian vision in which labour took its place as life's prime want. He took the ontological need for labour as a given so that his pragmatic model of historical development could explain the transition to communism without having to rely on 'utopian' conceptions of anything.

Whilst undoubtedly 'utopian' in nature, then, these 'visionary' descriptions of communism were not projected by Marx as the result of a conscious decision on his part to imagine what the 'ideal' form of humanity would look like. Instead, they entered his work as part of a completely different endeavour; the endeavour, that is, to devise a model of historical development that could guarantee the emancipatory nature of the future without requiring 'pictures' of it to be painted at all. In the sense, therefore, that this endeavour ultimately failed and *did* require the development of 'imaginary' categories which together form an 'imaginary' picture, Marx can rightly be termed a 'utopian'. In the sense, however, that these categories were developed in the midst of Marx's attempt to avoid, undermine and supersede the need for utopianism, Marx can ultimately be termed an 'accidental' utopian. Marx's utopianism, that is, was nothing more than an accidental by-product of his inability to get historical materialism to do the things that he wanted it to do.

Notes

1. For definitions of what a teleological explanation involves, see Cohen, 1978, p.278; Wood, 1981, p.107; and Elster, 1986, p.32. The obscure nature of many of these definitions is highlighted by Roy Bhaskar, who helpfully suggests that in a teleological explanation 'it is the prior or concurrent existence of a dispositional property which explains the existence or persistence mentioned in the antecedent of the tendency statement specifying the disposition' (1986, p.144).
2. It could be contended here that because the passage in question predates the 'discovery' of historical materialism, it could not have been developed in order to solve the problems associated with it. As we have already seen, however, the anti-utopian foundations of historical materialism had been laid as early as 1843, when Marx said that 'we do not anticipate the world with our dogmas, but instead attempt to discover the new world through the critique of the old' (Marx, 1975b, p.207). The problems involved in 'discovering' the new world without 'anticipating' it had thus been facing Marx since then. That the solution proposed in the *Manuscripts* predated the term 'a materialist conception of history' does not, therefore, mean that it was the solution to a different problem.
3. Marx identifies the existence of many tendencies within capitalism. Some of these, including the most famous of all — the tendency for the rate of profit to fall — are confined solely to the workings of capitalism and do not point to anything beyond it. Important though they are, these tendencies need not concern us here. What we are interested in are those tendencies which lead us towards communism.
4. Marx refers to the joint-stock company as 'the abolition of capital as private property within the framework of capitalist production itself' (Marx, 1959, p.427). He also refers to it as 'outright social property' and thus 'the abolition of the capitalist mode of production within the capitalist mode of production itself' (ibid., pp.428-429). Although Daniel Bell suggests that Marx was pre-empting the theories of post-industrialism and the notion of the decentralisation of capital (1973, p.40), it is more common to see Marx struggling to understand the development of a new *form* of capital — what Rudolf Hilferding was to call 'finance capital'. According to Hilferding, the

joint-stock company was symptomatic of the transformation of the bank into an industrial capitalist in its own right (1981, p.225). Lenin also argued that 'a personal link-up, so to speak, is established between the banks and the biggest industrial and commercial enterprises, the merging of one with the other through the acquisition of shares' (1968, p.196). A generous interpretation of Marx would therefore argue that he quite understandably failed to recognise the role played by joint-stock companies in developments that were to take another three or four decades to fully manifest themselves. A less generous interpretation would point to the realities of the joint-stock company as it existed in Marx's time (for an excellent study see Charles Freedeman, 1979) and would mock him for believing that it had anything to do with the development of 'outright social property'

5   I have termed this a pragmatic version of historical materialism because, as Stanley Moore suggests, Marx's 'position strikingly resembles Dewey's version of pragmatism' (1990, p.139). Whilst I do not know how far the specific parallel between Marx and Dewey can be taken, I think that its emphasis on the role played by practice in the constitution of knowledge, and more importantly on the fact that the practice itself becomes a part of that which is known, enables one to link Marx's model here to a pragmatism of sorts.

6   Marx's talk of alienation and the dialectics of labour have often been accounted for in terms of a simple Hegelianism on Marx's part. It could then be argued that the existence of an ontology of labour in Marx's works needs no explaining; it simply testifies to the fact that Marx appropriated lots of ideas from Hegel. Such a notion will not do, however, simply because it fails to account for the fact that Marx transformed Hegel's ideas to such a great extent. Thus, for Hegel, labour as objectification was alienation, and alienation was an ontological fact, whereas for Marx alienation could be overcome by recognising the ontological fact that labour is objectification. As Alasdair MacIntyre remarks: 'The concepts that dominate Marx's thinking are drawn from Hegel and Feuerbach; the use he makes of them is his own' (1969, p.29). Whilst this may be overstating the influence of both Hegel and Feuerbach, the point itself is well made. For what needs to be accounted for is not the influence of Hegel but rather the use to which Marx puts some of the ideas which he draws from Hegel and then transforms.

Conclusion: Marxism and Utopia

The relationship between Marxism and Utopia has become the source of much debate over recent years. This debate has taken an unusual turn in the sense that a stream of writers have actively sought to 'defend' Utopia against its traditional Marxist denigrators and have even gone so far as to suggest that the revitalisation of Marxism itself depends upon the rehabilitation of Utopia. Indeed, it would not be overstating the case to refer to the emergence of a 'pro-utopian' orthodoxy within contemporary Marxism, an orthodoxy typified by proclamations such as this:

> It is time Marxists (hopefully freed from the scriptural shackles of Engels' *Socialism: Utopian and Scientific*) take note of the concept of utopia divested of its pejorative connotations, and project and draw upon the utopian features of Marxism in the quest for an alternative vision for our time (Shiviah, 1994, p.305).

Time and time again over recent years we have been told that if Marxism's moribund body is to drag itself into the new millennium then it will have to capture the spirit and harness the energies of the utopian imagination. At a time when apathy and pessimism are the ruling passions, and in a world in which socialism is deemed to equal nothing more than the gulag plus bread queues, the very survival of Marxism is said to depend upon its being able to offer hope in the form of a vision of a better future. When Fukuyama says that 'we cannot picture to ourselves a world that is *essentially* different from the present one, and at the same time better' (1992, p.46), Marxism needs to be able to say 'yes we can'; when François Furet remarks that 'henceforth we must live in a closed political universe, with nothing beyond the horizon' (1995, p.80), Marxism needs to be able to say 'no we must not'; and for it to be able to say these things, it must think beyond the horizon of the present and paint a picture of a world that *is* essentially different from the present one and at the same time better. It must, in other words, construct a utopia.

Whilst arguments such as these possess a certain emotive appeal, the case for a Marxist utopianism is not, in my view, quite as straightforward as its proponents seem to suggest. What I want to do by way of conclusion, then, is broaden the scope of this book a little and, in the light of conclusions drawn from it, offer a critical evaluation of the grounds upon which contemporary socialists have sought to 'defend' the concept of Utopia. Before doing this, however, I will spend a little time discussing the specific implications that can be drawn from the central argument presented in the book, namely, that Marx was an 'accidental' utopian.

Marx's Accidental Utopianism – What does it Matter?

Many of the pro-utopians attach at least some importance to the claim that Marx himself was a 'utopian socialist'. Indeed, they go to great lengths to devise arguments which suggest that Marx was not, in fact, opposed to utopian speculation at all. For those seeking a *rapprochement* between Marxism and Utopia, the utility of the arguments constructed around means/ends and strategy/principle dichotomies is plain to see. For if one's readers can be convinced that 'it was not the ends that the utopian socialists sought that made them "utopian" in the Marxist sense, but rather the inadequacy of the means proposed to achieve those ends', then they can also be convinced that the construction of utopian 'ends' is not, because it never has been, antithetical to the Marxist project. Similarly, if one's readers can be convinced that when Marx *did* criticise the ends that the utopians sought he did so for 'strategic' reasons, then they can also be convinced that, contrary to popular opinion, Marxism was not founded on a 'principled' objection to discussing the nature of communist society.

What I have tried to argue in this book, however, is that Marx remained a vehement critic of utopianism – i.e., the activity of constructing utopian ends – throughout his life. And in spite of the fact that he developed certain categories which, when taken together, can be said to comprise a utopia, I have also emphasised the fact that it was never Marx's conscious intention to construct a utopian vision of the future. At the very least, this means that those who seek to find a utopian precedent in Marx would do better to look elsewhere. Marx's own vision of communism cannot, at any rate, be used in support of the claim that a *conscious* utopianism has always lain at the heart of Marxism. Marx would, indeed, have been mortified to have found himself being discussed as a part of the utopian tradition. As a man who consciously rejected utopian systems of *every* kind, the last thing he was attempting to do was construct one of his own.

The natural response to this, of course, would be to say 'who cares?' For the fact remains that Marx presented us with a utopia, and the issue of whether or not he consciously intended to do so could therefore be regarded as irrelevant. Marx's utopia has taken its place in the social, cultural and textual landscape and now constitutes an image or symbol to be drawn upon by anyone who considers it useful. Indeed, even commentators with little sympathy for Marxism have recognised the symbolic potency of Marx's utopia. Adam Ulam, for example, suggests that: 'Even in that least utopian of socialisms, in Marxism, it is the vision of the final and frankly utopian phase of social development, of communism, which is responsible for much of its appeal' (1973, p.117). And Frank E. Manuel adds that:

> Since there are many chambers in the house that Marx built, the ideal of physical and psychic self-actualization as an individual human right, embedded in the Marxist utopia and long repressed, may yet find a place as a moral statement acceptable to both a secular and religious humanism (1992, p.18).

However 'accidental' its construction may have been, it seems that Marx's utopia may have survived the historical blasts which destroyed the other chambers in his house. For this reason, it could perhaps be viewed as the foundation upon which the house itself can be rebuilt.

As has already been highlighted, contemporary Marxists have indeed been following this line and have increasingly come to view a renewed utopianism as the foundation upon which the Marxist project can be reconstructed. For the most part, however, the utopian imagination has been endorsed uncritically. This is not to suggest that utopianism should be viewed critically in deference to Marx's own views on the subject, for to define Marxism entirely in terms of what Marx himself said is nothing short of a useless theoretical fetishism. Marxism needs to adapt itself to changing social and historical conditions and Marx himself (as the pro-utopians are fond of pointing out) did not live through the Stalin era. Nonetheless, there are certainly reasons for doubting the emancipatory potential of the utopian 'spirit' and there are strong grounds for disputing the claim that Marx's critique lacks contemporary relevance. In what follows, therefore, I take a critical look at the laudatory claims made on behalf of Utopia within the growing body of pro-utopian socialist and Marxist literature. On the basis of a detailed examination of the various functions that have been ascribed to the concept, I argue that 'Utopia' cannot be divested of its pejorative connotations. What, however, do I mean by the concept of 'Utopia'?

The 'Utopian' Nature of Utopia

A utopia should describe in a variety of aspects and with some consistency an imaginary state or society which is regarded as better, in some respects at least, than the one in which its author lives. This is a good definition in the sense that it is flexible, i.e., it does not prescribe the degree of stasis, symmetry or perfection required by a description in order to be designated as 'utopian'. The definition also captures what I believe to be the very essence of utopia – its status as an *imaginary* state or society. For this is what the concept of Utopia is all about. The utopian escapes 'the constraints of empirical reality' (Goodwin, 1982, p.23) and describes a state or society that is both incongruous with and removed from the world as it presently stands. Not only will the state or society described by the utopian imagination lie outside the framework of existing reality, but its realisation will also be impossible within the framework of existing reality. Were it otherwise – i.e., were the description to lie within the framework of existing reality such that its realisation required modifications being made *to* reality – then the description itself would not be 'utopian'. It would merely constitute a programme for 'institutional reform' or 'cultural change'. A utopian description is utopian precisely because of its fantastic, abstract and incongruous nature as something Other.

This having been said, however, distinguishing between a utopia and a programme for reform can be problematic. For example, an alternative to the present may be regarded by its author as utopian whilst being regarded by others as little more than a proposal for piecemeal reform (and vice versa). This is the kind of problem one encounters when dealing with the phenomenon of 'market socialism', which *is* regarded by some as a 'utopian' alternative to the present whilst being regarded by others as a piecemeal compromise with reality in all of its immutable glory.

I will not debate the issue here. Instead, I will merely suggest that in some of its guises the concept of 'market socialism' *can* be incorporated into discussions concerning the role of utopianism within the contemporary socialist movement. For example, whilst Robin Blackburn accepts 'the necessity of the socialised market' (1991, p.227) he also thinks it necessary to develop 'a programme which could take us *beyond* capitalism' (ibid., p.173). This in turn will consist of something more than 'capitalism with a bit of social christian input', i.e., Eric Hobsbawn's (accurate) description of market socialism in some of its other forms (1991, p.322). Instead, it will involve a radical transformation of all the institutions and values upon which the present system is based; it will, that is, necessitate a degree of *qualitative* change that is unrealisable within the framework of present reality. Such a programme could therefore be described as 'utopian'.

To be perfectly clear, then, I am using the concept of Utopia to designate an imaginary state or society which is both incongruous with and unrealisable within the framework of reality as it presently stands. Whilst some elements of present reality may find their way into the utopian description, the realisation of the world depicted by the utopian will require radical qualitative change. This is the 'utopian' nature of Utopia.

Similar considerations apply to Utopia's function. For whilst liberal reformers may view utopia 'as a means to an end rather than an end in itself' (Holloway, 1984, p.180), i.e., as a means of suggesting directions for partial change *within* the framework of existing society, this fails to capture 'the whole spirit of Utopia' (Morrison, 1984, p.148). This spirit is captured instead by Mannheim's description of utopias as 'orientations transcending reality' which, 'when they pass over into conduct, tend to shatter . . . the order of things prevailing at the time' (1968, p.173). The spirit of Utopia lies in its ability to take us beyond the framework of existing society, not only in thought but also in reality. Once again this is the 'utopian' nature of Utopia. Fortunately, this insight has not been lost on contemporary pro-utopians within the Left, who do indeed view utopianism in terms of 'transcending reality' and moving 'beyond capitalism'. So what we need to ask now is how it is able to do this; what reality-transcending powers does Utopia possess?

Utopia as a Blueprint to be Realised

It has often been argued that utopias conceived as blueprints to be realised will involve nothing less than a messianic and authoritarian elitism. The most famous of these arguments was presented by Karl Popper, whose critique of 'Utopian engineering' centred around the claim that it 'is likely to lead to a dictatorship' because the utopian is almost certainly going to claim that his or her utopia represents the best world for all and is almost certainly, therefore, going to 'suppress' those who think otherwise (Popper, 1962, pp.157-168). Many others have expressed the same view (see, for example, Cioran, 1996, p.86; Hodgson, 1995, p.197; Barclay, 1993, *passim*) and Agnes Heller presents the case well when she remarks that 'superimposing one's own utopia on others as their panacea has become an outrage. Utopian imagination, so misused, becomes a weapon against the utopian imagination of others and kills their promise of happiness' (1993, p.57).

Whilst Marx and Popper make the most uncomfortable of bedfellows, there can be no doubting the similarities between their respective critiques of utopianism. Indeed, one could almost say that Popper's critique mirrors Marx's own. For Marx also believed that there is no rational means of determining what the 'ideal' form of society is, and he also believed that superimposing one's own utopia on others as their panacea is an outrage because he also believed that it was not the task of prophetic utopian messiahs to determine what the future should look like. Like Popper, then, Marx believed that such prophetic utopianism portended to an elitist philanthropy that was doomed from the outset to result in failure.

Interestingly, such views are also shared by contemporary supporters of the utopian imagination such as Krishan Kumar, who opines that:

> The attempt to realize utopias as a political project is fraught with danger. It is, at best, likely to bring about a society bearing only the slightest resemblance to the utopian conception and that in what may be its most superficial features. At worst it will create the opposite of utopia, an anti-utopia of authoritarian regimentation. This has been the experience of all so-called utopian communities and utopian societies, from the American communities of the nineteenth century to the socialist societies of the twentieth (1991, p.95).

The idea that the totalising impulse to *realise* Utopia is 'fraught with danger' is thus a popular one, not only with Popperians and 'traditional' or 'orthodox' anti-utopian Marxists, but also with contemporary pro-utopian socialists such as Kumar. The idea is also accepted by Barbara Goodwin, although in a rather unusual form. For whilst Goodwin concedes that utopians attempt to mould both society and individuals into a shape determined by their own particular theories (1982, p.24), and whilst she also accepts that the realisation of Utopia will involve 'authoritarian' coercion (ibid., p.25), she nonetheless offers a vigorous defence of utopianism. In *The Politics of Utopia*, her co-author Keith Taylor begins by forwarding this descriptive argument:

> Historically, the conviction that something positive can be done to transform existing conditions of misery into a new world of true harmony and happiness has invariably spread as the result of the deliberate efforts of various individual thinkers or groups of thinkers who have assumed the mantle of leadership, and have usually presented themselves as great intellectuals, prophets, revolutionaries or even messiahs (Goodwin and Taylor, 1982, p.139).

Goodwin then transforms this description into a prescription. In an exhilarating and refreshingly honest argument, she concedes that 'Utopia is the attempt of one individual to impose *his/her* world-view and his/her rationality on others' (Goodwin, 1982, p.24). She defends this practice, however, on the grounds that 'people owe the Good Life to their fellows' and should therefore be prepared to sacrifice 'a measure of personal freedom' in order to realise it (ibid., p.27). Because most people in liberal democracies are ignorant puppets of ideology, however, one cannot define this Good Life 'on the precarious basis of individual choice' (Goodwin and Taylor, 1982, p.225). And because the social elites within liberal society coerce people covertly, whilst maintaining that they are acting in the name of freedom, their definition of the Good Life is not to be trusted. Rather, the task of defining the collective good should be placed in the hands of a utopian, who will take on 'the mantle of leadership' of which Taylor spoke and lead the people into 'a new world of true harmony'.

For Goodwin, then, the utopian process will inevitably involve coercion and is intrinsically, therefore, 'authoritarian' in nature. If a utopia is viewed as a goal, a vision of the Good to be striven for and realised, then *of course*, we are told, it will involve an individual, or a group of individuals, assuming the mantle of leadership, presenting themselves as prophets or messiahs and imposing their vision of true harmony upon anyone who refuses to accept its inherent truth. For this is the only way that a utopian transformation of society *can* come about. In other words, if a utopia is *not* paraded as the best world for all then support for it will not be found and if it is *not* imposed then it will never be realised.

This line of argument poses problems for those who wish to see Utopia divested of its pejorative connotations. For whilst Goodwin mounts a strong defence of the utopian process, she stands alone in defending its 'authoritarian' nature. Indeed, the rebirth of utopia is more generally associated with a move *away* from authoritarian politics and its mechanistic rationalism and towards all manner of humanist virtues – Romanticism, thought and feeling, as Levitas describes them, which are then counterposed to Marxism's supposed reliance on Utilitarianism, knowledge and thought (1989, p.35). So the issue becomes one of whether the pro-utopians can offer an understanding of the utopian process which avoids the pejorative authoritarian connotations accepted by Goodwin and yet which can reasonably be expected to form the basis of an emancipatory socialist strategy. In other words, if it is not to be understood as a blueprint to be realised by authoritarian means, then how *is* the humanist process of utopian emancipation to be understood?

Utopia as a Mode of Critique

Carol Farley Kessler thinks that we should 'see the values of Utopia to be less a blueprint for change and more a reflection of social lack, less apolitical prediction than social criticism' (1989, p.120). Implicit here, then, is the claim that one can divorce Utopia as social criticism from Utopia as blueprint for change and thus rid utopianism of the authoritarian implications which follow from the latter. Whilst the distinction between blueprint and critique can quite clearly be made, I suggest here that making the distinction actually rids the utopian critique of any power that it may be said to possess.

Utopia as a Precondition for Critique

Paul Ricoeur presents the strongest case for Utopia as a mode of critique when he argues that:

> What we must assume is that the judgement on ideology is always the judgement from a utopia. This is my conviction: the only way to get out of the circularity in which ideologies engulf us is to assume a utopia, declare it, and judge an ideology on this basis. Because the absolute onlooker is impossible, then it is someone within the process itself who takes the responsibility for judgement (1986, p.xvi).

Ricoeur's is an interesting argument. For one of the many objections Marx had to utopianism was the fact that it implied someone standing 'outside' society and identifying 'the Good' which lay beyond and ahead of it. For Ricoeur, however, it is precisely because one *cannot* stand 'outside' society that utopias are essential. Because all ideas are social constructs, one has to construct one's own (a utopia) in order to criticise that constructed in order to maintain the social hegemony of the ruling elite (an ideology). In other words, utopianism becomes a precondition for social critique.

This is, in fact, an extreme version of a quite straightforward notion; the notion that one cannot criticise what exists without implicitly formulating a view of what *should* exist in its stead. Burke, Crocker and Legters present the same argument in a weaker form when they state that:

> It is a truism that one can criticise a given society without offering a blueprint for its replacement. But it is also clear that any but the most superficial criticism of existing society delimits the range of alternative societies that the

critic would find more congenial. These could only be societies lacking the feature that is the immediate target of criticism in the present society. Vague as it may be, a vision of a good society is, if nothing else, at least the hidden agenda of all social criticism (1981, p.1).

The suggestion here is that any critique of, say, exploitation will implicitly assume the idea of a non-exploitative society. This alternative society then becomes a utopian hidden agenda, reinforcing the notion that any critique of the present world will depend upon a vision of a different and better one.

Two things can be said in relation to this line of argument. The first is that, in its weaker form, the argument remains unconvincing. For it is both unhelpful and misleading to elevate to the status of 'utopia' the concept of a society 'lacking the feature that is the immediate target of criticism'. Whilst Burke, Crocker and Legters do not explicitly state that such a concept constitutes a 'utopia', they certainly imply some degree of equivalence. It is therefore important to stress that even the most rigorous of critiques need incorporate nothing more 'utopian' than a vague list of negatives. In other words, a 'utopian' vision of a good society (properly understood) is neither implied by social critique nor must it form an integral part of it.

The second thing to be said is that, in its stronger form, the argument is simply incorrect. For in order to criticise an ideology one *does not* have to declare a utopia. Without wishing to become embroiled in debates concerning the possibility of 'scientific' critique, it is clear that Ricoeur is mistaken in thinking that a non-utopian critique will depend upon the existence of an 'absolute onlooker'. It is, in other words, perfectly possible to criticise the present from *within* it and yet do so without descending into utopianism. One does not have to 'assume' a utopia in order to identify the structural contradictions of capitalism, nor does one have to 'declare' a utopia before one can say that these contradictions are responsible for real human misery.

Utopia as the 'Unmasking' of Reality

Most writers thankfully avoid the suggestion that utopianism is a precondition for social critique. What they do suggest, however, is that utopianism is the *best* form of critique. Whilst, that is, Marxism does not *need* to describe an alternative in order to criticise the present, it will be better equipped to do so if it does describe such an alternative. The reasoning behind such claims is eloquently presented by Vincent

Geoghegan when he describes the power of Utopia thus:

> Its alternative fundamentally interrogates the present, piercing through existing societies' defensive mechanisms — common sense, realism, positivism and scientism. Its unabashed and flagrant otherness gives it a power which is lacking in other analytical devices. By playing fast and loose with time and space, logic and morality, and by thinking the unthinkable, a utopia asks the most awkward, the most embarrassing questions. As an imaginative construction of a whole society, the utopia can bring into play the rich critical apparatus of the literary form and a sensitivity to the holistic nature of society, enabling it to mock, satirize, reduce the prominent parts, to illuminate and emphasize the neglected, shadowy, hidden parts — and to show the interrelatedness — of the existing system (1987a, pp.1-2).

Utopianism is a powerful mode of critique, then, because utopias 'pierce through' such 'defensive mechanisms' as common sense and realism, mechanisms which 'other analytical devices' supposedly reproduce. A utopia's very 'otherness' allows it to desymbolise ideological claims concerning the nature of the present in ways denied to more sober methods of critique. As Zygmunt Bauman puts it: 'If the reality-protecting ideology attempts to disguise history as nature, utopias, on the contrary, unmask the historical status of alleged nature' (1976, p.15).

The idea that utopias can and do serve a critical function will not be disputed here. What will be disputed, however, is the idea that utopianism serves a critical function *lacking in other analytical devices* if it is divorced from the attempt to realise the utopias produced. For one can assume that the pro-utopian socialists want their critique to be something more than mere coffee-table chat. One can assume, that is, that they strive to 'unmask' reality for a reason and that this reason (i.e., the aim of their critique) is to engender change. What hope does a utopia have of achieving change, however, if the alternative posed is not designed to serve as the form of change desired? What critical forces, in other words, can a utopia generate if, for example, its own author concedes that it is nothing more than an analytical device? Other analytical devices — mere observation in fact — can be used to mock and satirise the present, so what we want to know is what sets the utopian device apart; what makes it so special that Marxism cannot do without it? If it is something more than satire but less than a blueprint for change, then what exactly *is* the radical function served by utopian critique?

Darko Suvin supplies one possible answer when he argues that

> utopia is a *method* rather than a *state*, but I would add that it is a method

camouflaging as a state: the state of affairs is a signifier revealing the presence of a semiotic process of signification which induces in the reader's imagination the signified of a Possible World, *not necessarily identical with the signifier* ... In other words, even in the case of perfect stasis and closure in the signifier, the signifying process inscribed in or between the text's lines, and finally proceeding to contextual reference, will make for a larger or smaller opening of the signified (1990, pp.74-75).

Suvin goes on to claim that utopian discourse is a process which emphasises creative power rather than the created piece of work, a process which involves 'an ongoing feedback dialogue with the reader' (ibid., p.75). In other words, the power of utopia lies in its ability to induce the reader's imagination to contemplate the possibility of other worlds (irrespective of the form taken by the original signifier). This is what André Gorz had in mind when he described 'A Possible Utopia' in *Ecology as Politics*. Rather than representing *the* future or the *best* future, it was merely *a* possible future and 'its only function', said Gorz, was 'to liberate the imagination as to the possibilities for change' (1987, p.42).

So the force generated by a utopia which is not conceived as a blueprint to be realised is that which liberates the imagination as to the possibilities for change. By means of 'an ongoing feedback dialogue', the construction of a utopia creates an opening through which the reader enters the world of alternatives to the present. These alternatives may bear no resemblance to the original utopia encountered by the reader, but this does not matter, for if the utopia has made the reader aware that alternatives can be thought of then it will have succeeded in its task. This is, in fact, a powerful argument. It is difficult to see, however, how the ongoing feedback dialogue will liberate the imagination unless both the dialogue and the imagination are linked to the quest to *realise* the utopias they create. As Gorz remarks, utopias liberate the imagination as to *the possibilities for change*, and if this argument is to make any sense then surely the possibilities for change which the imagination has now conceived will be those informed by the utopian alternative it has either encountered or produced. The possibilities for change will be those presented by the utopia and change will be defined in terms of a movement towards realising this utopia.

Whilst, therefore, utopia may well be a method camouflaging as a state, what distinguishes it as a method (i.e., what sets it apart from other analytical methods) is the fact that the 'ongoing feedback dialogue' instils in the reader the desire to realise the state that the method is camouflaged as. Without this additional element of desire the method itself becomes nothing more than a reading exercise with no (or at least no radical or subversive) political implications.

Utopia as Self-Ironizing Deconstruction

Our attention has recently been drawn to a new breed of 'critical' or 'self-reflexive' utopias, utopias which abandon the blueprint format and thus avoid the authoritarianism associated with the 'traditional' utopia and yet which serve a subversive and critical function nonetheless. Michael Gardiner describes this new breed of utopia thus:

> They are not merely imaginary projections of ideal cities or societies, in that they are linked to actual socio-historical movements and the activities and desires of particular social groups. Moreover, they are reflexive in the sense that they are aware of the limitations of the dominant utopian tradition, but also in that they are self-ironizing and "internally" deconstructive. Accordingly, they attempt to realize the contours of a desired future society in their very textual form via the incorporation of elements of contradiction, ambiguity, and openness. In so doing, they disrupt the unified and homogenous narrative of the traditional utopia and demonstrate the multiplicity of possible futures. In sum, the critical utopia is a heterodox manifestation of a diffuse "utopian impulse" which steadfastly resists the systemization and closure characteristic of the traditional utopia and is ultimately concerned with the satisfaction of unfulfilled needs and the perennial human desire for autonomy and voluntaristic solidarity (1992, p.25).

By virtue of self-irony, internal deconstruction, ambiguity, contradiction and openness, the critical utopia resists systematisation and closure. More importantly, as Giuseppa Saccaro Del Buffa emphasises, critical utopianism rejects 'the pretension of possessing and imposing a universal truth' (1990, p.74). Instead, 'utopia must become a plural noun – utopias – which means . . . it has to propose a variety of projects, in order to suppress univocal social conventions, big, monotonous systems, and spatial-temporal homogeneities, in favour of a non-Euclidean political geometry' (ibid.). The key to 'critical' utopianism lies, therefore, in the plurality of utopias to which it gives rise and the refusal of each to claim for itself the status of 'truth'.

These utopias, it is claimed, arise out of current contradictions within the political unconscious and articulate the needs of actual socio-historical movements by means of incorporating the ambiguous and often contradictory nature of these needs into the Utopian text itself. The source of the critical utopia's subversiveness is deemed to lie in this very ambiguity — the ambiguous, ironic and contradictory form taken by the language and structure of the Utopian narrative supposedly disrupts the homogenous language by means of which the dominant social formation has hitherto been supported. Helen Kuryllo can subsequently argue that the factors which once made Elizabeth Gaskell's *Cranford* (1853) the source of ridicule — the fact that its narrative was clumsy and that it lacked any structure — now make it a radical and subversive force (1989, p.106).

A number of things need to be said about the 'critical' utopia. The first is that its proponents claim too much for it and are clearly confused if they think that elements of ambiguity and openness have not played their part in traditional utopias of the Morean kind. As Darko Suvin has argued, not even More's Utopia was unambiguous or closed (1990, pp.73-74). Secondly, in claiming that its link to actual socio-historical movements somehow sets the critical utopia apart from its traditional namesake, writers such as Gardiner ignore the socio-historical origins of 'traditional' utopian movements. Thirdly, one of the major socio-historical movements to which the critical utopia is linked is the Green movement, and yet the utopias produced by this movement are archetypes of the 'traditional' form they are supposedly disrupting. A simple glance at the language used by 'ecotopians' reveals that they are nothing short of social millenarians, proclaiming 'the dawn of a new age' (Goldsmith and Allaby, 1972, p.62) and professing to incorporate '*a different world view*' (Porritt, 1984, p.44), 'a new world view' (Goldsmith, 1992, p.xvi) and many other sins connected with 'totalising' discourse. Not only this, but they want, nay demand in apocalyptic tones, to be *realised*. As Andrew Vincent remarks: 'They usually want a total value change in society — a new age to be constructed, where the whole perception of the world and nature changes' (1993, p.265). Robin Eckersley adds that the Green movement aims to create a 'cultural, educational, and social revolution involving a reorientation of our sense of place in the evolutionary drama' (1992, p.59). In short, the ecotopians are for the most part precisely the type of people who hold onto the 'traditional' pretension of possessing and imposing a universal truth.

Finally, it is difficult to appreciate the subversiveness of those utopias which truly *are* self-reflexive and internally deconstructive. Listen, for example, to Naomi Jacobs as she tells us about Ursula Le Guin's *Always Coming Home*:

> There is thus quite literally no stasis and no symmetry in the book. The shifts between exposition, poetry, and narration continually destabilize a reader's

relationship with the writer and her characters. And the complexity of Le Guin's imagined world requires physical shifts between parts of the book; I began by diligently turning to the "back of the Book" for explanations and definitions, but eventually gave up on studying this textbook and simply browsed around in it, following Stone Telling's story as long as the hunger for narrative lasted, flipping randomly to other parts when I wanted variety, choosing a poem here, a drawing there, a recipe or map or dance or a chart of the system of lodges, and then returning to the narrative thread which weaves through the whole (1989, p.114).

On the basis of appraisals such as this, it would seem that the more 'intelligent' and 'self-reflexive' utopias *lose* their subversive critical power as a result of their very intelligence and self-reflexivity. Rather than acting as a political tool, they become 'social texts' which carry meaning only to those who understand how to deconstruct them. It seems, in fact, that the function of the 'critical' utopia is to provide a picture of a world so complex that intellectuals (who thrill in being 'continually destabilised' by a text) need to consult an appendix in search for explanations and definitions. Whilst this may render utopianism devoid of any authoritarian political implications, it also, I would suggest, renders it unable to interrogate the present in any truly useful way.

As I see it, then, Utopias which eschew the blueprint format and opt for internal deconstruction instead may enable academics to write esoteric tracts preaching the values of destabilising complexity but they will hardly help the rest of us to come to terms with the problems facing us in the present. And whilst 'traditional' utopias are able to interrogate the present in a useful way, the real power behind the utopian critique lies in its ability to generate utopian 'desire', i.e., the desire to see the alternative posed by the utopia *realised*. Without this, utopia becomes a mere imaginative fancy, just another analytical technique (and certainly not the best). I therefore agree with Alasdair Morrison when he remarks that

> utopia can, and often does, generate both enthusiasm and determination. It attracts supporters who will not be content with thought-experiments: they want the real thing. That indeed is what utopia is *for*: it is an inspiration and a goal (1984, p.144).

Only once a utopia has made the transition from thought-experiment to inspirational goal will it take on a function that somehow sets it apart from other modes of critique.

Utopia as an Inspirational Goal

Utopia as Political Psychology

According to Geoghegan, 'Marx and Engels failed to develop a psychology. They left a very poor legacy on the complexities of human motivation . . . A simple concept of the individual coexisted with simplistic socialist strategies' (1987a, p.68). One of the principal reasons for the current popularity of utopianism is that it claims to take the complexities of human motivation into account and thus seems to fill this particular gap within Marxism. With regards to the relationship between utopianism and the complexities of human motivation, Ivor Sarakinsky and Jürgen Habermas make similar claims:

> People are hardly receptive to dry conceptual discourse. However, they respond quickly to images, rhetoric and symbols. Utopian thought has all of these, and more. As a result, it has the potential to stir the emotions, get people involved and draw them together in hope of a better future (Sarakinsky, 1993, p.112).

> People do not fight *for* abstractions, but *with* images. Banners, symbols and images, rhetorical speech, allegorical speech, utopia-inspired speech, in which concrete goals are conjured up before people's eyes, are indeed necessary constituents of movements which have any effect on history at all (Habermas, 1986, p.146).

For both Sarakinsky and Habermas, movements require utopias because their symbolic imagery inspires action in a way that dry conceptual discourse and theoretical abstractions do not. This, in essence, is a rerun of the classic Reason versus Rhetoric debate, although Maurice Meisner adds another dimension to Utopia's appeal when he suggests that

> people must hope before they can act, and their hopes must be lodged in a vision of a better future if their actions are not to be blind and devoid of purpose. Indeed, it is an inherent and unique attribute of mankind that human actions are both purposive and future oriented. In this respect, the utility of utopias is obvious. Utopian visions of the future not only serve as critiques of existing social orders but offer alternatives to it, and thus not only make people aware of the imperfections of the present but also move them to transform it in accordance with the utopian ideal (1982, pp.20-21).

Utopias thus inspire people to act in a way that dry conceptual discourse cannot, not only because people are more responsive to their symbolic imagery and so on, but also because people are unlikely to act unless they have a *goal*. Utopias provide such a goal whereas rational critique does not. Utopias are therefore essential if a movement is to have any effect on history at all.

Utopia as post-Soviet Necessity

That the collapse of 'actually existing socialism' added a new dimension to the relationship between Marxism and utopianism hardly requires stating. Nor does the fact that the changing political landscape has changed the landscape of Utopia itself. Thirty years ago, for example, Leszek Kolakowski could declare that: 'The Left gives forth utopias just as the pancreas discharges insulin — by virtue of an innate law' (1968, p.70). No such declaration could be made today, however, as the Left appears to have become (in a predictable extension of Kolakowski's simile) diabetic. The innate law which drove the Left to discharge utopias has now been displaced by what Habermas terms 'the Exhaustion of Utopian Energies' (1989, p.48). Some go even further and argue that the events of 1989 and their aftermath rid Utopia of its last exhausted breath. Writing in 1991, for example, Wolf Lepenies remarked that 'two years of unbelievable political change in Europe have been sufficient to proscribe the use of the word 'utopia'. No one talks about utopia any more . . . Utopias are dead' (1991, p.8).

For many on the Left, such events have rendered Marx's critique of utopianism obsolete. In order to avert its impending death, it is claimed, socialism itself needs to talk about utopia, and talk about it a lot. The exhaustion of utopian energies is here equated with the exhaustion of the socialist project, and a thoroughgoing renaissance of utopian thought is said to be required if socialism is ever to recover. As Harry Brighouse puts it,

> socialists need more than a critique of the self-evident (and even the oblique) evils of capitalist society: they need to pose an institutionally viable alternative to capitalism which can plausibly be thought to avoid at least most of the evils of the no longer actually existing socialist societies (1994, p.569).

Given that people have seen something called socialism in action — and have had the idea that socialism = Stalinism etched deeply into their consciousness by the post-mortems which followed the demise of 'actually existing socialism' — socialists can no longer rely merely on critique. Instead, they need to provide alternative models of socialism with which to counter the things that people have seen. Gregory Elliott adds that the 'socialism = Stalinism' equation has only gained widespread acceptance because of 'the palpable absence of any feasible and desirable alternative to it as a non-capitalist societal future' (1993, p.7). Like many others, therefore, Elliott believes that socialists should take the time to offer a desirable alternative to Stalinism as a non-capitalist societal future. Indeed, for Daniel Singer, this is the *only* way that socialism can hope to gain mass support. For he argues that:

> After all that has happened, people may still be driven by their conditions to rebel, but they will not enter a coherent movement, will not join a potentially hegemonic bloc capable of long term action without knowing the goal and the route to be travelled (1993, p.253).

This is the crux of the pro-utopian argument. Marxism needs to embrace utopianism, we are told, not because of any critical powers it possesses, but because now, more than at any other time in its history, Marxism needs *more* than critique; it needs a revitalised sense of purpose — it needs a goal. The full force of this argument is brought home by a remark once made by Roger Scruton. 'Revolution is now unthinkable', he said: 'it is like murdering a sick mother out of impatience to snatch some rumoured infant from her womb' (1989, p.1-2). What those such as Singer are trying to point out is that people now need more than rumours before they will act. Never again will rumours or vague hints win any converts for socialism. People have seen what revolutions based on rumours produce — the spectre of 'actually existing socialism'. If, therefore, people are to join a socialist movement which aims at the radical transformation of society, they will now demand to *know* what socialism is, and this is why Marxism needs to be able to tell them. This is why, in other words, Marxism needs to develop its own Utopia.

The same point was made by many other writers in the aftermath of the collapse of the Soviet Union. Eric Hobsbawm, for example, suggested that we learn from the Bolshevik Revolution and substitute concrete goals for abstract rumours (1991, pp.316-317). Fred Halliday insisted that 'the starting point for a future politics has to be the critique of existing capitalist society and the laying out of alternatives that are both desirable and plausible' (1991, p.114). Robin Blackburn, too, emphasised the need for socialism to develop a goal, arguing that:

> Anti-capitalist movements can do valuable work checking particular manifestations of the divisive or destructive logic of capitalist organization.

But if they won sufficient support, what could they offer at the level of regional or national government? And if they are dissatisfied with the world pattern presided over by the Group of Seven, what would they have develop in its place? (1991, p.174).

Each of these writers and many more suggest that Marxism needs to embrace utopianism because it needs to provide a goal, in the form of an institutionally viable alternative to capitalism, that will inspire people to join a socialist movement capable of long-term action and will serve as the pattern to be introduced if and when the movement gains sufficient support to implement it. The form of utopianism advocated by all of these, then, is the act of drawing up a blueprint to be realised. There is no other way of interpreting their arguments: if Marxism needs a utopia because it needs a goal around which to mobilise support, and if it needs a utopia because it needs to provide a viable alternative to capitalism that could be implemented *as* an alternative, then surely Marxism is being told that it needs a utopia because it needs to formulate a goal to be realised. As we saw Maurice Meisner remark earlier, utopias are required in this context not only because they make people aware of the imperfections of the present but also because they move them to transform it *in accordance with the utopian ideal.*

Viewed as either a mode of critique or a means of inspiration, then, it is difficult to see how utopianism can be divorced from its function as a blueprint to be realised. Put another way, if a utopia does not inflame the desire to see itself realised then what *does* it do? It may provide entertainment, it may be studied as an interesting example of a literary genre, it may be viewed as a satirical comment and it may unmask the inadequacies of the present, but none of these things captures the essence of *political* utopianism. Rather, as Morris Zeitlin forcefully argues, the purpose of political utopianism is to 'reach, teach, inspire, and move masses of people . . . to follow us to a socialist future' (1996, pp.25-26). The purpose of political utopianism, in other words, is the realisation of Utopia.

Given this, the arguments for a Marxist utopianism need to come to terms with the various criticisms that have been levelled at Utopia conceived as a blueprint to be realised. If the socialist movement really is in need of a goal around which to mobilise support, a utopian conceptualisation of an institutionally viable alternative to capitalism, then whose goal is it to be and how is support for it to be mobilised? If the utopian process is not to be understood in terms of a single individual assuming the mantle of leadership and leading the people into a new world of harmony, then we must ask again, how is it to be understood?

Utopia from 'Above' or from 'Below'?

Daniel Singer remarks that socialism 'cannot be built thanks to a blueprint drawn at the top and imposed from above. The vision of a different society must be elaborated collectively and in the open . . . the project itself is bound to be flexible, provisional if socialist construction is seen as a conquest by the working people, advancing stage by stage and changing themselves as they change society' (1993, p.253). Singer thus adopts a gradualist, grass roots approach to utopian construction. It is to be a collective project, advancing stage by stage. Presumably, the utopian vision itself will change as people change themselves and openly elaborate their ideas concerning the different society to which their changing selves eventually hope to give rise.

On paper at least, this sounds fine — the gradual emergence of an openly debated vision based around a broad movement for social change seems a realistic means of both developing a vision worth striving for and of avoiding the elitist notion that such visions should emerge 'from above'. The problem is, however, that the very notion of a grass roots utopia belies the urgency with which Singer talks of the need for people to 'know *the* goal and *the* route to be travelled' *before* they will enter any coherent movement. For the whole gist of Singer's paper is to stress that people are no longer prepared to join a movement that does not have a clear and well-defined utopian goal. Given the horrors associated with past attempts to change the world, people will refrain from becoming involved in any future attempt if it involves uncertainties or risks. As such, a *knowledge* (the word is Singer's) of the goal and the route to be travelled is required by people in order to persuade them that *this time* there will be few uncertainties or risks.

Zeitlin presents a similar argument when he states that:

> To them ['most people'], the socialist promise of a noble society needs to be explicitly clear. They need to *see* not only why humanity got into the capitalist dead end and how it can get out of it but see also, in full colour, the promised future at the end of the road (1996, p.25).

With regards to why people need to see the promised future in full utopian colour, Zeitlin adds:

> To tend and fan the smouldering hopes of oppressed humanity, we need to put across our socialist ideal in more inspiring ways than we have of late. We need to pierce the seductive bubbles and babble of dominant ideology better than we have. It is long time to make explicit the full brilliance of the utopian promises implicit in Marxism (ibid., p.24).

What pro-utopian Marxists such as Zeitlin and Singer appear to be saying is that a concerted utopian effort is now required because the historical mechanisms which usually drive the utopian process have ground to a halt. These mechanisms were best described by Karl Mannheim when he argued that 'every "actually operating" order of life is at the same time enmeshed by conceptions which are to be designated as "transcendent" or "unreal" because their contents can never be realized in the societies in which they exist' (1968, p.175). He then suggested that some of these 'transcendent' conceptions absorb themselves into the consciousness of a social group and that this social group, on the basis of its new-found 'utopian mentality', translates the ideal into social action (ibid., pp.186-187). As far as the pro-utopians are concerned, however, the distinctive feature of the present historical juncture is that it lacks transcendent conceptions of life and subsequently lacks the basis upon which utopian mentalities are constructed. As a consequence, they see it as their own personal task to rebuild the utopian base of society (or at least to 'tend and fan' it) in order to regain the imperative for social action. At the same time, however, the utopian base needs to be stronger and firmer than it has ever been before precisely because people will no longer allow themselves to be carried away on the basis of a mere transcendent conception of life. Instead, they require a map (drawn in full colour by those who parade their thoughts as *knowledge*) which not only tells them where they are travelling but also gives them detailed directions of how they are going to get there.

This not only introduces an element of *deceit* into utopian discourse (discussed below), it also highlights the tension underlying much pro-utopian thought. For a people lacking hope in the possibility of a socialist future are less than likely to formulate a vision which embodies and supposedly fosters the realisation of this alternative future (not even via a process of 'ongoing feedback dialogue'). Whilst, therefore, the pro-utopians want their Marxist utopia to emerge from within a broad-based movement for change, they also believe that a people lacking hope in the possibility of a non-capitalist future will need to be given a vision of it before they will consider joining such a movement. Implicit here, then, is the concomitant belief that a vision of a better future will not emerge from within the masses if the masses lack hope enough to believe that an alternative to the present is possible. Hope has to come from 'above' or from 'outside' the everyday world that most people live in, and if hope depends upon a vision of a better future then this vision too will have to come from above or outside. No amount of lip-service to the notion of a grass-roots utopia will hide the fact that a people lacking hope in the future, which for the pro-utopians is the same as saying a people lacking a vision of a better alternative, cannot be expected to formulate their own vision.

The tension underlying pro-utopian thought, therefore, is this: that whilst they argue that the exhaustion of radical hope has rendered utopianism more necessary now than ever, the utopianism they advocate will of necessity take a top-down form because the exhaustion of radical hope precludes the possibility of utopianism emerging from below. In short, their very justification for a renewed utopian spirit emphasises the lack of utopian hope within contemporary society. As such, their arguments cannot help but imply that a revitalised utopian spirit needs to be instilled into society by those few who still possess hope. With regards to the goal that socialism so desperately needs, therefore, this will be constructed from above by those with hope and vision enough to think beyond the confines of the present.

Utopia as Deceit

The pro-utopians are fond of making a certain anthropological generalisation, one which claims that people are more inclined to react to positives than they are to negatives. This, they then suggest, lends support to the idea that utopias inspire people in a way that scientific and rational discourse do not. Whilst this may well be true, a caveat needs to be added, and it is this: that whilst utopias may inspire people in a way that rational discourse does not, they do not inspire people unless they are declared to be something *other* than a utopia. Put another way, people will not join a coherent movement if they know that the goal for which it strives is *merely* a utopia; a personal, subjective construct which possesses no more truth-value than any other 'utopian' vision.

This can also be looked at from the perspective of the utopian. For if utopianism is to serve as a political tool such that people are motivated into action by the utopias produced, then the authors of these utopias will inevitably be led to argue that *their* utopias are *right*. If one's theoretical premises lead one to conclude that revolutionary hope depends upon people being given a picture of an alternative to the present, then one is more than likely going to prioritise and filter the various alternatives on offer. And if one goes to the trouble of writing one's own alternative then one is more than likely going to explain why it, as opposed to other alternatives, best serves the interests of revolutionary hope.

This certainly applies to the three thinkers from whom utopian guidance is often sought – William Morris, Ernst Bloch and Herbert Marcuse. For whilst Morris subtitled *News From Nowhere* 'some chapters from a Utopian Romance', there can be no doubt that he considered it to be something more than merely *a* utopia – he considered it the best. Indeed, the book itself was written 'in indignant response', as Kumar puts it (1993, p.133), to the vision of socialism presented to the proletariat in Edward Bellamy's *Looking Backward*. More specifically, *News From Nowhere* was written with the intention of providing the proletariat with a vision that was right. This was made clear in Morris' review of *Looking Backward* in which he summarised the issues at stake in the conflict between himself and Bellamy. For he said that 'there is a certain danger in books such as this', and the danger is that potential socialists, 'accepting its speculations as facts, will be inclined to say, 'If *that* is Socialism, we won't help its advent, as it holds out no hope to us'' (Morris, 1994, p.420). Concluding his review, Morris then adds that 'incomplete systems impossible to be carried out but plausible on the surface are always attractive to people ripe for change, but not knowing clearly what their aim is' (ibid., p.425). What was at stake, then, was the *right* way of holding out hope to the masses and the *right* way of showing people ripe for change what their aim is. If Morris sought 'to teach desire to desire, to desire better, to desire more, and above all to desire in a different way' (Thompson, 1977, p.791), then he sought to do so by teaching desire to desire what *he* (and certainly not Bellamy) thought it right for it to desire.

What was mainly implicit in Morris becomes explicit in Bloch. For Bloch's project, much like Morris', was one of 'educating' the hope of the 'little man'. For Bloch, the dreams of most people were both 'full of false hope' (1986, 1, p.351) and yet 'teachable' (ibid., p.3). The issue then became one of teaching these dreams in such a way as to fill them with true hope. In a statement which neatly captures the essence of his thought, he remarks: 'Nobody has ever lived without daydreams, but it is a question of knowing them deeper and deeper and in this way keeping them trained unerringly, usefully, on what is right' (ibid.). Bloch, of course, knew what was 'right' and he encapsulated this in *The Principle of Hope*, that enormous, sprawling attempt to pinpoint where 'true' hope actually lies. As it happens, true hope was found to lie in the cultural realm; in philosophy, novels, architecture, pieces of music and works of art. Not all works of the 'cultural superstructure' embodied hope, however, so Bloch took it upon himself to separate those which prefigured the realm of freedom (and were therefore concretely utopian) from those which did not (which were therefore reactionary). Whilst hidden beneath a bewilderingly complex set of categories, Bloch's method for distinguishing the concrete from the abstract and reactionary boiled down to nothing more than distinguishing between his own personal likes and dislikes. Thus, concrete utopia could be found in Beethoven's Ninth Symphony but not in Jazz, in Baroque but not in Bauhaus, in classic theatre but in *nothing* American. The emancipation of humanity thus came to depend upon the dreams of the little man being trained to focus unerringly on what *Bloch* thought was right, and this meant ignoring Jazz and rejecting Hollywood whilst capturing the spirit and the feeling of Beethoven, Goethe and Baroque architecture. Whatever his merits, therefore, Bloch represents a stereotypical example of the utopian parading his own pedantic cerebrations as the best world for all.

Marcuse presents an even more extreme case in that he never (to my knowledge at least) even *once* conceded that his vision of the emancipated society was a utopia (which of course it certainly was). In 'Protosocialism and Late Capitalism', he did argue that his conception of socialism was a 'concrete utopia' (1980, p.25), but by this he merely meant that socialism was 'an already existing, real possibility — indeed a necessity' (ibid., p.26). And whilst he once remarked, in a lecture entitled 'The End of Utopia', that 'we must face the possibility that the path to socialism may proceed from science to utopia and not from utopia to science' (1970, p.63), this was merely phrasing 'in a provocative form' his basic claim that socialism was no longer a utopia at all (ibid.). More often than not, in fact, when Marcuse refers to 'utopia' he is deriding those who continually refer to socialism in such terms. He could thus state that:

> It may well be that precisely in those aspects of socialism which are today ridiculed as utopian, lies the decisive difference, the contrast between an authentic socialist society and the established societies, even the most advanced industrial societies (1969c, p.20).

Marcuse's point here, then, was not that *he* endorsed a utopian conception of socialism. Quite the contrary. What he meant was that he endorsed a conception of socialism that was ridiculed by *others* as utopian. This was, indeed, a standard defence mechanism employed by Marcuse. In order to allay any fears concerning the utopian nature of his vision, he claimed that it could only be derided as utopian by those who wished to preserve the present system. Thus: 'What is denounced as "utopian" is no longer that which has "no place" and cannot have any place in the historical universe, but rather that which is blocked from coming about by the power of the established societies' (1969a, pp.3-4). Sometimes he went even further, in fact, and claimed that *because* his vision was derided as utopian, this indicated that it was the truth: 'When truth cannot be realized within the established social order, it always appears to the latter as mere utopia. This transcendence speaks not against, but for, its truth' (1968, p.143). Whatever others thought of it, then, the fact remained that the society he envisioned was not a utopia. Even in *Eros and Civilization* Marcuse makes it clear that: 'The notion of a non-repressive civilization will be discussed not as an abstract and utopian speculation' (1969b, p.24). Emphasising the distinction between the society he envisages and a Utopia, he then informs us that 'Utopias are susceptible to unrealistic blueprints; the conditions for a free society are not. They are a matter of reason' (ibid., p.181). Whilst, therefore, Marcuse's views on other matters changed quite dramatically during his life, the one thing that remained constant was his attempt to mobilise support around a 'utopian' vision that was variously paraded a matter of reason, necessity and at one stage even 'an objective truth' (1969d, p.103).

All of which serves to highlight the fact that utopianism, conceived as a political tool rather than a mere literary genre, contains an implicit danger not readily conceded by its advocates. This danger was identified a century and a half ago by a certain Karl Marx and his findings are still applicable today. For Marx, socialism in its utopian form brought with it a prophetic messianism, such that the utopians claimed for themselves the status of prophets who knew what was right and they claimed for their utopias the status of New Jerusalems. For the utopians, the key to the riddle of history lay in their plans, if only others would realise it. Their plans were the truth and the emancipation of humanity awaited their implementation. This was the spectre of deceit which Marx himself tried so hard to exorcize – the spectre which sees the cerebrations of the individual pedant paraded as the best world for all and the fantasies of the human brain heralded as knowledge of 'what is right'; the spectre which forecloses the future and regards the masses as singularly unable to determine where their own emancipation lies.

The messianic nature of utopianism is not, of course, implicit in the actual act of constructing a utopia. There is nothing implicitly messianic in a writer describing, in a variety of aspects and with some consistency, an imaginary state or society which he or she regards as better, in some respects at least, than the one in which he or she lives. To claim otherwise would be bizarre. Utopianism *is* implicitly messianic, however, if it is regarded as a political tool. For if one believes that the revolutionary hope of the masses depends upon a vision of a better future then one will be led to proclaim that this vision is *not* a utopia, and one will be led to proclaim this because, quite simply, the revolutionary hope of the masses has never been ignited by a *mere* utopia. Any utopia that has had any effect on history at all has had such an effect only because its author, or its author's followers, have proclaimed it a truth to be realised. Any utopia that has had any effect on history at all has had such an effect only because its author, or its author's followers, have proclaimed that the emancipation of humanity depends upon its realisation. No utopia will have any effect on history at all if its author concedes that it is a product of the purely subjective imagination, one possible vision among many, and maybe not even the best.

When the pro-utopians eulogise the inspirational power of the utopian imagination they would do well to remember this. When they argue that Marxism needs to take note of the concept of utopia divested of its pejorative connotations, they would do well to take note of Goodwin and Taylor's analysis of the utopian process. For they were convinced that utopians can, do, and have inspired hope. In Taylor's quite accurate words, however, they have managed to do this only because they 'have assumed the mantle of leadership, and have usually presented themselves as great intellectuals, prophets, revolutionaries or even messiahs'. When contemporary Marxists tell us to embrace utopianism, they can begin by pointing out the utopians to whom this does not apply.

So Utopia conceived as a political process that will take us beyond capitalism and into the socialism it describes can, in my view, be nothing other than the elitist process of messianic prophetism so powerfully described by Marx. The reason why so many writers have been drawn into defending this process stems, I believe, from their acceptance of a number of underlying premises. If we take a look at these then perhaps we can begin to formulate an alternative to utopianism as a means of transcending reality and moving beyond capitalism.

The Premises Underlying Contemporary Pro-Utopian Thought

The basic premises upon which contemporary pro-utopian socialism stands were best articulated by Maurice Meisner when he said the 'people must hope before they can act, and their hopes must be lodged in a vision of a better future if their actions are not to be blind and devoid of purpose'. There are three basic claims being made here, two explicit and one implicit. The two explicit claims are that people must hope before they can act and that purposeful hope is dependent upon a vision of a better future. The implicit claim is that people at present lack purposeful hope. Indeed, it is precisely because people at present lack purposeful hope that the pro-utopians talk about utopianism in the first place — as a means of both igniting hope and of providing it with a purpose.

Of the three claims, two can be accepted without argument — the claims that people at present lack hope in the future and that people must hope before they can act in any purposeful and constructive way. With regards to the first of these, a MORI poll conducted in April 1995 asked: 'Do you think that the kind of world that today's children will inherit will be better or worse than the kind of world that children of your generation inherited, or about the same?' In response, 60% of people answered 'worse'. A similar poll conducted by Gallup in March-April 1995 asked: 'Do you think that children today have a better future in front of them than you had when you were a child, a worse future, or about the same?' This time 63% answered 'worse' (Jacobs, 1996, p.3). On the basis of such evidence one would seem justified in concluding that people in general, at the present time at least, lack hope in the future.

The claim that people must hope before they can act is a little more contentious in the sense that other factors also motivate people to act — fear being the most obvious example. Given, however, that a complex socio-psychological investigation into the historical bases of political action is beyond the scope of this book, I will simply accept as a generalised premise the seemingly reasonable claim that purposive political action requires Hope as its basis.

In addition to these, two further things can also be accepted. The first is that radical hope cannot, as Marx himself believed, be fuelled solely by a critical analysis of the material conditions of the present. The second is that, conversely, radical hope needs to be fuelled by something *in addition to* the critical analysis of the material conditions of the present. In other words, socialists do indeed need 'more than a critique of the self-evident (and even the oblique) evils of capitalist society' (although they *do*, I would strenuously add, need such a critique).

The problems begin to arise, however, when one considers the third of the claims mentioned above – the claim that purposeful hope depends upon a vision of a better future. For underlying this claim is the contention that visions of a better future are required if radical political action is to be something more than blind adventurism, and it is this contention which signals a fundamental flaw in the arguments for Utopia. For what the pro-utopians seem so often to be suggesting is that the construction of utopias somehow prevents radical political action from becoming adventuristic. The term 'adventurism' has, indeed, acquired all sorts of pejorative connotations and has itself become a 'dirty word' to be avoided at all costs. Thus asks Iakov Pevzner:

> If you do not know what the new society will be like, is it reasonable to call for the destruction of the existing society? Is such an appeal not adventuristic? (1994, p.8)

The only possible answer to this question is that of course it is, simply because all calls for the destruction of the existing society will be adventuristic. For Pevzner is quite wrong if he thinks that one can make an appeal that is *not* adventuristic if one presents people with pictures of what the new society will 'be like'. Indeed, Pevzner's language is indicative of the central problem here, for he quite plainly states that the key to avoiding adventurism lies in one's being able to *know* what the new society will be like, when, of course, no such knowledge is ever going to become available to anyone. What Pevzner's question leads to, in fact, is one of two perverse conclusions. The first is that because one can never 'know' what the new society will be like, all calls for the destruction of the existing society will be adventuristic and therefore open to censure. This, then, is nothing short of ultra-conservatism. The second is that if one needs to 'know' what the new society will be like before one can avoid charges of adventurism, then one will proclaim that one *does*, in fact, know what the new society will look like. This, however, is nothing short of the prophetic messianism that so many utopians adopt and which is rightly open to censure.

The language of knowledge versus adventurism is, I believe, symptomatic of the fact that the pro-utopians are vainly attempting to get utopianism to do the comforting things that 'science' once did but no longer can. It is no coincidence that contemporary support for utopianism first began to emerge in the early 1970s, just as the omnipotent powers of 'science' were being subjected to the most rigorous of critiques. For whilst the 'inevitability' of socialism had long been questioned within the Left, it was only during the late '60's-early '70's that it became clear to everyone that there was no scientific basis upon which the final victory of socialism could be proclaimed. Understandably, the fact that socialism had now become just one possibility amongst many caused all sorts of anxieties within the Left, and it is these anxieties that led many to turn to utopianism as a source of comfort.

Unfortunately, however, via a strange process of substitutionalism, utopianism became burdened with a whole host of unreasonable expectations. Prime amongst these was the idea that utopias could somehow provide the sense of security that science had previously done. Faced with the 'evitability' of socialism and the uncomfortable thought that its realisation would involve an element of 'adventurism', the comforts of science were untidily transposed onto utopianism: the utopian imagination would now guide and direct us, providing us with a concrete purpose and ensuring a minimum of risk and singular lack of adventure, in exactly the same way that the iron logic of historical development used to do.

Utopias, however, possess no intrinsic powers by which our actions can be guided and directed without risk of adventurism. Indeed, the very notion that utopias provide the only basis for purposive action can be criticised on the grounds that it is based upon a false equation; that which suggests that 'people are purposive creatures *therefore* people need visions of a better future'. For to claim that human beings are purposive creatures is to claim nothing more than people generally act only when they feel that their action serves a purpose. Now, as far as I can see, there is nothing in this to suggest that the purpose of mass political action can be supplied *only* by a 'vision of a better future'.

This, however, is a common theme. Sometimes, in fact, the arguments are taken even further so that utopianism is referred to as the *embodiment* of hope. So intractable does this idea appear to be that one finds support for utopianism arriving from the most unexpected quarters. Listen, for example, to Milan Simecka when he says of utopias that:

> Being as a rule the fruit of elite aspirations and minority dreams, they automatically provoke attempts to inculcate forcibly the minority's ideals in the majority. Attracted by the lure of an abstract good, they easily succumb to the view that the end justifies the means, thus taking a direct part in the history of violence, dictatorships and slaughter in the name of a better future (1984, p.172).

Karl Popper could not have said this any better. 'And yet', continues Simecka, 'let us try to imagine a world without utopias . . . A world without utopias would be a world without social hope, a world of resignation to the status quo and the devalued slogans of everyday political life' (ibid., pp.174-175). He thus concludes: 'Today the world is in such a state that it needs new utopias' (ibid., p.176). Arguments such as these are strange to say the very least — although utopias are the fruit of elite aspirations whose realisation will involve a select minority imposing its views upon the majority by means of violence and slaughter, utopianism is socially necessary because *only* utopis can offer hope.

Such claims are, in fact, the product of a popular misconception. Frank E. Manuel provides the archetypal rendering of this misconception when he remarks that 'to attack utopias is about as meaningful as to denounce dreaming' (1973, p.95). The misconception, then, is that utopianism is somehow inextricably linked to the process of dreaming; it is dreaming writ large. Writers such as Lyman Tower Sargent even go so far as to *define* utopianism as 'social dreaming' (1994, p.9). What, however, does this mean? Dreaming in the company of others? Many people sharing the same dream? The implication, of course, is that social dreaming involves dreaming *about* society. Are utopian thoughts about society really comparable to dreams, however? Sargent seems to think so and goes on to defend his definition on the grounds that 'utopianism is a universal human phenomenon' (ibid., p.3). He then adds:

> I do not think it necessary to assume a common "human nature" to conclude that the overwhelming majority of people — probably it is even possible to say all — are, at some time dissatisfied and consider how their lives might be improved (ibid.).

Whilst this is undoubtedly so, I think it almost self-evident to say that the ways in which people imagine improvements being made to their lives are almost never 'utopian'. Most people think in terms of winning the lottery, or in terms of sexual conquests, and rarely in terms of lucid descriptions of imaginary states. And yet writers keep on claiming that utopias are comparable to dreams; that they embody our hopes, desires and aspirations in much the same way. This then leads critics like Simecka into the false belief that those who oppose utopianism are somehow opposed to all forms of hope and are secretly plotting some wild scheme to eradicate dreams from the world. A world without utopias would be 'a world of resignation to the status quo', he argues, as if utopianism is the only possible way of challenging the status quo and the only possible source of social hope.

To be clear, then, utopias are not a universal expression of social hope lodged somewhere deep inside the collective human psyche. They are imaginary states constructed in the minds of a few scattered individuals. And the idea that purposeful hope depends upon a vision of a better future is not a claim based upon a detailed understanding of the complexities of human motivation — as a claim it is founded on a fallacious anthropological generalisation whilst as the premise underlying pro-utopian thought within the Left its contemporary popularity can be viewed in terms of the attempt to locate a new source of non-adventuristic comfort to replace that once offered by Marxism's historical 'science'. A world without utopias is not a world without hope and utopianism is certainly not the best means of 'giving' hope to those who lack it. Political utopianism so conceived is, as Marx so perceptively argued, 'deliberate deception on the part of some; self-deception on the part of others, who give out the world transformed according to their own needs as the best world for all'.

In Search of the Spirit of Adventure

Radical political action is inherently adventuristic, and neither science nor utopia can prevent it from being so. This is a point that needs to be emphasised, repeated and emphasised again. There are quite simply no guarantees — those once provided by science have now been eclipsed and utopianism, no matter how hard its advocates try, can offer no replacements. Socialism is now nothing more (but importantly nothing *less*) than an adventure. Rather than hide from this fact, I think it necessary for socialists to actively seek 'the *spirit* of adventure'. This is the willingness to risk everything without guarantees, to destroy the present in the name of a future that is not and cannot yet be known. It is, quite literally, the willingness to step into the *un*known.

If this sounds overly-adventuristic then it might be useful to point out that the general lack of popular hope which the pro-utopians rightly emphasise is due less to a lack of alternative visions than it is to the feeling that subjective action *does not* serve any purpose. The mistake made by the pro-utopians is that they equate 'lack of hope' with 'lack of utopias' and then declare that the solution lies in 'abundance of utopias'. This, however, misses the point. For by virtue of the fact that subjective action is now deemed to serve no purpose, people are unlikely to join a movement whose aim is to realise — by means of subjective action — a vision of a new and different world. People tend to be wary of new and different worlds and describing an abundance of them will do nothing to alter this.

Whilst, therefore, socialists do need more than a critique of the self-evident (and even the oblique) evils of capitalism, this something more is not an abundance of utopias. What socialists do need, however, is to convince people that subjective action can and does serve a purpose — that one can act in the world and change it for the better. What needs to be emphasised, therefore, is the immense scope for change that exists in the present and the fact that human beings can intervene and collectively alter the world around them. Utopian images will not do this because, quite simply, until people think and believe that radical change is possible, no radical 'alternative' will inspire them. And as soon as they *do* think that change is possible, utopian images become irrelevant because people themselves can be entrusted with the task of deciding what the alternative will be. Indeed, the notion that radical political action requires a utopian guide underestimates the extent to which people are capable of acting on their own volition, *once, that is, they believe that their actions can actually serve a purpose.*

It is thus the task of socialists to show that human intervention does not always result in catastrophe. It is the task of socialists to emphasise the power of subjective action. It is the task of socialists, armed with a critique of the present and pointing to successes achieved by human beings in the past, to ignite the spirit of adventure. It is no use denying that the future is an adventure away, nor that its creation will involve time, effort, problems and risks. No amount of science and no number of utopias will enable one to do this. It is a matter of kindling the will to take risks and to embark on an adventure.

There is therefore still a world to gain; but this is not an abstract utopian world, existing in the ether of the present, nor a 'concrete' utopian world, disguised as 'the truth' or 'what is right'. It is a world whose nature is as yet unknown, indeed is unknowable *now*, but whose nature will be known to us in the future because it will be our own creation. Because the realisation of socialism cannot be guaranteed, nor its nature predicted, by either 'science' or 'utopia', this will involve an adventuristic leap into the unknown. This leap will, in turn, only be taken by a people imbued with the spirit of adventure, a people willing to take risks in return for the opportunity to act in and upon the world.

Bibliography

Adamiak, R. (1970) 'The "Withering Away" of the State: A Reconsideration', *Journal of Politics*, 32 (1), pp.3-18.

Alexander, P. and Gill, R. (eds.) (1984) *Utopias*, London, Duckworth.

Annenkov, P. V. (1968) *The Extraordinary Decade: Literary Memoirs*, Ann Arbor, University of Michegan Press.

Avineri, S. (1968) *The Social and Political Thought of Karl Marx*, Cambridge, Cambridge University Press.

Avineri, S. (1973) 'Marx's Vision of Future Society and the Problem of Utopianism', *Dissent*, Summer, pp.323-331.

Bahro, R. (1978) *The Alternative in Eastern Europe*, London, New Left Books.

Barclay, M. W. (1993) 'Utopia and Psychological Theory', *Theory and Psychology*, 3 (2), pp.173-190.

Bauman, Z. (1976) *Socialism: The Active Utopia*, London, Allen and Unwin.

Beauchamp, G., Roemer, K. and Smith, N. (eds.) (1987) *Utopian Studies I*, New York and London, Jonathan Cape Ltd.

Bell, D. (1973) *The Coming of Post-Industrial Society*, New York, Basic Books.

Bender, F. L. (1990) 'The Ambiguities of Marx's Concepts of "Proletarian Dictatorship" and "Transition to Communism"', in B. Jessop and C. Malcolm-Brown (eds.), *Karl Marx's Social and Political Thought*, Volume 3, pp.355-383.

Berki, R. N. (1983) *Insight and Vision: The Problem of Communism in Marx's Thought*, London and Melbourne, J. M. Dent and Sons.

Berland, O. (1990) 'Radical Chains: The Marxian Concept of Proletarian Mission', in B. Jessop and C. Malcolm-Brown (eds.), *Karl Marx's Social and Political Thought*, Volume 2, pp.278-97.

Berneri, M. (1971) *Journey Through Utopia*, New York, Schocken Books.

Bhaskar, R. (1986) *Scientific Realism and Human Emancipation*, London, Verso.

Blackburn, R. (ed.) (1991) *After the Fall: The Failure of Communism and the Future of Socialism*, London, Verso.

Blackburn, R. (1990) 'Marxism: Theory of Proletarian Revolution', in B. Jessop and C. Malcolm-Brown (eds.), *Karl Marx's Social and Political Thought*, Volume 3, pp.235-272.

Blackburn, R. (1991) 'Fin de Siècle: Socialism after the Crash', in R. Blackburn (ed.), *After the Fall*, pp.173-249.

Blanchette, O. (1990) 'The Idea of History in Karl Marx', in B. Jessop and C. Malcolm-Brown (eds.), *Karl Marx's Social and Political Thought*, Volume 2, pp.17-48.

Bloch, E. (1986) *The Principle of Hope* (3 volumes), Oxford, Basil Blackwell.

Brighouse, H. (1994) 'Transitional and Utopian Market Socialism', *Politics and Society*, 22 (4), pp.569-584.

Buber, M. (1988) *Paths In Utopia*, New York, Collier Books.

Bultmann, D. R. (1957) *History and Eschatology*, Edinburgh, The University Press.

Burke, J. P., Crocker, L. and Legters, L. H. (eds.) (1981) *Marxism and the Good Society*, Cambridge, Cambridge University Press.

Burke, J. P., Crocker, L. and Legters, L. H. (1981) 'Introduction', in J. P. Burke, L. Crocker and L. H. Legters (eds.), *Marxism and the Good Society*, pp.1-6.

Carver, T. (1988) 'Communism for Critical Critics: *The German Ideology* and the Problem of Technology', *History of Political Thought*, 9 (1), pp.129-136.

Carver, T. (1998) *The Postmodern Marx*, Manchester, Manchester University Press.

Cioran, E. M. (1996), *History and Utopia*, London, Quartet Books.

Cohen, A. (1995) 'Marx and the Abolition of the Abolition of Labour — End of Utopia or Utopia as an End', *Utopian Studies*, 6 (1), pp.40-50.

Cohen, G. A. (1978) *Karl Marx's Theory of History: A Defence*, Oxford, Clarendon Press.

Colletti, L. (ed.) (1975) *Karl Marx, Early Writings*, London, Penguin in association with New Left Review.

Crocker, L. (1981) 'Marx, Liberty, and Democracy', in J. P. Burke, L. Crocker and L. H. Legters (eds.), *Marxism and the Good Society*, pp.32-58.

De George, R. T. (1981) 'Marxism and the Good Society', in J. P. Burke, L. Crocker and L. H. Legters (eds.), *Marxism and the Good Society*, pp.7-31.

Derrida, J. (1994) *Specters of Marx*, London and New York, Routledge.

Draper, H. (1987) *The 'Dictatorship of the Proletariat' from Marx to Lenin*, New York, Monthly Review Press.

Draper, H. (1990) 'Marx and the Dictatorship of the Proletariat', in B. Jessop and C. Malcolm-Brown (eds.), *Karl Marx's Social and Political Thought*, Volume 3, pp.289-315.

Durkheim, E. (1959) *Socialism and Saint-Simon*, London, Routledge and Kegan Paul.

Durkheim, E. (1960) *The Division of Labour in Society*, Illinois, The Free Press of Glencoe.

Eckersley, R. (1992) *Environmentalism and Political Theory*, London, UCL Press.

Eliade, M. (1987) *The Sacred and the Profane*, New York, Harcourt Brace and Co.

Elliott, G. (1993) 'The Cards of Confusion: Reflections on Historical Communism and the "End of History"', *Radical Philosophy*, 64, pp.3-12.

Elster, J. (1986) *An Introduction to Karl Marx*, Cambridge, Cambridge University Press.

Engels, F. (1962) 'The Housing Question', in K. Marx and F. Engels, *Selected Works in Two Volumes*, Volume 1, pp.557-635.

Engels, F. (1968a) 'Preface to "The Peasant War In Germany"', in K. Marx and F. Engels, *Selected Works In One Volume*, pp.235-241.

Engels, F. (1968b) 'Introduction to *The Civil War in France*', in K. Marx and F. Engels, *Selected Works in One Volume*, pp.248-259.

Engels, F. (1968c) 'Socialism: Utopian and Scientific', in K. Marx and F. Engels, *Selected Works In One Volume*, pp.375-428.

Engels, F. (1968d) 'The Origin of the Family, Private Property and the State', in K. Marx and F. Engels, *Selected Works in One Volume*, pp.449-583.

Engels, F. (1973) 'The Magyar Struggle' in D. Fernbach (ed.), *Karl Marx: The Revolutions of 1848*, pp.213-226.

Engels, F. (1976) 'The Principles of Communism', in K. Marx and F. Engels, *Collected Works*, Volume 6, pp.341-357.

Engels, F. (1978) *Anti-Dühring: Herr Eugen Dühring's Revolution in Science*, Moscow, Progress.

Engels, F. (1979), 'Introduction to *The Class Struggles in France*', in K. Marx, *The Class Struggles in France 1848 to 1850*, pp.7-29.

Fernbach, D. (ed.) (1973) *Karl Marx: The Revolutions of 1848, Political Writings Volume 1*, London, Penguin in association with New Left Review.

Fernbach, D. (ed.) (1974) *Karl Marx: The First International and After, Political Writings Volume 3*, London, Penguin in association with New Left Review.

Fischer, E. (1970) *Marx in His Own Words*, Harmondsworth, Penguin Books Ltd.

Fourier, C. (1996) *The Theory of the Four Movements*, Cambridge, Cambridge University Press.

Freedeman, C. (1979) *Joint-Stock Enterprises in France, 1807-1867*, Chapel Hill, The University of North Carolina Press.

Fukuyama, F. (1992) *The End of History and the Last Man*, London, Penguin.

Furet, F. (1995) 'Europe After Utopianism', *Journal of Democracy*, 6 (1), pp.79-89.

Gardiner, M. (1992) 'Bakhtin's Carnival: Utopia as Critique', *Utopian Studies*, 3 (2), pp.21-49.

Geoghegan, V. (1987a) *Utopianism and Marxism*, London and New York, Methuen.

Geoghegan, V. (1987b) 'Marxism and Utopianism', in G. Beauchamp, K. Roemer and N. Smith (eds.), *Utopian Studies I*, pp.37-51.

Geoghegan, V. (1990) 'Remembering the Future', *Utopian Studies*, 1 (2), pp.52-68.

Goldsmith, E. (1992) *The Way: An Ecological World View*, London, Rider.

Goldsmith, E. and Allaby, M. (1972) *Blueprint for Survival*, London, Penguin.

Goodwin, B. (1982) 'The "Authoritarian" Nature of Utopia', *Radical Philosophy*, 32, pp.23-27.

Goodwin, B. and Taylor, K. (1982) *The Politics of Utopia*, London, Hutchinson.

Gorz, A. (1987) *Ecology as Politics*, London, Pluto Press.

Gramsci, A. (1971) *Selections From The Prison Notebooks*, London, Lawrence and Wishart.

Habermas, J. (1973) *Theory and Practice*, Boston, Beacon Press.

Habermas, J. (1986) *Autonomy and Solidarity: Interviews*, London, Verso.

Habermas, J. (1989) *The New Conservatism: Cultural Criticism and the Historians' Debate*, London, Polity Press.

Halliday, F. (1991) 'A Reply to Edward Thompson', in R. Blackburn (ed.), *After the Fall*, pp.110-114.

Hammen, O. J. (1990) 'Alienation, Communism and Revolution in the Marx-Engels *Briefweschel*', in B. Jessop and C. Malcolm-Brown (eds.), *Karl Marx's Social and Political Thought*, Volume 1, pp.421-444.

Harvey, D. (1989) *The Condition of Postmodernity*, Oxford, Blackwell.

Heller, A. (1974) *The Theory of Need in Marx*, London, Allison and Bushy Ltd.

Heller, A. (1993) *A Philosophy of History in Fragments*, Oxford, Blackwell.

Hilferding, R. (1981) *Finance Capital*, London, Routledge and Kegan Paul.

Hobsbawm, E. (1991) 'Out of the Ashes', in R. Blackburn (ed.), *After the Fall*, pp.315-325.

Hodgson, G. M. (1995) 'The Political Economy of Utopia', *Review of Social Economy*, 53 (2), pp.195-213.

Holloway, M. (1984) 'The Necessity of Utopia', in P. Alexander and R. Gill (eds.) *Utopias*, pp.179-188.

Holton, R. J. (1981) 'Marxist Theories of Social Change and the Transition from Feudalism to Capitalism', *Theory and Society*, 10 (6), pp. 833-867.

Honderich, T. (1982) 'Against Teleological Historical Materialism', *Inquiry*, 25, pp. 451-469.

Horne, A. (1981) *The Fall of Paris*, Harmondsworth, Penguin Books.

Hunt, E. K. (1984) 'Was Marx a Utopian Socialist?', *Science and Society*, 48 (1), pp. 90-97.

Jacobs, M. (1996) *The Politics of the Real World*, London, Earthscan.

Jacobs, N. (1989) 'Beyond Stasis and Symettry: Lessing, Le Guin, and the Remodelling of Utopia', in M. S. Cummings and N. Smith (eds.), *Utopian Studies II*, pp.109-117.

Jameson, F. (1976) 'Introduction/Prospectus: To Reconsider the Relationship of Marxism to Utopian Thought', *The Minnesota Review*, NS VI, pp.53-58.

Jessop, B. and Malcolm-Brown, C. (eds.) (1990) *Karl Marx's Social and Political Thought* (4 Volumes), London, Routledge.

Johnstone, M. (1971) 'The Paris Commune and Marx's Conception of the Dictatorship of the Proletariat', *The Massachusetts Review*, XII, pp.447-462.

Kellner, D. (1973) 'Introduction to "On the Philosophical Foundation of the Concept of Labour"', *Telos*, 16, pp.2-8.

Kessler, C. F. (1989) 'Women Daring to Speak: United States Women's Feminist Utopias', in M. S. Cummings and N. Smith (eds.), *Utopian Studies II*, pp.118-124.
Kolakowski, L. (1968) *Toward a Marxist Humanism*, New York, Grove Press Inc.
Kolakowski, L. (1978) *Main Currents of Marxism* (3 volumes), Oxford, Clarendon Press.
Kumar, K. (1986) *Prophesy and Progress: The Sociology of Industrial and Post-Industrial Society*, London, Penguin Books.
Kumar, K. (1987) *Utopia and Anti-Utopia in Modern Times*, Oxford, Blackwell.
Kumar, K. (1991) *Utopianism*, Milton Keynes, Open University Press.
Kumar, K. (1993) 'News From Nowhere: The Renewal of Utopia', *History of Political Thought*, 14 (1), pp.133-143.
Kuryllo, H. (1989) '"A Woman's Text in the Wild Zone:" The Subversiveness of Elizabeth Gaskell's *Cranford*', in M. S. Cummings and N. Smith (eds.), *Utopian Studies II*, pp.102-108.
Lasky, M. J. (1977) *Utopia and Revolution*, London, Macmillan.
Lenin, V. I. (1968) *Selected Works*, Moscow, Progress Publishers.
Lepenies, W. (1991) 'Hope derailed on way from utopia', *The Times Higher Education Supplement*, December 27, p.8.
Levin, M. (1990) 'Marx and Working-Class Consciousness', in B. Jessop and C. Malcolm-Brown (eds.), *Karl Marx's Social and Political Thought*, Volume 2, pp.299-314.
Levitas, R. (1979) 'Sociology and Utopia', *Sociology*, 13 (1), pp.19-34.
Levitas, R. (1989) 'Marxism, Romanticism and Utopia: Ernst Bloch and William Morris', *Radical Philosophy*, 51, pp.27-36.
Levitas, R. (1990) *The Concept of Utopia*, Hemel Hempstead, Philip Allen.
Lichtheim, G. (1969) *The Origins of Socialism*, London, Weidenfeld and Nicolson.
Lichtheim, G. (1971) *From Marx to Hegel and Other Essays*, London, Orbach and Chambers.
Longxi, Z. (1995) 'Marxism: From Scientific to Utopian', in B. Magnus and S. Cullenberg (eds.), *Whither Marxism?*, pp.65-78.
Löwith, K. (1949) *Meaning in History*, Chicago and London, Chicago University Press.
Lukes, S. (1984) 'Marxism and Utopianism', in P. Alexander and R. Gill (eds.), *Utopias*, pp.153-167.

MacIntyre, A. (1969) *Marxism and Christianity*, London, Gerald Duckworth.

McLellan, D. (ed.) (1977) *Karl Marx, Selected Writings*, Oxford, Oxford University Press.

McLellan, D. (1969) 'Marx's View of the Unalienated Society', *Review of Politics*, 31 (4), pp.459-465.

McLellan, D. (1980) *The Thought of Karl Marx* (Second Edition), London and Basingstoke, Macmillan.

Magnus, B. and Cullenberg, S. (eds.) (1995) *Whither Marxism?*, New York and London, Routledge.

Mandel, E. (1977) *From Class Society to Communism*, London, Ink Links Ltd.

Mannheim, K. (1968) *Ideology and Utopia*, London, Routledge and Kegan Paul.

Manuel, F. E. (ed.) (1973) *Utopias and Utopian Thought*, London, Souvenir Press.

Manuel, F. E. (1956) *The New World of Henri Saint-Simon*, Cambridge Mass., Harvard University Press.

Manuel, F. E. (1973) 'Toward a Psychological History of Utopias', in F. E. Manuel (ed.), *Utopias and Utopian Thought*, pp.69-100.

Manuel, F. E. (1992) 'A Requiem for Karl Marx', *Dædalus*, 121 (2), pp.1-19.

Manuel, F. E. and Manuel, F. P. (1979) *Utopian Thought in the Western World*, Oxford, Blackwell.

Marcuse, H. (1968) *Negations*, London, Allen Lane.

Marcuse, H. (1969a) *An Essay on Liberation*, London, Allen Lane.

Marcuse, H. (1969b) *Eros and Civilisation*, London, Sphere Books.

Marcuse, H. (1969c) 'The Realm of Freedom and the Realm of Necessity: A Reconsideration', *Praxis*, 5 (1-2), pp.20-25.

Marcuse, H. (1969d) 'Repressive Tolerance', in R. P. Wolff, B. Moore Jnr. and H. Marcuse, *A Critique of Pure Tolerance*, pp.93-138.

Marcuse, H. (1970) *Five Lectures*, London, Allen Lane, The Penguin Press.

Marcuse, H. (1973) 'On the Philosophical Foundation of the Concept of Labour in Economics', *Telos*, 16, pp.9-37.

Marcuse, H. (1980) 'Protosocialism and Late Capitalism: Toward a Theoretical Synthesis Based on Bahro's Analysis', in U. Wolter (ed.), *Rudolf Bahro, Critical Responses*, pp.25-48.

Marx, K. (1946) *Capital, Volume 1*, London, Allen and Unwin.

Marx, K. (1959) *Capital, Volume 3*, Moscow, Foreign Languages Publishing House.

Marx, K. (1960a) 'The Indian Question — Irish Tenant Rights', in K. Marx and F. Engels, *On Colonialism*, pp.50-55.

Marx, K. (1960b) 'The Indian Question', in K. Marx and F. Engels, *On Colonialism*, pp.125-129.

Marx, K. (1962) 'The British Rule in India', in K. Marx and F. Engels, *Selected Works in Two Volumes*, Volume 1, pp.345-351.

Marx, K. (1968a) 'Theses on Feuerbach', in K. Marx and F. Engels, *Selected Works in One Volume*, pp.28-30.

Marx, K. (1968b) 'Wage Labour and Capital', in K. Marx and F. Engels, *Selected Works in One Volume*, pp.71-93.

Marx, K. (1968c) 'The Eighteenth Brumaire of Louis Bonaparte', in K. Marx and F. Engels, *Selected Works in One Volume*, pp.96-179.

Marx, K. (1968d) 'Second Address of the General Council of the International Working Men's Association on the Franco-Prussian War', in K. Marx and F. Engels, *Selected Works in One Volume*, pp.264-270.

Marx, K. (1968e) 'The Civil War in France', in K. Marx and F. Engels, *Selected Works in One Volume*, pp.271-309.

Marx, K. (1968f) 'Critique of the Gotha Programme', in K. Marx and F. Engels, *Selected Works in One Volume*, pp.311-331.

Marx, K. (1969) *Theories of Surplus Value, Volume 2*, London, Lawrence and Wishart.

Marx, K. (1970) *A Contribution to the Critique of Political Economy*, London, Lawrence and Wishart.

Marx, K. (1971a) *Theories of Surplus Value, Volume 3*, London, Lawrence and Wishart.

Marx, K. (1971b) 'Revelations Concerning the Communist Trial in Cologne', in K. Marx and F. Engels, *The Cologne Communist Trial*, pp.57-119.

Marx, K. (1973a) *Grundrisse*, London, Allen Lane in association with New Left Review.

Marx, K. (1973b) 'The Bourgeoisie and the Counter-Revolution', in D. Fernbach (ed.), *Karl Marx: The Revolutions of 1848*, pp.186-212.

Marx, K. (1974a) 'Provisional Rules of the International', in D. Fernbach (ed.), *Karl Marx: The First International and After*, pp.82-84.

Marx, K. (1974b) 'Instructions for Delegates to the Geneva Congress', in D. Fernbach (ed.), *Karl Marx: The First International and After*, pp.85-94.

Marx, K. (1974c) 'First Draft of "The Civil War in France"', in D. Fernbach (ed.), *Karl Marx: The First International and After*, pp.236-268.

Marx, K. (1974d) 'Political Indifferentism', in D. Fernbach (ed.), *Karl Marx: The First International and After*, pp.327-332.

Marx, K. (1974e) 'Conspectus of Bakunin's *Statism and Anarchy*', in D. Fernbach (ed.), *Karl Marx: The First International and After*, pp.333-338.

Marx, K. (1975a) 'Comments on James Mill', in K. Marx and F. Engels, *Collected Works*, Volume 3, pp.211-228.

Marx, K. (1975b) 'Letters from the *Franco-German Yearbooks*', in L. Colletti (ed.), *Karl Marx, Early Writings*, pp.199-210.

Marx, K. (1976a) *Capital, Volume 1*, Harmondsworth, Penguin Books Ltd.

Marx, K. (1976b) 'The Poverty of Philosophy', in K. Marx and F. Engels, *Collected Works*, Volume 6, pp.105-212.

Marx, K. (1976c) 'Moralising Criticism and Critical Morality', in K. Marx and F. Engels, *Collected Works*, Volume 6, pp.312-340

Marx, K. (1976d) 'The *Débat Social* of February 6 on the Democratic Association', in K. Marx and F. Engels, *Collected Works*, Volume 6, pp.537-539.

Marx, K. (1977a) *Economic and Philosophical Manuscripts*, Moscow, Progress Publishers.

Marx, K. (1977b) 'Towards a Critique of Hegel's *Philosophy of Right*: Introduction', in D. McLellan (ed.), *Karl Marx, Selected Writings*, pp.63-74.

Marx, K. (1977c) 'Critical Remarks on the Article: "The King of Prussia and Social Reform"', in D. McLellan (ed.), *Karl Marx, Selected Writings*, pp.124-127.

Marx, K. (1977d) 'Letter to Vera Sassoulitch', in D. McLellan (ed.), *Karl Marx, Selected Writings*, pp.576-580.

Marx, K. (1977e) 'Comments on Adolph Wagner', in D. McLellan (ed.), *Karl Marx, Selected Writings*, pp.581-582.

Marx, K. (1979) *The Class Struggles in France 1848 to 1850*, Moscow, Progress Publishers.

Marx, K. (1980) 'Speech at the Anniversary of *The People's Paper*, London, April 14th 1856', in K. Marx and F. Engels, *Collected Works*, Volume 14, pp.655-656.

Marx, K. (1981) 'Herr Vogt', in K. Marx and F. Engels, *Collected Works*, Volume 17, pp.21-327.

Marx, K. and Engels, F. (1960) *On Collonialism*, London, Lawrence and Wishart.
Marx, K. and Engels, F. (1962) *Selected Works in Two Volumes*, Moscow, Foreign Languages Publishing House.
Marx, K. and Engels, F. (1965) *The German Ideology*, London, Lawrence and Wishart.
Marx, K. and Engels, F. (1967) *Manifesto of the Communist Party*, Harmondsworth, Penguin Books Ltd.
Marx, K. and Engels, F. (1968) *Selected Works in One Volume*, London, Lawrence and Wishart.
Marx, K. and Engels, F. (1969) *Selected Correspondence*, Moscow, Foreign Languages Publishing House.
Marx, K. and Engels, F. (1970) *The German Ideology, Volume 1*, London, Lawrence and Wishart.
Marx, K. and Engels, F. (1971) *The Cologne Communist Trial*, London, Lawrence and Wishart.
Marx, K. and Engels, F. (1973) 'Address of the Central Committee to the Communist League (March 1850)', in D. Fernbach (ed.), *Karl Marx: The Revolutions of 1848*, pp.319-330.
Marx, K. and Engels, F. (1974a) 'The Alleged Splits in the International', in D. Fernbach (ed.), *Karl Marx: The First International and After*, pp.272-314.
Marx, K. and Engels, F. (1974b) 'Circular Letter to Bebel, Liebknecht, Bracke, *et al.*', in D. Fernbach (ed.), *Karl Marx: The First International and After*, pp.360-375.
Marx, K. and Engels, F. (1975) *Collected Works*, Volume 3, London, Lawrence and Wishart.
Marx, K. and Engels, F. (1976a) *Collected Works*, Volumes 5-6, London, Lawrence and Wishart.
Marx, K. and Engels, F. (1976b) 'The German Ideology, Volume Two', in K. Marx and F. Engels, *Collected Works*, Volume 5, pp.453-539.
Marx, K. and Engels, F. (1980a) *Collected Works*, Volume 14, London, Lawrence and Wishart.
Marx, K. and Engels, F. (1980b) *The Holy Family*, Moscow, Progress Publishers.
Marx, K. and Engels, F. (1981) *Collected Works*, Volume 17, London, Lawrence and Wishart.

Meikle, S. (1979) 'Dialectical Contradiction and Necessity', in J. Mepham and D.-H. Ruben (eds.), *Issues in Marxist Philosophy*, Volume 1, pp.5-36.

Meisner, M. (1982) *Marxism, Maoism and Utopianism*, London and Wisconsin, University of Wisconsin Press.

Mepham, J. and Ruben, D.-H. (eds.) (1979), *Issues in Marxist Philosophy* (4 Volumes), Brighton, Harvester Press.

Moore, S. (1980) *Marx on the Choice Between Socialism and Communism*, Cambridge MA, Harvard University Press.

Moore, S. (1990) 'Marx and the Origins of Dialectical Materialism', in B. Jessop and C. Malcolm-Brown (eds.), *Karl Marx's Social and Political Thought*, Volume 1, pp.138-146.

Morris, W. (1994) 'Looking Backward', in N. Salmon (ed.), *William Morris, Political Writings*, pp.419-425.

Morrison, A. (1984) 'Uses of Utopia', in P. Alexander and R. Gill (eds.), *Utopias*, pp.139-152.

Niebuhr, R. (1949) *Faith and History*, New York, Charles Scribner's Sons.

Oliver, W. H. (1971) 'Owen in 1817: The Millennialist Moment', in S. Pollard and J. Salt (eds.), *Robert Owen, Prophet of the Poor*, pp.166-187.

Ollman, B. (1977) 'Marx's Vision of Communism: A Reconstruction', *Critique*, 8, pp.4-41.

Owen, R. (1963) *A New View of Society and Other Writings*, London, J.M. Dent and Sons Ltd.

Pevzner, I. (1994) 'Socialism: Utopia or Science?', *Problems of Economic Transition*, 37 (3), pp.5-20.

Plekhanov, G. V. (1969) *Fundamental Problems of Marxism*, London, Lawrence and Wishart.

Pollard, S. and Salt, J. (eds.) (1971) *Robert Owen, Prophet of the Poor*, London and Basingstoke, Macmillan.

Popper, K. R. (1962) *The Open Society and Its Enemies, Volume One: The Spell of Plato*, London, Routledge and Kegan Paul.

Porritt, J. (1984) *Seeing Green*, Oxford, Blackwell.

Rattansi, A. (1982) *Marx and the Division of Labour*, Atlantic Highlands NJ, Humanities Press.

Ricoeur, P. (1986) *Lectures on Ideology and Utopia*, New York, Columbia University Press.

Ruben, D.-H. (1979) 'Marxism and Dialectics', in J. Mepham and D.-H. Ruben (eds.), *Issues in Marxist Philosophy*, Volume 1, pp.37-86.

Saccaro Del Buffa, G. (1990) 'The Second International Congress on Utopias and the Problem of Modernity', *Utopian Studies*, 1 (1), pp.73-76.

Saint-Simon, C. H. (1976) *The Political Thought of Saint-Simon*, Oxford, Oxford University Press.

Salmon, N. (ed.) *William Morris, Political Writings*, Bristol, Thoemmes Press.

Sanderson, J. (1969) *An Interpretation of the Political Ideas of Marx and Engels*, London and Harlow, Longmans.

Sarakinsky, I. (1993) 'Utopia as Political Theory', *Politikon*, 20 (2), pp.111-125.

Sargent, L. T. (1975) 'Utopia — The Problem of Definition', *Extrapolation*, 16 (2), pp.137-148.

Sargent, L. T. (1994) 'The Three Faces of Utopianism Revisited', *Utopian Studies*, 5 (1), pp.1-36.

Sayer, D. (1990) 'The Critique of Politics and Political Economy: Capitalism, Communism, and the State in Marx's Writings of the Mid-1840's', in B. Jessop and C. Malcolm-Brown (eds.), *Karl Marx's Social and Political Thought*, Volume 1, pp.662-691.

Sayers, S. (1994) 'Moral Values and Progress', *New Left Review*, 204, pp.67-85.

Schaff, A. (1990) 'Marxist Theory on Revolution and Violence', in B. Jessop and C. Malcolm-Brown (eds.), *Karl Marx's Social and Political Thought*, Volume 3, pp.217-223.

Sciabarra, C. M. (1995) *Marx, Hayek and Utopia*, Albany, State University of New York Press.

Scruton, R. (1989) *The Meaning of Conservatism*, Basingstoke and London, Macmillan.

Selucký, R. (1979) *Marxism, Socialism, Freedom*, Basingstoke and London, Macmillan.

Shiviah, M. (1994) 'New Realities, New Utopia: A Perspective on Convergence of Radicalisms', *Economic and Political Weekly*, 29 (6), pp.305-312.

Shklar, J. (1973) 'The Political Theory of Utopia: From Melancholy to Nostalgia', in F. E. Manuel (ed.), *Utopias and Utopian Thought*, pp.101-115.

Simecka, M. (1984) 'A World With Utopias or Without Them?', in P. Alexander and R Gill (eds.), *Utopias*, pp.169-178.

Singer, D. (1993) 'In Defence of Utopia', *The Socialist Register*, pp.249-256.
Spencer, M. C. (1981) *Charles Fourier*, Boston, Twayne Publishers.
Stedman Jones, G. and Patterson, I. (1996) 'Introduction', in C. Fourier, *The Theory of the Four Movements*, pp.vii-xxvi.
Suvin, D. (1976) '"Utopian" and "Scientific": Two Attributes For Socialism From Engels', *The Minnesota Review*, N.S. VI, pp.59-70.
Suvin, D. (1990) 'Locus, Horizon, and Orientation: The Concept of Possible Worlds as a Key to Utopian Studies', *Utopian Studies*, 1 (2), pp.69-95.
Thompson, E. P. (1977) *William Morris: Romantic to Revolutionary*, London, Merlin Press.
Torrance, J. (1995) *Karl Marx's Theory of Ideas*, Cambridge, Cambridge University Press.
Tsuzuki, C. (1971) 'Robert Owen and Revolutionary Politics', in S. Pollard and J. Salt (eds.), *Robert Owen, Prophet of the Poor*, pp.13-38.
Ulam, A. (1973) 'Socialism and Utopia', in F. E. Manuel (ed.), *Utopias and Utopian Thought*, pp.116-136.
Vincent, A. (1993) 'The Character of Ecology', *Environmental Politics*, 2 (2), pp.248-276.
Wagner, Y. and Strauss, M. (1969) 'The Programme of The Communist Manifesto and its Theoretical Foundations', *Political Studies*, 17 (4), pp.470-484.
Walker, A. (1978) *Marx, His Theory and Its Context*, London, Longman.
Walliman, I. (1981) *Estrangement: Marx's Conception of Human Nature and the Division of Labor*, Westport, Greenwood Press.
Wilson, E. (1972) *To The Finland Station*, London, Macmillan.
Wolff, R. P., Moore, B. Jnr., and Marcuse, H. (1969) *A Critique of Pure Tolerance*, Boston, Beacon Press.
Wolter, U. (ed.) (1980) *Rudolf Bahro, Critical Responses*, White Plains, M. E. Sharpe.
Wood, A. (1981) *Karl Marx*, London, Routledge and Kegan Paul.
Zeitlin, M. (1996) 'In Defence of Utopia', *Monthly Review*, 48 (7), pp.23-28.

Index

Adamiak, R. 45
Adventure, spirit of 3, 164, 165, 167-168
Alienation 127, 128, 135, 137n
   and the development of radical needs 129-130, 137n
Annenkov, P. 26
Association of producers 43, 44-45, 59-60, 62-63, 67, 70, 128
Avineri, S. 19, 45, 57n, 83

Babeuf, G. 82-83, 88
Bauman, Z. 147
Bell, D. 136n
Bender, F. L. 41-42
Berki, R. N. 58, 118
Berland, O. 101
Berneri, M. 9-10
Bhaskar, R. 136n
Blackburn, R. 103, 141, 154
Bloch, E. 159-160
Brighouse, H. 153
Buber, M. 10

Cabet, E. 24, 25, 32, 65
Capitalism
   and emergence of utopian socialism 22-24, 28, 34
   class structure 99-100, 101-102
   creation of transcendent needs within 126-132
   development within lower phase of communism 38, 40-41, 42, 43, 46, 50, 51, 54, 56
   structural contradictions 40, 91-92, 121-122
   tendencies towards communism 118, 120-122, 123, 125, 136n
   transition from feudalism to 96-97, 136n
Carver, T. 2, 61
Circulation, sphere of 41, 54
Cohen, A. 73
Cohen, G. A. 108n, 136n
Communism (higher phase) 36-37, 50, 54, 58-77
   ambiguous nature of Marx's description 61-63, 65, 66-68, 70, 75, 77
   and self-determination 60, 68-69, 123-125
   development of the all-round individual 71-72, 74, 109, 121-122, 124-125, 135
   distribution 53, 64, 65
   Dream of the Whole Man 70-71, 74, 109, 113-114, 117, 135
   economic, social and political structure 58-63
   extension of free-time 72, 74, 131
   ontological necessity of labour 72-74, 109, 129-130, 132, 133, 135
Communism (lower phase) 36-57
   as a stage of capitalism 38, 42, 44, 51, 54
   non-utopian nature of 42, 55-56
   transition to higher phase 37, 43, 50, 53-54, 56
Communism (movement)
   and the classless society 92-99
   and the material conditions for emancipation 85-90, 116
   and the proletariat 99-105
   and utopian socialism 22-24

Community of free individuals 62,
    63, 67, 68
Crocker, L. 33

De George, R. T. 6
Derrida, J. 2
Dictatorship of the Proletariat, *see*
    Communism (lower phase)
Division of labour
    abolition of 53, 60-61, 69, 72, 77,
        93, 124
    and the fully-developed
        individual 121-123
Draper, H. 39, 45-46, 57n
Durkheim, E. 122

Eckersley, R. 150
Elliott, G. 154
Engels
    and theory of permanent
        revolution 57n
    critique of utopian socialism 20-
        21
    on distinction between Marxism
        and utopian socialism 86
    on the return to an original state
        of unity 114-116
Essentialism 119-120

Fischer, E. 71
Fourier, C. 11, 13-14, 18-19, 32, 63
Fukuyama, F. 138
Furet, F. 138

Gardiner, M. 149
Geoghegan, V. 7, 8, 32, 33, 106,
    147, 152
Goodwin, B. 11, 93, 143-144, 162
Gorz, A. 148
Gramsci, A. 120
Green movement, utopianism of
    150

Habermas, J. 116, 152, 153
Halliday, F. 154

Hammen, O. J. 66
Harvey, D. 122
Hegel, G. W. F. 111, 112, 115, 117,
    137n
Heller, A. 127, 130, 132, 142
Hilferding, R. 136n
History, materialist conception of
    and Marx's accidental
        utopianism 116-117, 125-
        126, 132-133, 135
    and proletarian mission 99-105
    and the spirit of revolution 90,
        106
    as a non-utopian framework 85-
        90, 110, 116-117, 117-118,
        125, 126, 131, 133, 134-135,
        136n
    forces/relations model 91-99,
        105, 124
    pragmatic model 126-132, 137n
    Russian exceptionalism 97-98
    structural model 117-123
    teleological model 110-116
Hobsbawm, E. 141, 154
Holton, R. J. 96, 97
Hope
    contemporary lack of 157-158,
        163, 167
    purposive 152-153, 163, 165
    radical 2, 107, 158, 162
Horne, A. 45, 50
Hunt, E. K. 77

Jacobs, N. 150
Jameson, F. 5
Johnstone, M. 45
Jones, G. S. 27

Kautsky, K. 67, 68
Kessler, C. F. 145
Kolakowski, L. 153
Kumar, K. 71, 72, 77, 114, 143, 159
Kuryllo, H. 150

Lasky, M. J. 66

Lassalle, F. 51, 52, 54
Lenin, V. I. 36, 67, 68, 137n
Levin, M. 92
Levitas, R. 4, 5, 6, 7, 8, 32, 77, 144
Lichtheim, G. 80, 96
Lukes, S. 1, 59, 77

MacIntyre, A. 137n
Mannheim, K. 142, 157
Manuel, F. E. 15, 55, 140, 166
Marcuse, H. 160-161
Market socialism 141
Marx, K.
    accidental utopianism 2, 76, 107, 109-110, 116-117, 125-126, 132-133, 135-136, 140
    anti-utopianism 1, 2, 4, 12-13, 26-28, 33-34, 61, 66, 68, 76, 77-78, 79, 84-85, 107, 117, 134-135, 139, 143, 161
    concept of 'class' 101-102
    critique of utopian socialism 19-20, 21-22, 24-28, 30-33, 68, 80, 87, 106-107, 162
    humanism 33, 74, 76, 77, 134
    messianism 101
    'multiple' Marxes 2, 134
    on English and French Revolutions 81-84
    on materialism 126-127
    on proletarian disunity 104-105
    on 'radical' needs 128-132, 133
    project of 2, 107, 126, 133-135
    theoretician of the proletarian class 89, 90, 91, 107, 133
    theory of progress 95-99
    'vision' of communism 70-74, 77, 109, 135, 140
    womb metaphor 118-120, 125
Marxism
    pro-utopian orthodoxy 138, 140, 146-147, 152-153, 156-158, 162-167
    and collapse of actually existing socialism 153-155

Materialistically Critical Socialism 12, 13, 79-90
    failings of 91-106, 107, 109
    see also History, materialist conception of
McLellan, D. 75, 77
Means/Ends interpretation of Marx 5-9, 26-27, 30, 35n, 139
    critique 9-12, 23, 27, 29, 31, 33
Meisner, M. 5, 152, 163
Money, abolition of 65
Moore, S. 36, 37, 43, 137n
Morgan, L. 114-115, 116
Morris, W. 159
Morrison, A. 151

Needs, radical 126, 127, 130, 131, 132-133

Ollman, B. 10, 11, 59, 66, 75, 76, 77
Owen, R. 11, 14, 17-18, 32, 63

Paris Commune 28-29, 44-47, 48-51, 62
Patrick, J. M. 1, 13
Patterson, I. 27
Pevzner, I. 164
Plekhanov, G. 126
Popper, K. 142, 165
Pragmatism 126-127, 132-133, 135, 137n
Private property
    abolition of 44, 49, 50, 58, 59, 71, 77, 93, 124, 129
    and the proletariat 102-105, 116
    transformation into socialised property 120-121
Proletariat
    alienation of 128
    and radical needs 129-130, 131
    and utopian socialism 22-24, 25, 28-29, 30, 34, 81-83
    antithetical relation to private property 102-105, 106, 116, 129

as ruling class 39-40, 41, 44, 49, 53, 56
creative novelty of 33
divisions within 104-105
historical mission 93, 99-102, 111
revolutionary consciousness of 91-92
self-determination 32-33, 60, 68-69, 77, 79, 90, 94, 106, 109, 116, 124, 125, 131, 132, 133, 135
self-emancipation 24-25, 26, 27, 30, 32, 33, 79, 90, 106, 109, 133, 135
Proudhon, P. 11, 19, 87

Revolution 8, 24, 30, 66, 112, 118, 150
Bolshevik 154
bourgeois 37, 38, 39, 42, 44, 47, 48, 49, 53, 56, 98
English 81-82
French 16, 81-82, 83-84
permanent 37-38, 39, 42, 43, 48-49, 56, 57n
proletarian 16, 17, 27, 35n, 37, 38, 39, 46, 49, 83, 88, 89, 91, 99, 100, 101, 103
spirit of 2, 79, 85, 90, 106, 109, 117, 133, 135
Ricoeur, P. 145, 146
Robespierre, M. 82, 83
Ruben, D.-H. 119, 125

Saccaro Del Buffa, G. 149
Saint-Simon, C. H. 11, 14-17, 32, 63, 64-65, 94
Sanderson, J. 75
Sarakinsky, I. 152
Sargent, L. T. 162
Sayers, S. 127
Schaff, A. 118
Sciabarra, C. M. 108n

Science 19-21, 64, 80-81, 87, 88-89, 106-107, 113, 114, 119, 125, 146, 164, 165, 167
Scruton, R. 154
Selucký, R. 67-68, 78n
Shklar, J. 10
Simecka, M. 165, 166
Singer, D. 154, 156, 157
Stalinism 153-154
State, the
in the higher phase of communism 62, 63, 64-65, 69
in the lower phase of communism 39, 41, 54-55
Stirner, M. 12
Strauss, M. 40-41
Suvin, D. 7, 8, 21, 32, 147-148, 150

Talmon, J. 83
Taylor, K. 8-9, 11, 143, 162
Teleology 110-117, 127, 136n
Terror, the 16, 83
Torrance, J. 35n

Ulam, A. 140
Utopia
and deceit 157, 158-162, 167
and desire 148, 151, 155, 159, 166
and dreaming 166
and hope 152-153, 157-158, 162, 163-164, 165-166, 166-167
and ideology 145, 147, 157
and messianism 143-144, 161-162, 164
and political adventurism 164-165, 167
and psychology 152
and science 164, 167
and truth claims 15-18, 20-21, 34, 149, 150, 156, 158-161, 164, 168
as a mode of critique 145-149
as an inspirational goal 152-156, 163-164

blueprint function 142-144, 155
'critical' utopias 149-151
defined 1, 141-142
grass roots construction of 156-158
Marx's definition of 12-13, 23-24, 30, 34
rhetorical power of 152-153, 158
Utopian mindset 26-28, 31, 32, 34
Utopian Socialism
and revolution 11, 30-31
and science 13-15, 20, 22
and the proletariat 64, 99
as political anachronism 22-24, 28-30, 31, 34, 80, 87
distinction between Marx and 55, 86, 88, 107
influence on Marx and Engels 63-65
messianic elitism of 15-19, 25-26, 32, 34

Vincent, A. 150

Wagner, Y. 40-41
Walker, A. 98, 118
Weitling, W. 11-12, 25, 26, 32, 35n
Wilson, E. 26

Zeitlin, M. 6, 155, 156-157